Inside
Heaven's Door

THE TRUE LIFE STORY OF ONE WOMAN'S JOURNEY
INTO HER EXTRAORDINARY SPIRITUAL AWAKENING

SHIRLEY ST. MICHAEL

BALBOA.PRESS

A DIVISION OF HAY HOUSE

Balboa Press books may be ordered through booksellers or by contacting:

Balboa Press
A Division of Hay House
1663 Liberty Drive
Bloomington, IN 47403
www.balboapress.com
844-682-1282

Because of the dynamic nature of the Internet, any web addresses or links contained in this book may have changed since publication and may no longer be valid. The views expressed in this work are solely those of the author and do not necessarily reflect the views of the publisher, and the publisher hereby disclaims any responsibility for them.

The author of this book does not dispense medical advice or prescribe the use of any technique as a form of treatment for physical, emotional, or medical problems without the advice of a physician, either directly or indirectly. The intent of the author is only to offer information of a general nature to help you in your quest for emotional and spiritual well-being. In the event you use any of the information in this book for yourself, which is your constitutional right, the author and the publisher assume no responsibility for your actions.

Any people depicted in stock imagery provided by Getty Images are models, and such images are being used for illustrative purposes only. Certain stock imagery © Getty Images.

Print information available on the last page.

ISBN: 978-1-5043-5814-9 (sc)
ISBN: 978-1-5043-5815-6 (hc)
ISBN: 978-1-5043-5839-2 (e)

Library of Congress Control Number: 2016908332

Balboa Press rev. date: 12/07/2023

DEDICATION

To the healer that lives within all of us.

"The Universe is responding to all of our heart's desires and needs; if only we were open to embrace the many ways by which the answers come.

My story is, in many ways, the story of all of us. The message is that spiritual consciousness is working in our lives every day. We don't have to travel to far-off places to find it. In fact, everything we need for this to awaken is right within ourselves."

Shirley St. Michael

Preface

The course I developed, entitled "The Power Within," focused on educating counselors and health professionals in human potential, spiritual consciousness and integrative healing modalities, teaching them how to better counsel and coach their clients towards wellness. My course did not particularly focus on the healings my clients experienced, but to illustrate one of the spiritual concepts I taught, I used as an example, the story of a woman I had helped who had a debilitating disease, that had no cure.

Because of my knowledge base in working with energy and consciousness, I no longer used the, hands on healing method. Instead, I incorporated education in my coaching services that taught my clients the understanding of human energy systems and how to find the factors that hindered or helped them in their pursuit for health, happiness, fulfillment and success in life. As with others, these spiritual concepts, helped to awaken them to their wisdom within that transformed them forever.

When I had finished with the story, a man, whom came as a guest with one of the psychotherapists, raised his hand with a question. He asked me if I would be open in helping him heal his hands the way I had helped the woman in the story. He had undergone several painful treatments, one of which was the severing of some of some his sweat glands, but the warts always grew back. He went on to explain that after many treatments, he encountered great difficulty flexing and using his hands because of constant pain. After a moment of self-inquiry, I accepted to assist him in his healing.

The gentleman listened intently to what I was saying as I explained that this would be a cooperative experience. I prepared him by asking if he was willingly open to having his hands completely healed. After his emphatic "yes," I then asked him to participate by visualizing his hands completely free of warts and to know that his hands were healthy, as well as pain free.

As others in the class looked on, I took the man's hands in mine while I silently prayed. Prayer is my way of making a conscious bridge to the healing energy and divine wisdom that resides within me. As my heart and my mind became aligned with one another, I began to feel a tingling sensation from a source deep within me that resonated down my arms and hands to my fingertips. I then proceeded to listen to my intuition for guidance on what I should do next.

After several minutes of the laying on of hands approach, the tingling sensation subsided, and we disengaged from one another. As I observed him looking down at his hands, I shared with him the importance of visualization and purposeful intention. "Visualization is your God given gift to create an image in your mind of what you want to create in life. Purposeful intention involves focusing not only on the result but why you want this particular result to happen."

"Hold in your heart your desire for your hands to be completely healed. Envision this in your mind and consciously focus on doing this for a period of time daily." Listen to your intuition regarding other changes you are guided to make in your life to complete this healing."

He graciously thanked me, and I then returned to finishing the evening's class.

In the beginning of the following week's class the same gentleman asked if he could speak. I agreed, and with his eyes beaming, he held up his hands for all of us to see. There were audible gasps as we observed that most of his warts had vanished, except for the two largest, which were now dramatically reduced in size and, as he said, "getting smaller every day."

He demonstrated the greater flexibility he now had in his hands, which were smoother, softer, and he added, "practically pain-free." He said he believed that taking part in his own healing was one of the most profound experiences he had ever had in his life, and that he would continue the healing exercise until his hands were completely healed.

As the gentleman took his seat, one of the students suddenly stood up and asked to speak. She gazed around the room and then looked back at me.

*   *   *

"Why aren't you working as a healer?" she asked fervently. "Isn't it your duty to use your abilities to cure the sick, as you did with this man?"

What she said took me by surprise. No one had ever questioned why I chose not to use the "Hands-on-Healing" method anymore in my work.

As I stood in front of approximately sixty people, I paused and said something to this effect; "This ability to heal exists within all of us. The primary reason for my giving this class is to help enable you to connect and experience your own divine connection by focusing on the dynamics of your unique energy."

My words had a powerful impact on the class. After that experience, everyone became more intent than ever to engage in understanding the power they have within themselves. From this event they learned that it is one thing to study the concepts of healing and transformation, and clearly another to experience them.

This woman, by having the courage to ask this one question became, what I call, a "living angel," giving the message about the importance of sharing our experiences and knowledge so we may all learn and grow from one another. Because of this important message, I am sharing my story with you.

My purpose in writing this book is not just to tell you a story, but to engage you in your own transformation. I encourage you to find for yourself those beliefs and practices you believe to be true and in what way they strengthen and guide you in your life.

My spiritual awakening shared in this book was a journey that took place over a period of 10 years. Even though these stories are factual, some of them have been placed according to the topic in the chapters and not necessarily by the actual time they occurred. Other aspects of this story have been omitted to honor the privacy of others.

Also, I have been given permission with great enthusiasm to use the real names of many who were involved. Those whom I was not able to locate I have used pseudonyms. I have also chosen to omit the names of famous people, whom I have worked with, in order to keep the essence of this book focused on spiritual consciousness and transformation.

Please remember while reading this book I use the term God in respect to other terms such as universe and source. That my belief system is that we are all from one divine creator and that there are many ways we can connect to the same divine source.

I also want to share that everything I experienced as my own truth, I found assistance to understand in a more comprehensive manner from information that I studied in spiritual and human consciousness, research findings in printed materials from books, websites, video's, tele-classes and spiritual programs.

To access book club and group discussion questions to begin your transformation please visit Inside Heaven's Door at www. shirleystmichael.com

Introduction

Did you ever have an extraordinary time in your life when everything was going so good how could anything possibly go wrong? I was a junior in high school. It was a great year. I was such a lucky girl. My friends, school, job, and boyfriend; everything was perfect. Then something happened that changed it all.

Ten years later . . . . . .

I was twenty-five years old and I was your average American suburban housewife, the mother of two beautiful young daughters, Melyssa and Krystine and happily awaiting the arrival of our third child. My husband, Jake, was my childhood sweetheart, my best friend and confidant whom I had known since fifth grade.

Life was wonderful—or so I believed. With the money my brother Billy had loaned us for the down payment on a house, we finally moved out of our cramped apartment and into a home of our own. The house was old and in need of repair but it was reasonably priced and was located in Auburn, a town next to Worcester, Massachusetts where all of our family lived.

After settling into our new home and adjusting to life with our newborn daughter Laurie, Jake and I got busy with remodeling our broken-down house. What we really loved about this house was the property. The big backyard reminded Jake and me of a neighbor's yard where we played kickball and other sports as children. First, we began by restructuring the landscape and extending the driveway back behind the house so our children could safely play and ride their bikes. The worn grey shingles that covered our house were replaced with a pretty pale yellow siding. New concrete sidewalks and stairs gave a fresh new look to this sixty-year old home. Jake and I loved working together. I was quite happy being a stay-at-home mom. For me, life was wonderful.

But for Jake, things were very different. He was working full-time as a computer analyst for the Air National Guard Reserve unit in Worcester, Massachusetts, and part-time for a paint and wallpaper store. Most of his time was spent working these two jobs, in an effort to ensure our financial stability and pay for the remodeling of our home. Even though we had our share of disagreements, I felt our life was blessed.

We had been living in our new home for almost a year when Jake's boss offered him a position with the Northeast Phased Array Warning System, known as PAVE PAWS, in the town of Sagamore, Massachusetts, located in the region known as Cape Cod. Jake would be working with the only radar system on North America's East Coast that warned our government about incoming sea-launched and intercontinental ballistic missile attacks.

After several days of discussion, Jake decided to accept the offer for the new position. This move would give Jake the opportunity to make his dream, of owning his own sailboat, come true. I was excited for him and for our family because of the amazing opportunity this afforded us to raise our children in a beautiful, natural environment near the ocean.

Our family and friends accepted the fact of our impending move. And I, not wanting to deal with my feelings about leaving everyone I loved, chose to focus on the excitement of living near the ocean. There the children could learn about its natural environment and the rest of our family and friends could visit and enjoy its beauty.

Of course, there was a certain amount of stress involved in making this decision. For one, we would be moving almost 200 miles away from our family and friends and Jake would have to begin his new job before we were able to get our house on the market. So we decided that the children and I would stay in Auburn until our house was sold, and Jake would come home on weekends to help pack for our eventual move.

So, like I said, life was wonderful … until.

Jake left on a Sunday afternoon to return to Otis Air Force Base located in Falmouth, Massachusetts, to begin his training on Monday morning. That evening, after I had tucked the children into bed, I myself had fallen asleep very quickly and had a dream that was so vivid and real that I awoke startled. I very seldom recall my dreams, but here's what I remember as my thoughts raced from one place to another and images slipped in and out of my consciousness. This dream would be the beginning of my life unraveling. This would be the beginning of a journey that would transform me forever.

The Dream...

I was in a sterile, white room, looking out into darkness. In this room there was no ceiling, no floor, no windows or doors, and I was floating aimlessly in the middle of it. In this place, I felt a sense of calm and peace that I never experience when I'm awake. The air that filled this space was the purest air I had ever breathed, and everywhere I looked, I could see tiny points of light and glistening particles dancing around, some merging together, while others floated in slow motion as if lying dormant just waiting to be awakened. I felt like this is how it would feel if I was out in cosmic space, yet I was deeply inside myself, more than I had ever been before.

There are no boundaries or directions here, I thought. *Have I lost my compass?* Then, with that question, I saw at a far off distance what I thought was an opening. *"Is that a door?"* I asked myself.

As I cautiously tried to move toward this tiny image, I began to panic. The air suddenly became stagnant and I began to lose my ability to breathe. My body felt heavy and denser as I began to swirl around and around until finally a question came up in my mind.

"Where am I?" I shouted.

"Heaven," a voice replied.

"Heaven!" I replied back.

"Why am I here?" I then asked.

The voice answered, "The Truth."

I felt my chest expand slightly as the word "Truth" kept running through my mind. I began to breathe more easily again, and my whole body began to move effortlessly. It was then that I realized my compass was made up of my thoughts, and my feelings were the fuel that moved me forward. With this awareness, I was able to direct myself toward this object.

As I drew closer, the vision I had, looked less like a door and more like a dust particle. *That darn dust particle*, I thought. *What is it about you that I am so attracted to?* As I moved even more closely, I could hear a humming sound coming from within it, and with that, it floated into my mind, bringing with it, thoughts of Jake that gave me a horrible feeling in the pit of my stomach that quickly awakened me.

I awoke in darkness. It was after 2 a.m. It took just a second to forget what my dream was about, but the urge to call Jake was so commanding that hesitation was not an option. So why was I calling him? I actually didn't remember until Jake answered the phone, and that's when a horrible thought emerged from deep within me.

After he realized the importance of my calling him so early in the morning, I asked earnestly, "Jake, do you love me?"

"Of course I do Shirl," he said sleepily. "What's the matter?"

I gulped as I tried to hold back my tears. "Then will you tell me the truth?" I asked.

With hesitation in his voice, he said, "Yes, absolutely."

I took a deep breath, closed my eyes, and asked, "Are you happy in our marriage?"

The silence on the other end of the phone was deafening. My heart felt like it was going to leap out of my chest, and then I took another breath. With my eyes closed, I waited for Jake's reply. Still sitting in the darkness of my bedroom, I heard him say, "No...no, I'm not."

Chapter 1

Welcome to Life 101

Life would never be the same again for Jake, the children, and me. We finally sold our home in Auburn and moved away from the community we had known so well throughout our lives. All the support we had ever known was there: our parents; our sisters; my brother, and all of our wonderful friends.

Our family and friends were a loving group of fun and supportive people. We saw them almost every day. We took vacations together, went on day trips together, and celebrated birthdays and holidays together.

What Jake had revealed to me was devastating. I was scared and unable to make rational decisions. Do I move or do I stay? How could I have missed the indications that something was terribly wrong? I had no idea how this was going to turn out, so I prayed like I had never prayed before.

* * *

We finally rented a house in Pocasset, a quaint, picturesque community on the western side of Cape Cod, where we could walk to the beach. During our first few months in our new surroundings, what Jake had revealed weighed heavily on my mind. With more of his truth being told, my reality of our wonderful happy life turned into confusion and chaos in my mind. It was difficult for me to handle to say the least. Out of respect for our privacy, we had decided to tell no one and to work through our marital problems in therapy.

Meanwhile, talking to my family and friends as if everything was going well was one of the most difficult things I had ever done. I was usually an open book, and most of the time when I was dealing with things that bothered me, I would just become quiet. So hiding the truth made me feel fragmented, to say the least. Here I was acting excited and happy about the move while deliberately hiding the pain and torment I was feeling inside. This was the first time in my life that I forced myself to act as if I was happy but in truth I was torn apart.

Dealing with the facts Jake had revealed about his unhappiness, I began to feel incredible, uncontrollable anxiety. As much as I tried to move through each day with a positive attitude, I just couldn't seem to extract myself from my emotional swings. I couldn't eat, I hardly slept, and I didn't know what to do with all my thoughts.

My imagination ran wild. I screamed, I cried, I even tormented Jake with questions and accusations, but nothing helped to end the emotional roller coaster ride I was on. I was losing grasp of reality. Who was this person that was showing up in my life--meaning me? Finally, I wore myself out. Then, depression set in.

* * *

One afternoon while the children were napping, I laid down to rest. I was gazing at the ceiling of our bedroom when I suddenly felt a presence in the room. I quickly sat up to see if one of the girls had awakened early from her nap and had come downstairs, but there was no one there. Then, as I looked around the room, I could faintly see the reflection of a figure standing next to the bed.

Startled, I pulled back in fear and asked out loud in a commanding voice, "Who are you?" Anxiously, I waited for an answer then asked, "What do you want?" Still, no one answered.

I jumped up towards this figure but was quickly pushed back down on the bed by the power created by our two forces colliding. As I half lay on the bed with my feet dangling off to the side, a gentle feeling came over me. Then a slight fragrance of roses began to fill the air, bringing with it thoughts of my grandmother, who had passed away when I was only eleven years old.

Thoughts of my childhood filled my mind. I remembered a time when I was eight. One evening while I was sleeping over at my grandmother's house she allowed me to stay up later than usual to watch a movie about angels. After the movie ended, she sat me down at the kitchen table for a bedtime snack. She asked me if I understood what the movie was about. I must have given her a confused look because she went on to explain that there were good angels but also other angels that had fallen away from God's plan. She said that we are all angels of God, and how we live our lives is how we become angels of goodness or angels whom have fall away from goodness.

"There are also angels that God sends to watch over, guide, and protect us," she said. "They are our guardian angels."

"I see angels, Grammy," I said.

"You do?" she said, surprised.

I nodded my head yes.

"Shirley, when have you seen an angel?" she asked.

"Here, Grammy." I answered.

"Here in this house?" she asked.

"Does this angel have wings?" She asked, as if she was delighting in the movie we just watched.

"Uh, no," I said in a smaller voice than I usually speak from. "He is a big man with white hair, and he wears baggy pants with straps that go across his shoulders," I answered as I lifted up my eyes to meet hers.

My grandmother began to smile.

"Hmmm," she exclaimed. "I believe he is your grandfather. He passed away before you were born, but he loves you very much, and I know he watches over us from heaven."

As my thoughts returned to the present moment I noticed that the fragrance of roses and the spirit-like figure disappeared. I shook my head to dismiss my confusion then got up to check on the children.

* * *

As time went on, the days began to get a little easier to awaken to. We had enrolled our first born, Melyssa, in the grammar school located on Otis Air Force Base. At the first parent teacher conference Melyssa's teacher told Jake and I that she was intellectually ahead of her classmates and had become bored with the first-grade curriculum. Because of her comprehension level, she suggested that Melyssa read advanced material, and we agreed.

While Melyssa was in school, Krysie and Laurie spent most of their time playing together. It was always a special treat when the elderly couple who lived across the street, Mr. and Mrs. Childs, would take the girls for walks around their yard, teaching them about nature and building their excitement toward springtime when they could pick strawberries that grew wild on their property.

All three of our children adjusted well to the changes in their lives. As for Jake and me, we began marriage counseling and worked earnestly toward understanding the problems we had created in our relationship.

In our first counseling session, our therapist explained that during life transitions, many couples go through a time of re-evaluation of their life and goals independently from one other. Often what seems to happen is that couples may not share their inner thoughts and deeper feelings, which can lead to subtle deceptions. What happened to us was only the exterior event that mirrored a deeper issue. We both lacked important skills that are needed for a healthy relationship.

The therapist also pointed out that the only behaviors we knew were the ones we were conditioned to, which began in early childhood as we observed how our families and others around us behaved. He explained that our beliefs and behaviors were instilled unconsciously in our minds, and these beliefs determine how successful, or unsuccessful, our lives would be unless we became aware of our behaviors that created turmoil in our lives.

This made all the sense in the world to me. I remembered as a child how I would go to my father for advice. Instead of giving it he would send me to talk to my mother. When I talked to my mother, she would hug me and tell me everything would be fine. Believing that my problem would not just disappear, I was left alone to figure out the solution on my own or dismiss the problem altogether.

As for Jake, his parents divorced when he was young. He took over as the responsible man in the family, even though he was only twelve years old. He would "suck up" his feelings in order to meet his responsibilities, without taking the time to express his own needs, leaving him with unfulfilled dreams for his own happiness.

From these discussions, I knew that education was the important factor in changing my well-adapted behaviors in order to become the type of person I wanted to be, instead of living my life out of adapted unconscious behaviors. At that time, I had no idea what form this education would take or the turmoil this would bring to my life.

* * *

The children, Jake and I, even though it was difficult at times, had a glorious first year on Cape Cod while waiting for our new home to be built. From everything we had learned in therapy we chose to incorporate books that would instill in our daughters that which we ourselves had learned in our weekly therapy sessions. We joined a small Catholic church. We visited museums and sites that the Cape is well known for. The gorgeous fall season quickly turned into a brilliant white winter and then it was spring before we knew it.

We found a beautiful piece of land that was just perfect for building our new home. Sandwich is the name of the town we would live in. It is known as the oldest town on Cape Cod and we loved its beauty and picturesque qualities. The children loved visiting the museum of the famous author, Thornton Burgess, a well-known conservationist and author of children's books. Because of the town's location on the ocean shore there were children's educational programs on marine wild life given at the Green Briar Nature Center where families from all over the world would visit.

One breezy, sunny, spring day, Jake the children and I had plans to meet with the building contractor over at our new house to review the plans that were to be presented to our bank in order to receive the next stage of funding. As I walked up the back steps leading into what would be the kitchen area, I remember feeling uneasy. My stomach was quivering and my whole body became alert as if danger was close by. My mind was racing with thoughts and scenarios of times in the past when I had encountered similar feelings.

I became calm as if I detached from my surroundings. Physically, I was standing near Jake in the kitchen of our half-built home. I could hear Jake talking with the builder, while I was at a distance from them, as I was watched my children play between the wall studs on the first floor. I felt as if I was somewhere else, observing reality with a sense of detachment.

I then heard a voice inside me say, "Don't forget your feelings."

"What do you mean, don't forget my feelings?" I responded in my mind.

Suddenly, I thought of the dream that had alerted me about the problem in our marriage. I remembered what I had learned in therapy; that in my life, I often disassociated from my feelings. Now I understood. This, too, could be dismissed and forgotten, washed away from my consciousness, never to be understood.

I must choose to be aware my feelings, I thought.

My thoughts were interrupted by the sound of Jake's voice. My body slightly shifted and I became conscious of my surroundings again.

"Shirl, what do you think?" Jake asked.

"What do I think about what?" I asked slowly, my mind still a little foggy.

"Honey, are you okay?" Jake asked.

It was obvious to Jake that something was wrong with me.

"I'm sorry, I didn't hear what you were saying," I slowly responded. Still, the thoughts of my unusual experience lingered.

"Never mind," Jake responded with a somewhat concerned look. "I'll go over the plans with you later."

I became physically weak as Jake and I listened to the details the builder was explaining about the next steps his crew would take in finishing the house. It was as if a cloud had come over me and was sapping every bit of strength I had. Try as I may, I couldn't shake off this strong sense of danger.

"Jake, I'm not feeling very well," I said.

At that moment, a voice inside me whispered, "Pay attention, pay attention to what is happening here!"

As soon as I heard the builder's car pull out of the driveway, I once again became alert to the feeling of danger and blurted out hysterically, "He's going to take our money!"

Jake responded, "Who is going to take our money? What are you talking about?"

I looked at Jake and said, "The builder! The builder is going to take our money!"

Frustrated, Jake replied, "Of course he is Shirl, he's building our house."

I could hardly breathe and was straining with every breath to get my point across to Jake.

"No!" I stated more frantically. "He's going to take our money, and he will not come back to finish our home!"

I'd finally said it, except I didn't know why I had said what I did. I just blurted out those statements without logical thought and without understanding.

My body finally felt released from the constriction I had been feeling. I could breathe easier again, and I felt more present.

Jake shook his head and walked away.

I must have been wrong, I thought.

What was I thinking? Oh God, please help me!

Confusion set in once more. All I wanted to do was forget this ever happened.

*   *   *

A few days had passed when the builder told Jake he was going on vacation, but assured him that his construction crew would be at our house to work while he was away. Every day they worked on our house, and I worked alongside them, carrying supplies, sweeping up sawdust and picking up nails so the girls would not get hurt while we inspected the progress.

I often thought of why I had those feelings of the builder running off with our money. As I thought again on these things, something still didn't feel right to me. I still couldn't shake this feeling. Then a series of flashbacks came streaming through my mind from my childhood.

*   *   *

Royal Road was the street that many of us children walked up to get to the grammar school. The incline on this road was very steep, and the houses that lined it were small but neatly groomed.

I was about ten years old and while I was walking to school a vision came to my mind. In this vision, I saw children walking up Royal Road to school when a car parked on the top of the hill began to roll down the hill directly into the path where the children were walking. Traumatized by the sight, they could not move as the out-of-control car came toward them.

"No!" I screamed out loud. I could feel the intensity of the accident that was about to happen. I ran all the way to the end of Knox Street, where I lived, to Edlin Street, and then to the bottom of Royal Road until I came to a clearing from where I could see the top of the hill. There was no car coming down the road out of control. There were only my friends and their brothers and sisters walking up the road to school like they did every school day.

What just happened to me? I asked myself. *Why did I think this?*

This thought kept ruminating in my mind until one day I couldn't stand it any longer. It was making it difficult for me to focus in school and, I didn't even want to go out and play with my friends. One night as I was saying my prayers, I remembered something I had learned from my catechism teacher. "God can help us with our thoughts, the good thoughts and the bad ones." she said. So I prayed to God.

"God, take these thoughts away from me," I said. "Don't let this happen."

I prayed this same prayer over and over again, at bedtime and even while walking to school, until the thought of this horrible sight ceased to exist in my mind.

About two weeks later, I again was walking to school. The air was still and I noticed that I couldn't see my sisters and friends walking in front of me. I felt something must be wrong.

I must be late for school, I thought.

So I ran until I reached the bottom of Royal Road. None of my friends were on the steep road, but I could see the figure of a man at the top of the hill. Then he disappeared out of sight.

I was halfway up the hill when it happened. A car parked on the side of the hill began to roll into the street, gaining speed. There was no sound of a car engine running and no one in the driver's seat. I was the only one walking up the hill. I was frozen still, unable to move, standing in harm's way.

When the car was within a few houses from where I was standing, it veered into the middle of the street. I gasped in shock fearing it was going to hit me! Then suddenly, it careened off to the right, rolled over a small embankment, and crashed, head on, into Mrs. Samuels' driveway. I walked away unharmed.

I began to realize that these flash backs were situations that had occurred to me that I could never make sense of. Many of these past experiences I couldn't understand. And here they are again. Leading me down a path to where?

* * *

The construction crew worked for the next two weeks, but then everything came to a screeching halt. No builder, no workers, no more progress on our house. After making numerous phone calls to the builder's office with no reply, Jake finally started to inquire in town. The landscaper working on our property told Jake that he had heard the builder had filed for bankruptcy. Jake was astounded. I had been right.

I remember asking myself, *"What does this mean?" How did I know this even though, at the time, it didn't make sense to me?*

Something important is happening here! I thought. I began to recognize that this was a direct connection to an awareness that I didn't understand.

* * *

The lease on the home Pocassett that we were renting was about to expire. We had only one month to prepare for the move into our unfinished home. At this point, most of our loan from the bank had been distributed to pay the builder, and there was very little left in reserve.

Back at the house we were renting, I received a phone call from my mother.

"Shirley, what's wrong?" she asked.

I told her about the dilemma we were having with building our house. My mother had always been a fortress of support, even though she had no idea what Jake and I had to work through in our relationship. She was so concerned about us, especially her three granddaughters.

She jumped in and asked, "Shirl, why don't you and the children come and stay with your father and me until this mess has been cleaned up?" My mother didn't understand. There was absolutely no one to clean the mess up except for Jake and me. No one knew us in town. We were the first family to have built our home in our development. There was no one else for miles.

Looking at our newly built house from the outside, everything seemed just perfect. Rows of new cedar shingles covered the sides of the house, and red and brown colored bricks covered the front. The natural setting of trees and blueberry bushes gave an appealing beauty to the front yard, and tall trees gave privacy to the bay window in the living room.

However, from the inside, it was a different story. Walking through the house you could see that we had plumbing but no fixtures except for the toilets. The floors were still in their roughened condition before the finished floors would be laid. The kitchen was completely open with no cabinets, no sink, just carpenter tools all over the place. Some of the walls had been plastered while others were still bare. It felt so deserted, so empty. We had no other options. We had to move into our unfinished home.

Jake, the children, and I looked fine, but we were far from being whole. Here we were, living in one of the most beautiful places in Massachusetts; where we had built our home on a beautiful site. From the top of the house we had a beautiful view of the ocean and the center of Sandwich; but we were living as if we were on a camping trip.

I knew we were living on a wish and a prayer when the inspectors turned their heads to the fact that we were living in the house without an occupancy permit. They never once said a word.

We worked feverishly, day and night, to make the house somewhat livable. We sold our car and used some of the money to buy an old, run down, rusty, green station wagon to transport materials. We saved the rest of the money to purchase whatever else we needed to survive. As a result of these stressors, Jake and I both had lost a good amount of weight. The children though were in their own world of play and looked at this as an exciting adventure, which I believed kept them healthy and well.

Because we had no running water to the showers and sinks, Jake took his showers at work while I was able to bathe the children daily by bringing water into the house from the outside faucet. As for myself, even though I bathed from the basin as well, I just couldn't handle it any more. I don't recall why but we knew where the realtor's key was kept for the model home across the street. One evening I went across the street to this vacant house and took a shower.

How good it felt to be clean again. In a moment of frustration I had decided that it was more important for me to be clean than to abide by my own jurisdiction over my ethics and morals. My need for cleanliness won the battle.

*   *   *

We were exhausted from working night and day on completing our home. Physically and mentally, we had no more energy to give. My head was constantly foggy, my body felt heavy, and I couldn't get myself motivated to do much of anything. This was my life.

Other thoughts started drifting into my mind. *Having a foggy mind is a part of the aging process,* I thought. *Having no motivation is just a part of life's big challenges. Just work, work, and work, go to bed then get up the next morning and start all over again. Was this how illness and aging sets in?* I thought.

"This isn't what I want my life to be like!" I said out loud. I forced myself to shake off these negative thoughts every time they came into my mind. Then I willed myself to accomplish more, something, anything!

Days went by without Jake or me saying much to each other, only what was necessary. We had no TV, no radio, and I had no one to talk to except for Jake and the children. In this silence I began to realize that there was something more going on inside of me. In the depths of my mind I could faintly hear a conversation.

This reminded me of when I was sixteen years old, and my friends and I went on a spiritual retreat with our church's youth organization. At the retreat, we had to sit still for two hours a day while we talked to God. I thought the silence would kill me! What do you mean, sit quietly for two hours and talk to God? I can't even sit still for five minutes! I remember thinking of what I went through in high school; a hopeless dilemma that I had no answers to and because of this I was thrown into a state of internal confusion. How I tried to look normal. How I tried to keep my thoughts on my school work and everything in my life. Even God couldn't help me then. But now, I had more important issues to deal with. Okay God, where are you now?????

* * *

It still amazes me that when you have given all you can and you have nothing else to give, God somehow brings you hope. For us, that hope came from a group of military men who were away from their own families while being trained at the PAVE PAWS site where Jake worked. As Jake got to know them, he mentioned our situation. Much to his surprise, they immediately volunteered to help. In three weeks' time, they transformed our "campsite" into a beautiful, livable home. Our house was finally ready for inspection. It passed with flying colors, all due to the unselfish giving of the soldiers that were stationed at Otis Air Force Base in Falmouth.

I had never experienced such kindness from strangers before. This experience changed my life forever. I was amazed how these acts of kindness opened a door for me to understand unconditional love.

Jake, the children and I were finally able to enjoy things we formerly had taken for granted. Electricity, running water, and other necessities needed to survive in the modern world. Now that our home was coming together, I had a renewed surge of energy!

* * *

One evening while Jake was working the night shift, I was busy finishing up some odds and ends in the kitchen. The time was about one a.m., when I heard a subtle sound that seemed to create a swirling motion in the air. And there, in the center of the energy, appeared a figure of a little girl in the doorway of the foyer.

"Krysie? Krysie, is that you?" I asked out loud. I then closed my eyes for a brief moment and then opened them again, only to find the form of a little girl fading in and out of my vision. I knew then she was not Krysie.

The little girl in spirit was wearing a burlap-textured dress that was tattered and dirty. Her face was beautiful yet smudged with dirt. Her eyes were brown, and her dirty blonde hair was tangled and in disarray; I could hear her call out, "Mama, Mama," and then she disappeared.

I was stunned. With the little energy I had left, I quickly passed by the place where I saw the little girl spirit. My heart was beating fast as I ran upstairs to my bedroom. Scared, I jumped into bed fully clothed and pulled the covers over my head.

I awoke again at 4:30 a.m. "Oh, my God!" I remember saying out loud. I threw the covers off me, only to remember that I had fallen asleep with my clothes on. I jumped out of bed, ran around the house picking up clothes, and then ran downstairs to the laundry room in the basement, trying to forget what I had seen the night before. I was pushing desperately against these thoughts of the little girl in spirit, as if I was trying to hold back a dam of information from entering my mind.

As I entered the basement where the framed off laundry room was, images of the little girl, once again, started to enter my mind. This time I tried to think of other things but it didn't work. I dropped the clothes I was carrying and leaned against the washing machine for support. More images moved in and out of my consciousness. Then a scene became clear: a little girl around four to five years old was walking up a narrow path. She was crying out, "Mama, Mama!"

This vision disappeared when flashes, once again, moved through my mind of similar events that had already occurred in my life: the memory of the experience of seeing my grandfather in my grandmother's house, the precognition of the runaway car, the visitation from a spirit that reminded me of my grandmother, and now this, a little girl in spirit in our new home.

I could only hope that, if this was true, this little girl somehow would find her way to heaven, but for me it was a different story. I felt like I was losing my sense of reality. I had to force my mind to focus on something else . . . Oh yes, the laundry.

* * *

The rest of the summer was quite peaceful, and the beginning of the school year was fast approaching. I feared mentioning my experience to anyone. I finally concluded I must have been delusional from the long hours of working with little sleep. Every time my thoughts slipped back to that evening, I would command my mind to be redirected to other things. This was successful.

It was about a week away from the end of school vacation when we decided to visit our parents since it would be awhile before we could enjoy their company again. We had so much fun that weekend, and the children loved spending time with their grandparents and cousins. My mother and father pitched in to purchase the children's school supplies so they would have what they needed. New school clothes, shoes, notebooks, pens, and pencils filled our car as we drove back to our new home in Sandwich. We were all very happy.

The children were already asleep in the backseat of the car as we approached our house. I looked over at Jake as we pulled into our driveway and felt a sense of hesitation from him. He was eyeing our house in the dark as if he was trying to see something.

"Jake, are you okay?" I asked.

He hesitantly answered yes.

Then he said, "Shirl, I have something to tell you."

My breathing became shallow as I tried to stay as still as possible, trying to quiet the anxiety that began to crop up from inside of me.

"When I'm working in the house," he began pausing to clear his throat, "I feel like something is watching me."

My thoughts of the little girl spirit entered my mind.

I asked, "Do you have any idea what it is?"

"I believe it is a spirit. I can feel a presence, as if someone is looking over my shoulder when I am sitting at my desk. I even turned my head to see if you or one of the girls was there but there was no one." Perhaps it was our Catholic upbringing, but it was not unusual for both Jake and me to use the word, "spirit" as compared to "ghost" or "apparition".

This was a defining moment. I had to say something to him about what had happened to me only a few weeks prior.

"Do I say something or don't I?", I said to myself.

Flashes of my high school days came into my mind. Fun, laughter, then fear turning into confusion.

"No! Not again!", I thought. I tried with all my might to speak, but the words wouldn't come . . . then, I broke through.

I took a deep breath and replied, "Jake, I had an experience about a month ago when I was working in the kitchen one night." Jake then turned to me, more intently on listening to what I had to say.

"For a brief moment, I thought I saw a little girl and I thought I heard her call out for her mother." "Mama, Mama," she said." I went on and told Jake the rest of the story.

He reached over and took my hand. In the darkness, we sat in the car, for what seemed like eternity, while our children slept in the back seat untouched by it all.

The next morning, Jake and I didn't speak of this. We went about our daily routine as if nothing had happened, but I was left with a burning desire to understand this unusual experience. Something was happening here!

Chapter 2

Seek and You Shall Find

After the girls settled into their routine of school, new friends, and extracurricular activities, I decided to complete the courses I needed for my nursing degree. I enrolled in three courses at Cape Cod Community College, in Hyannis. Previously, I had been enrolled in a nursing program at St. Vincent School of Nursing in my hometown of Worcester, Massachusetts, but I left after the first semester, choosing to rethink my choice in career.

Usually, I liked getting the most difficult courses out of the way first, like chemistry and physics, but this time I wanted to enjoy my first semester back in school, so I chose to take English, Psychology and Biology II.

My classes were going well, I had great teachers, and I was making friends with other students. One day after a meeting with my guidance counselor, I noticed a flyer on a campus bulletin board announcing a six-week, non-credited course in psychic phenomena. The teacher was Pat McKenna, a local psychotherapist and medium.

I, hesitantly, chose to attend. Even though I was hesitant, I chose to attend hoping this would help me understand what had happened to Jake and me. *This might be the beginning of understanding a whole new level of spirituality.* I thought.

I was born and raised Catholic and was baptized and married in the same Catholic Church. I've always had a great respect for other belief systems and I believe we all have a moral compass and that at the core of us we all know right from wrong.

So here I was, excited but nervous for the first class. Pat was a very warm and intelligent woman. Her knowledge was based on scientific research, and her degree in Psychology. The first class was quite informative about consciousness and the workings of the mind. At the end of the first class, Pat explained that in our next class we were going to examine our own psychic abilities. I was hesitant about this. *"Why would I need to know about my own psychic ability?"* I asked myself. All I want to do is understand the phenomena that happened in our lives.

Reluctantly I went to the second class. After Pat gave a twenty-minute lecture she began the psychic exercise. The premise was to be able to describe her house by only giving us the street address and town she lived in.

"Close your eyes and concentrate your thoughts on my house. Try to be as specific as possible," she said. "How many rooms are there; is it a ranch style home or a home with two floors, and how are these rooms furnished?" As we did this, we were to write down what we saw in our minds.

As I began focusing my thoughts on her home, I could feel my mind searching for the answers deep within myself. The energy around me began to change. I sensed I was somewhere different. I could no longer feel the presence of the other students in the room. I was also surprised to find that I couldn't even feel the chair beneath me. It was like my dream where I was floating in an eternal ocean of energy, except this time my compass was directed at Pat's home and my feelings, well . . .

I began to feel increasingly anxious. I understood my feelings to be the fuel for the direction of where my thoughts were taking me, but this time they were telling me something different. It was clear to me that that this was wrong for me to do. So I opened my eyes and wrote down a stream of random thoughts, just to get through the exercise.

While I waited for the exercise to be over, my mind flashed back to a class retreat I had taken in high school, where we broke up into groups for an exercise in personal growth. We were told to share our feelings about what we liked about each other. A few weeks later, my girlfriends and I decided to repeat this exercise on our own. But instead of sharing what we liked about one another, we agreed to tell what we didn't like and how we could help each other become better friends.

When my turn came, I suddenly found myself sharing facts about my friends I didn't realize I knew. The words began spilling from my mouth. I said that one friend was taking drugs and another friend was cheating on her boyfriend. Boy, this didn't go over very well, to say the least! Immediately, an argument started over who had broken a confidence. The fact was, nobody had. I said I didn't know how I came across the information. I just knew it. None of them accepted this. As close friends would have it, we eventually forgot about this experience as we began to make plans for our summer vacation.

My focus shifted back to the classroom when Pat asked the class to share the visions we had written down. Since my paper was filled with random information, I kept my hand down.

At the end of the exercise, Pat described her house and its furnishings for us to see how close we had come to describing it. To my shock, I had instinctively described her home down to the last detail, except I had described it from the opposite direction. Everything she described on the left side of the house, I had written down was on the right and vice versa.

* * *

What I had experienced about myself was bewildering and a little frightening. But one thing I was sure of, I didn't want to develop any psychic abilities of my own. I knew then that I would never return to her class.

* * *

Our finances were becoming more challenging as Jake and I tried to finish our home the way it was supposed to have been completed by the builder. A second semester of school for me was out of the question. I had to focus on getting a job that would benefit our family, and hopefully, I would find one in the health field.

Around the corner from the Catholic Church we attended was a new office that had just opened. "Dr. Ben Siding," the sign read "Chiropractor." *Because he was new in town, Dr. Siding might be looking for help,* I thought. So I decided to see if there was any chance of being hired as his assistant.

This was important. I had to be prepared to walk into his office and present myself the best way I knew how. My wardrobe for the past year had been mostly cut-off jeans, men's V-neck T-shirts, and most importantly, a pair of red sneakers. How I loved those sneakers. They had saved me more than once from falling off ladders or stubbing my feet on wooden planks and builder's tools that had been scattered around our house.

I had lost so much weight that my good clothes just hung off me. I decided that it was time to shop. I ended up buying a pair of beige dress pants and a purple blouse. There was something about putting these clothes on that made a world of difference to me. They were not too dressy and not too casual. And even though they were bought from a lower end store, they fit me better than anything that I had ever worn before.

Dr. Siding was standing at the front desk when I walked into his office. He was a tall, handsome man who looked to be a couple of years younger than Jake and me. The diplomas hanging on the waiting room wall indicated he had just graduated from chiropractic school.

I walked up to him, held out my hand, and introduced myself, saying, "Hi, Dr. Siding, I'm Shirley Beauman." We shook hands, and I added, "I was wondering if you have any positions open for an assistant or receptionist."

"Well, not right at this moment," he said. "I'm able to handle the incoming calls and tend to my patients at this point."

I hesitated for a moment almost turning around to leave when a thought came to me. "What will it take for you to give me a job, even if it's part time, to show you how I can help your business grow?"

After pausing for a few moments, he asked, "What will you do to accomplish this?"

I asked him how many patients he was booking weekly. He handed me his schedule, and I noticed that his appointment book was sparse.

"How many appointments would you like to book weekly?" I asked.

He responded, "About one hundred and twenty."

"It looks to me from what I'm seeing here that you would have to triple the amount of appointments in order to make that number."

"Yes, I would!" he exclaimed.

I explained to him that word of mouth was the best way to sell his services. If he would take me on as a patient while I worked for him, I could personally tell others about the benefits of his treatments.

He looked at me, surprised, and said, "You're hired. But I'll have to see how well you do on a part-time basis before hiring you full time."

I agreed and I was thrilled. I couldn't wait to get home and share this great news with Jake. Not only would I be getting a weekly paycheck, but also I would learn about holistic health and chiropractic care.

Since I found a job, our finances were back on track again. Jake and I felt more relaxed and decided it was time for all of us to participate in community activities. Jake and the children auditioned for one of the yearly community plays and were given main roles.

For my participation, I came across an ad, seeking people to teach adult evening courses at our town's high school. These were non-credited classes opened to the public to teach. My nutritional classes from nursing school and my interests in natural foods gave me the expertise I needed to apply.

Jake and I had joined a whole foods cooperative and the girls put on a brave face and did their best to adapt their taste buds to the new organic meals I was serving. It was great to learn the benefits of healthy foods. Unbeknownst to me, in order to persuade the girls to at least try our new way of eating, Jake made a deal with the girls that if they did their best to eat healthier, he would take them out on weekends to their favorite ice cream stand.

Finally my proposal to teach the natural foods class was accepted; I was excited about the prospect of teaching what I loved and meeting with other like-minded people. The classes went well, with everyone participating and sharing recipes.

On the last evening of the course, three women approached me with a question, a question I found to be quite unusual.

"Shirley, how do you know so much about us?" One of the women asked. I thought to myself, *they must mean how do I know so much about natural foods and healthy eating.* So I began to tell them about my interests in health, when one of the women quickly interrupted me and said, "No. That's not what we mean."

Then she asked, "How do you know so much about our personal lives when we haven't shared details about them with you? Like when you said to our class, "When your children are picky about vegetables and your son won't eat corn or can't stand the taste of milk, they may be trying to tell you that they have a food allergy."

I looked back at her in astonishment.

"Well," she went on, "you were looking right at me, and what you said is exactly what my son does, except I never thought he might be allergic to these foods!"

"Oh, I was just giving an example," I said.

Another woman chimed in and said, "Well, what about the time when you directly said to me that my little girl might be having a difficult time falling to sleep because she may need more calcium for her nervous system? I never said anything to you about her sleeping problem."

I was confused and I began to feel dizzy. I couldn't think of what to say. The third woman, Joanie Wisher, sensed I needed help, so she glanced at the other women and they quickly changed the subject and thanked me for giving the course. Joanie asked if she could meet with me later to continue the discussion. I agreed and even looked forward to meeting with her.

* * *

Joanie and I met the following week at my house. We sat at the kitchen table, drinking tea and talking about food and health. She knew so much about nutrition by just investigating information on her own. Joanie also had a deep interest in paranormal phenomena, which went back to experiences she had in her childhood.

"Shirley, do you understand what's meant by the term 'psychic'?" she asked.

"Yes, somewhat," I responded hesitantly. Truthfully, I didn't know all that much, since I had dropped out of Pat McKenna's course after only two classes.

"Well, I believe you have advanced psychic abilities," Joanie said.

At this point, something took over from inside of me. It was something very familiar to me, a self-defense mechanism that kicked in whenever I felt I was being threatened.

"No, I don't believe I do," I said, all along knowing that I was trying to avoid the question for fear she might find out something that I was unwilling to share.

She opened her purse and took out a book.

"I brought you this book," she said. "I believe it will help you understand what I'm talking about and why after class we asked you those questions."

She handed me, *The Sleeping Prophet*, by Jess Stearn. Joanie said it was about a healer named Edgar Cayce, an extraordinary psychic who lived in the early twentieth century. He was renowned for his ability to diagnose ailments with astonishing precision despite his lack of formal medical training; he could give underlying reasons for an illness along with information that might help to cure it. The book described Cayce's journey: his discovery of his incredible talent, his initial misgivings about it, and then his acceptance of it as a way to help others.

As Joanie was leaving, I thanked her for the gift, but I have to admit, I felt a sense of relief when she walked out the door. Yet, little did I know how much I would need her guidance within a short period of time.

* * *

Jake had not yet returned home from the night shift when I was suddenly awakened by a scream, in fact, two screams simultaneously coming from the room of my two youngest daughters. Krysie and Laurie had both awakened at the same time from a nightmare. As they both were trying to tell me about their dreams, I realized they each had a similar experience.

They dreamt they were playing in the basement of our home when suddenly a little girl appeared to them. The three of them started playing together when quite suddenly something startled them. The little girl ran away, and both my daughters woke up screaming.

The fact that they had shared this dream, at the center of which I believed was the same little girl's spirit I had seen in the foyer, truly disturbed me. I started to add everything up. First, the appearance I saw of the little girl in spirit; then Jake's feeling that someone was watching him at his desk; and, now my girls having the same dream and waking from it at the same time. Since I had no idea how to deal with this situation, I needed the perspective of someone else, someone who might have the answers. I called Joanie.

"I know someone," she said. "She is the reverend of the Plymouth Spiritualist Church where I attend. I know she would be able to help you and your family. Her name is Reverend Irene Harding."

I was concerned about my girls and knowing that a minister of a church could help us eased my fear, so I reached out and called her. Because I wasn't interested in learning about my own psychic abilities I believed this woman could explain to us why these paranormal experiences were happening without involving any connection to us.

When I first met Reverend Harding, I thought I had met an angel. Her eyes were light blue and clear. Her blonde hair was radiant, and her skin was translucent. As she entered through the back door of our house, she pointed to the basement door, asked where the door led to, then began to descend the basement steps, closing the door behind her.

When she returned she took a seat at our kitchen table and gestured for both Jake and me to sit down. She then took a deep breath and said,

"The little girl's name is Amelia. She is about four years old. She has brown eyes and dirty blonde hair, and she is searching for her mother."

Reverend Harding went on to explain that Amelia hadn't crossed over to the next level of consciousness. She remained close to the earth.

"I believe this happened in or around the mid-1800s," she said.

"But what about all the years between her death and now?" I asked.

"In the spiritual realm, there is no sense of time," she explained. "All she understands is she's looking for her mother who, I believe, walked up this hill many years ago to where your home stands now."

"Why doesn't her guardian angel help her?" I asked.

"Spirits, like people, only see what they want to see," she said. "Her guardian angel is around her, but Amelia may not be able to see or hear those from the angelic kingdom. Her reality is in the search for her mother, who she believes is still here."

Jake asked, "What can we do about this? Can you help us with this little spirit?"

"Yes, I can," Reverend Harding, responded. "But Amelia is drawn to your wife."

She looked directly at me and said, "Shirley, you can help her."

"Me?" I said, shocked. "I don't know what to do. Trust me, I can't help her."

Reverend Harding responded matter-of-factly, "Yes you can, and I believe you will, in time."

She proceeded to walk through the rest of our home, blessing every room with sage and holy water. This was comforting to me, as I knew the importance of a blessing such as this. During the traditional Catholic Mass, the priest will bless the altar with incense and holy water. Even my mother would bless our home every year on New Year's Eve to signify that Jesus Christ was the first and most important guest in our home, to forever be with us, guide us, protect us, and bring us health and prosperity.

During the next few days, Jake and I were very quiet. It was as if our home had been turned into a spiritual sanctuary. Here within the fabric of our lives was a child in spirit, searching for her way back home.

My thoughts then turned to what I had been taught in catechism; that there are souls in purgatory and it is just as important to pray for the dead as it is for the living. Could this be what purgatory is, a spiritual place that is part of heaven but not the level of heaven, where peace and tranquility exist?

Without telling Jake, I decided to go down to Sandwich City Hall and search the records for a child by the name of Amelia who died in the mid-1800s. I was surprised to find that records went back that far in their archives. There to my surprise was a child born in 1860 who had died of scarlet fever at the age of six. Her name was Amelia Atkins. Reverend Harding was right.

The fact that I was able to find the evidence that this child existed helped to open my mind that there are different levels of consciousness living in and around us. Whether we give it a name such as purgatory, a level in between the life we know and heaven as I was taught, the truth is Amelia exists and I wanted to help her. So I walked around the house with a constant prayer for little lost Amelia, until one morning I felt compelled to go downstairs into the basement.

As I sat on a basement step, looking into the heaviness of its air, I started to hear a humming sound. My body began to vibrate subtly and the basement air began to lighten. In the middle of the light, Amelia appeared, surrounded by subtle points of brilliant light and transparent forms, which I believed to be angels. *What a beautiful sight!* I thought. And as the darkness of the basement returned, Amelia, and the angels disappeared. She had crossed over into the light.

* * *

Our first winter in our new home was filled with new beginnings. The play that Jake and the children were in was a big hit with the community and our family from Worcester came to Sandwich to see it. The holidays were the best ever with us hosting Thanksgiving and celebrating Christmas at my parents home. We had made it into a new year with no more strange occurrences. From what I could tell, Krysie and Laurie seemed to have no lingering effects from their dream that brought our attention, once again, to little Amelia.

During that winter our children spent much of their time at Sandwich library. In the spring, our oldest daughter, Melyssa, entered a contest called "The Best Sandwich Contest in the Town of Sandwich." All the children's sandwich recipes were creative and theme provoking. Besides her creative talent with pineapple, cottage cheese, lettuce, tomato and Syrian bread, she added to the ingredients label: "The best part about making a sandwich is when you share it with a friend." She won!

Our children, like most parents believe their children to be, exceptional. Melyssa, our first born, was a highly intellectual and caring child. She would take on complex projects that required skills and wisdom beyond her years. As for her caring side, injured animals and young children always found their way to her. She always wanted to find a solution to help others. By being still and objective she always came up with logical solutions.

Krysie, our second born, was a child of great heart. Everybody loved her. She had the gift of acting like a clown and loved to make everyone laugh. She made friends easily and was sensitive to the feelings of others. She loved to play with her friends in the neighborhood and had incredible sensitivities and instincts. She was the peacemaker in our family. Childhood allergies seemed to be her greatest challenge, so we kept a close watch on what she ate and her reaction to different foods to ensure that she stayed healthy.

Laurie was a child filled with determination and courage. No matter what, she was determined to do everything her older sisters did. That meant she would run a little faster, hit the tennis ball a little harder and challenge herself to take on activities that may be too advanced for her age but she always achieved her goals. She was sensitive to such a degree that she would know what was happening in someone's life before they even told her.

* * *

Cape Cod had so many exciting things to do, and I was looking forward to summer. The children had already signed up for nature walks and we planned to go to the annual rodeo when it came to town. Every summer, the 4-H club sponsored one of the biggest events with awards for livestock, carpentry, crafts, and food. I could feel the excitement building!

One of the best things about living on Cape Cod was that friends and family always wanted to visit. That summer, my brother Billy, his children, and his girlfriend, Rita, came for a visit. My brother was a fun loving guy, always joking with the children and making sure everyone in our family was doing well. Our conversations ran the gamut from how our children were doing to the successful growth of his business, what new ventures he was involved in and of course how his golf game was going.

This would be our first time in meeting Billy's girlfriend. Rita was a warm, caring person who lit up a room when she walked into it. She was a successful businesswoman and had the ability to make others feel comfortable in her presence. This visit turned out to be very unusual for both Rita and me.

While the children played outside, Rita and I sat at the kitchen table talking when I found myself staring at one of her wrists.

I looked up at her and asked, "What's wrong with your wrist?"

She looked at me and calmly replied, "How do you know there's something wrong with my wrist?"

"Oh, my brother told me about it," I answered.

Rita looked at me, quite surprised, and said, "Shirley, your brother couldn't have told you because I haven't told him about my wrist yet."

I had no idea what to do next. I truly believed my brother must have told me so I blurted out, "He must have told me or how else would I have none?"

The way she reacted surprised me. She was listening intently to what I said then . . . there was a pause that seemed to last forever. My hands started to tingle and I had an urge to hold her wrist.

She went on and explained that she was having trouble rotating her wrist. A couple of years earlier, she had suffered a compound fracture. Even after extensive physical therapy, she had limited wrist movement. She had just recently spoken to a surgeon, who told her that one of the joints in her wrist would have to be removed in order for her to regain her mobility. She then must have sensed my confusion.

"What is it Shirley?" she asked.

"I don't know why, but I want to hold your wrist," I said.

"Okay," she replied. Rita then extended her hand outwardly so I could touch her more easily.

An intense struggle began between my thoughts and what my instincts were telling me to do. I finally let go and my instincts took over. I began to calm down and a gentle energy began to flow from my hands. I don't know how long this lasted but as soon as the sensations in my hands stopped I knew it was complete. For a moment, we sat quietly, not saying a word to one another.

Then Rita smiled and asked, "Are you feeling better?"

I nodded yes.

*   *   *

We decided to take a drive to Hyannis to go shopping with the children while Bill and Jake opted to stay home. I had no problem putting out of my mind what had just happened. In fact, I was really good at this. I had worked all winter at controlling my thoughts so I could forget what happened with the little girl spirit and the events that followed. One little slip wasn't going to ruin my day.

When we arrived in Hyannis, both Billy's children and mine decided they wanted to venture in different stores than one another so we split up and planned to meet back at the car when we were done. My children and I were first to return to the car. From a distance, I could see Rita and Billy's children walking toward us. She had a surprised look on her face.

"What?" I asked, with a sense of curiosity in my voice.

She took my hands firmly in hers and said, "Shirley, my wrist! I can move my wrist!"

On the drive home, Rita talked excitedly about a man named Napoleon Hill, who had written several books on the power of our minds, and our personal ability to create success. I nervously told her about what had happened during the natural foods class.

After this experience with Rita, I knew I needed to educate myself on these concepts. I decided to begin by purchasing Napoleon Hill's book, *Think and Grow Rich.*

* * *

The next week I called on my new friend Joanie and told her about the healing experience with Rita. "Can you explain what happened?" I asked.

"Well," she said with a slight laugh, "in our church we call this, 'Laying on of hands.' This is considered to be one of the gifts of spirit, and every Sunday in the beginning of the service, lay people in the church stand and place their hands on the shoulders of others for healing. Why don't you come to one of the services at my church?"

I had never heard of "laying on of hands," and I was not ready to take the next step out of my comfort zone to go to a service in another church. However, I was curious to find out what the two books I had in my possession could teach me about, psychic energy and the power of our minds. So in between working, caring for the children, and household chores, I read the books, *The Sleeping Prophet* and *Think and Grow Rich.*

Edgar Cayce was a Christian who became known for his ability as a psychic to channel answers to questions while in a sleep state or as we know this now as an altered state of consciousness. He read the Bible daily and realized through self-observation that his extrasensory perception worked best when he kept close to his belief in the traditional Christian faith.

On the other hand, Napoleon Hill was an American author who was one of the first experts in the field of personal success; he lectured on the power of the mind. Hill interviewed over five hundred successful Americans in his time to discover the characteristics and behaviors that helped to create their success. He later wrote books on this subject, selling millions of them globally.

I was absolutely astonished by the ideas these books were advocating. Were such mental abilities real? Can people actually have capabilities beyond what we are taught to believe? After I absorbed the information from both books, one particular story often came to mind about Edgar Cayce about a woman who had been suffering from Scleroderma. I started thinking about Cyndy Niblett, a young woman whom after taking my natural food's class asked me if I would coach her on changing her diet for health reasons. She had Scleroderma, as well.

Then I asked myself, "*Could I, Shirley Beauman, an ordinary housewife with three children, a woman people may think, to put it nicely, a little bit odd if I told anyone about my experiences, could I actually help Cyndy with more than just her diet?*"

What a dilemma this was for me. I had no clue how to help myself, let alone someone else. Do I actually believe what I read?

I had a great fear that "psychic phenomena" was an area I dare not get involved in. I was struggling with the same concerns that Edgar Cayce had, that my traditional Catholic religion would frown upon my unorthodox approach to healing, never mind the other unusual events I had experienced.

"Boy, I better not think about this anymore." I said out loud. I had learned that every time I would give deep thought to an issue something would occur that was unexpected in my life.

As soon as I said this, I heard a voice reply, "Belief."

"What did you say?" I asked.

"Belief," the voice repeated.

I thought for a moment. Then a surge of emotion welled up from within me. I then said out loud, "Belief? I'll tell you what my belief is! I will lose my family and friends, ruin my marriage, be looked upon as mentally unstable, and that's just the beginning!"

I was in a high emotional state, but as soon as I shouted out my fears, a feeling of calmness came over me.

Then, I heard the voice again say, "Belief."

I searched my mind for a logical thought. Once again, a feeling deep inside me arose and I shouted out, "How can a person like me even fathom this idea of being powerful enough to heal and become successful. I am not buying into this!"

At this point, I was exhausted from all my emotional turmoil when I heard the voice again say, "Belief."

Visions from when I was a child began to fill my mind. I remembered sitting in the front row in church as a child. I remembered looking with awe at the light shining through a specific stain-glass window that encased a picture of an angel.

Then it hit me: *I believed what I heard at Mass*, I thought. I believed what he said. Jesus, I mean. Jesus said that we would do these things and more. Well, that's how I remembered it, anyhow.

What he actually said from the King James Bible is: "Verily, verily, I say unto you, he that believeth in me, the works that I do shall he do also; and greater than these shall he do; because I go unto my Father" (John 14:12).

"Oh, my God!" I said, surprised. "I actually bought into what he said!"

My heart started racing and I could feel myself wanting to block this out of my mind, but instead I paused, then shouted out loud, "Okay God, what do I do now???"

Chapter 3

Dare to Love

I began to think of the possibility of Cyndy being healthier. As soon as I thought this way, fear began to emerge. It was as if I had turned on a switch and my mind began to think of negative scenarios of what might happen if I chose to help her like I did with Rita. I struggled with this for days.

Then I decided to think of the potential for Cyndy to be healed and what that would be like for her. Again, as quickly as I had those thoughts, I was back thinking of my own fears. This was annoying this yo-yo feeling as if I couldn't make up my mind. So I willed myself to think of her as totally well, seeing in my mind a happy Cyndy with the full ability to accomplish anything she wanted, and, ironically, from choosing these consistent thoughts, my fearful thoughts began to diminish.

Cyndy was a petite lady with beautiful dark hair and a smile as radiant as the sun. In addition to progressive Systemic Scleroderma, she had Raynaud's disease. Though Cyndy eagerly wanted to become a mother, her doctor told her that she would never conceive because of the prognosis of her debilitating disease. Cyndy and her husband had tried for thirteen years to conceive a child, so you can imagine how devastating this news must have been.

Systemic Scleroderma is a disease that has no medical cure. It causes the connective tissue, layers of skin, blood vessels, and internal organs, to harden and tighten, eventually damaging these organs. In Cyndy's case, she had developed ulcers on her fingertips and elbows; her feet would consistently swell, and unbeknownst to me, she had developed knotted scar tissue across her chest, which made it difficult for her to breathe. Cyndy became depressed as the use of her hands gradually deteriorated. This is why she chose to take my nutrition class in the hope that a change in her diet might help her condition

After the natural foods class was over, I counseled Cyndy a couple of times to help her put together a diet that would alleviate some of her breathing discomfort. She began eating mostly raw foods with a small amount of fish, chicken, dairy and whole grain products. Almost immediately she found that she had more energy, and the swelling in her feet disappeared.

One day, it just happened. I was thinking about Cyndy and a calm feeling came over me. I decided to take a big step forward and dare to love. I picked up the phone and called her.

"Hello," Cyndy said as she answered the phone.

"Hi, Cyndy, this is Shirley Beauman," I said, with a nervous voice. After discussing how she was progressing with the changes in her diet, I began to relax, and it then became easier for me to tell her why I was calling.

"Would you be open to meeting with me to see if there is another way I can help you with your healing?" I asked.

"But how?" she replied.

"By working with spiritual energy," I said.

Not at all put off by the suggestion, Cyndy agreed to come to my home for one session.

The first initial healing session with Cyndy was awkward for me. I felt like I had a healing capacity but did not have the knowledge on how to implement it so we sat in my living room for some time without my knowing what to do. I had requested this meeting, whereas with Rita, the urge to place my hands on her wrist was spontaneous. But both Cyndy and I were willing to try.

This is what she wrote about her first healing experience: 4/26 *"What I remember about this first channeling session was that I became warm very quickly, but this was not new for me, as I had previously warmed up quickly and stayed warm during nutrition counseling, when the temperature of her house was about 65 degrees. This is extremely unusual for me, as I need a temperature of 75 degrees to be completely comfortable due to the Raynaud's Syndrome.*

Before her second session I decided to change rooms where we would meet and decided to use our dining room instead of our living room. It was the dining room that I enjoyed the most when we had finally finished building our home. I had made the drapes and the covers for the dining room chairs. Our best china was displayed in our glass hutch and I loved serving my family on the china pieces that came from a dear friend who was serving our country overseas. Many of the serving dishes were gifts from our family and friends, all of whom had no idea of what had transpired in our lives. There was so much love put into this room that I felt this is where we should meet for her healing.

As Cyndy sat in one of the dining room chairs, I pulled up a chair to sit in front of her, took her hands in mine, and silently prayed the Lord's Prayer.

Then, I paused and asked God to be with us, and again I began to feel my hands tingle.

I stood up and was compelled to place my left hand on Cyndy's left shoulder and move my right hand down her spine until I came to an area where I suddenly stopped. I paused and took a deep breath, held this breath, and then slowly released it. I found myself leaning in closer to her body, as if my hands wanted me to listen to something.

Then I asked silently, *"What am I supposed to be listening for?"*

A voice inside of me answered, "The Truth."

Out of the quiet came a very subtle sound, waves of energy seemed to be telling me a story, a story that was impossible to physically hear, yet some part of me knew exactly what these waves of energy were saying. Then it came to me that this communication was coming from a deeper level within her. I was being given permission to enter into another world. This world was beyond my physical senses. This was a world of vibrations and subtle sounds, and that's when Cyndy's inner world and mine began communicating.

I moved my hands across different parts of her body. My fingertips would tingle more intensely in some areas more than others. At times my hands would switch from warm to cool then back to warm again. I recognized I was breathing more deeply than usual, as if the energy from my fingers was connecting to a deeper level within my body. Sometimes, I would hold my breath, pause, and then let out the breath. When I did this, I could feel parts of her body, that were cool and constricted, begin to expand and warm up.

As this was happening, I would listen to my intuition and the inner cues it was giving me. Through my sense of touch, there seemed to be a subtle level of energy, more deeply within her, that felt fragmented, like that of a communication network that had been compromised. I could not see or feel this physically but I knew a connection to this system was being healed from a place deep within her. And I felt I was moving more deeply within myself as well.

After the second session, Cyndy and I were both amazed how her hands appeared. Her hands, which before this session looked like the hands on a mannequin, became visibly softer, and we began to notice her veins, which were not noticeable before. We both looked at each other in awe. After a long pause, I laughed, and said, "Maybe we should do this again."

She smiled and nodded yes. As soon as Cyndy and I said our good-byes, my feeling of joy turned into fear. A force of energy that came from deep inside of me traveled up into my chest, leaving me gasping for air. I was having an anxiety attack! Without thinking, I opened the front door of my home and forced myself to run as fast as I could down the street toward the woods. As I ran, I kept saying to myself, "*I have to get away from this. How do I get away from this?*" I ran into the thickness of the woods that surrounded our home and I finally collapsed on my knees and cried.

* * *

This is what Cyndy wrote about her second healing session: 4/29 *Blood veins/arteries became noticeable through the skin on back of hands. Skin was also a little softer in that area. Circulation and color of hands much better especially during channeling. Able to make a fist better with right hand, but left pointing and middle fingers have stiffened.*

* * *

During our third session I decided to pay close attention, so I could understand what had happened in the previous session. I remember trying to focus my thoughts exclusively on the healing of Cyndy's hands so that she could use them without the pain and limited mobility she had known for so long. But every time I focused on applying my hands to her in accordance with those thoughts, it was as though my hands refused to listen. They seemed to have a mind of their own. I realized that there was something greater than my mind guiding me where I needed to go. As I paid closer attention to where I was being guided, I realized it was to the areas where her energy was blocked located lower in her body.

I made sure, after this realization to pay close attention to shift from where I thought I should place my hands to where I was being guided intuitively to place my hands. And, I wanted to know where this guidance was coming from. Was it from outside of me? Was it from inside of me? How was this healing occurring? After a while, it made all the sense in the world to me. This ability to heal was coming from a source within me yet at the same time it was coming from Cyndy as well. This source had incredible wisdom and knowledge, and it allowed me to communicate to the knowledge and wisdom Cyndy's body held.

This session went as well as the previous session, and we both saw improvements right away.

Here are Cyndy's notes from her third session: "*Outline of bones appearing on back of hands. Skin wrinkling and becoming pliable. Neck range of motion improved, able to bend knees better.*" We were both very happy with the progress that was being made.

From paying attention to these first three sessions, I became aware that our body is made up of energy that holds information about our lives and how to heal. First, I always prepared for the healing session with the Lord's Prayer, and I would focus my thoughts and intentions on helping Cyndy to heal. Second, while praying, I would sit and hold her hands so I could consciously make a connection to Cyndy's body and the information it held. Third, I would listen to my intuition, which guided my hands to where I should place them. Fourth, when my hands began to hover over a certain area of her body, I would consciously engage in focusing on the energy emanating from that area. Fifth, I would listen to the humming sound that was coming from this emanation and what it was telling me. Sixth, I would then become more aware of the times when I sensed a constriction or a congested sensation in Cyndy's body; my breathing automatically changed as if it was assisting the energy flow in that specific area. Seventh, I would feel a release of the constriction, and a flow of energy would pulsate through to other parts of Cyndy's body. Then my hands would stop tingling.

In order for this to work, Cyndy had to become a conscious participant in her own healing. She would tell me what the feeling was like and what emotions she wanted to share, which varied depending upon where the focus of her energy was in her body. The thoughts, emotions, and sensations she had in her body played a vital role for her to understand herself and where her life force was suppressed or hindered. Cyndy would ask specific questions in order for her to know the next steps she needed to take in working with her new awareness.

Finally, I would give thanks to God for the healing that had occurred.

After the healing session was over, Cyndy and I would review every step taken and what she needed to do next in order to improve her health and life.

The joy I felt after each experience was tremendous. Not only was Cyndy's healing amazing to me, but I also realized that this was an energetic dance with three partners, Cyndy, an invisible source and me. The books that I had read about the power we possess were beginning to make sense.

After her fourth healing session was over, something unexpected happened. We found no outward signs or any indications of a physical change. I did not know what had happened. The last two times brought about wonderful changes right in front of our eyes. Yet this time no visible signs of healing had taken place . . . or so we thought.

However, late that same afternoon, I received a phone call from Cyndy. "Shirley, I hope I'm not bothering you," she said, "but I have something to tell you. When I was undressing this afternoon, my husband noticed that the knotted scar tissue that runs across my chest, well, it's totally gone!"

At first I didn't understand what she was saying. "What scar tissue?" I asked. Then she explained to me that the scleroderma had left a large ropelike scar across her chest to underneath her arms, and that scar tissue restricted her mobility and her ability to breathe properly.

This is what Cyndy wrote about her fourth healing session when we thought nothing had progressed:

> 5/1 *"Discovered scar tissue on sides from shoulder/ armpit area was gone. The "cord" I could feel was no longer there and the skin was a normal color as it had been darker in that area. Able to raise my arms higher though still tightness in that area".*

Cyndy and I continued our sessions together, eight in all. I have provided a copy of the original legal documentation of her healing in the appendix of this book. Here is the rest of what Cyndy had written on her physical transformations.

> 5/2 *Swollen, darkened area on back of hands close to and through wrist [is] smaller.*
> 5/3 *Face rash improving.*
> 5/4 *Skin on forearms very pliable and soft. Especially noted wrist area palm side on left arm.*

> *5/8 Face looks fuller. Skin between pointing finger and thumb [is] softening and also at bend of elbow.*
>
> *Elbows have completely healed except for a small scab on the right one. The skin in that area is more pliable.*
>
> *No more indigestion or reflux. [I am] able to sleep with only one pillow, although if I eat late, I will use two pillows.*

Extreme cramping and discomfort with menstrual cycle which necessitated the use of Motrin, probably 10 tablets over 2 [-] 3 days has gone to the point of slight discomfort for ½ a day and 1 Motrin tablet.

During channeling I always experience tingling in my hands, feet and face, especially lips due to the flow of energy. I also have experienced intense tingling sensation in the spine, stomach, intestines and rib area and have had pressure in my ears and a rapid heartbeat. Around mid May, I got to the point where my entire body has the tingling sensation during healing and I feel warm all over. This is due to all blockages being opened up and the energy is able to flow throughout my body.

One such block was a torn ligament in my right knee. I had pulled this last fall while exercising. I never told Shirley about this but she picked up on it psychically. She has worked on this area greatly and I think it is healing. I still experience pain in this area if I sit for a long time or if the weather is cold and damp. This fear limited some exercises I used to do, but I am gradually starting to improve in that area.

Finally, she concluded, *"Shirley has told me that in order for the healing energy to flow better I must deal with some emotional blocks due to low self-esteem. I must see that I am important. I must do what I feel is the right thing to do, not what I feel others will expect me to do. She is helping me to cope with a stressful job and mood changes which I have difficulty controlling. She has gotten me to think about what I want to do in the future and I am started in that direction with hopes to enroll in a nursing program [in the fall]. I feel 100 percent improved since last Fall and have God, Shirley, and myself to thank for this. Shirley is a wonderful, dedicated, self-sacrificing and courageous woman and I feel so fortunate to have met her."*

* * *

Cyndy's healing was remarkable to say the least; but what was most important to me was what we had both learned together. Cyndy understood that it wasn't just one specific area in her life that she had to change. She looked at every aspect of her life—diet, attitude, her thoughts, and her feelings—and chose to be aware of her actions every day.

This to me was the most important notation Cyndy wrote on June 17, about two months after our last healing session: *"I experienced my own healing energy and tingling in my hands, feet, and face. I should be able to do this if I can get myself in a quiet and relaxed state and think positive thoughts. I have been able to do this a few times since [our last session]."*

Cyndy had a debilitating disease yet walked away empowered to take charge of her own life.

June 14th was Cyndy's first checkup with the physician who was treating her for Scleroderma, since we began working together. She couldn't wait to show him how much she had improved. She told me later that he couldn't believe what he had seen.

"He listened as I explained what I had been doing and said he wanted to follow my case more closely." She said. "But when I told him that I had been working with you and that you would be open to meet with him, he became reluctant. I'm sorry Shirley, he told me that he would prefer to just document the physical changes."

Since I had attended nursing school and had worked on hospital floors with doctors, I knew that medical professionals were trained to follow proper procedures without deviation. So I had an understanding of why her physician declined her invitation to meet with me. Needless to say, not all physicians feel this way about alternative methods of healing. I would later meet a doctor who was totally open to my working with his patients.

But at this time, I began questioning the purpose in having a healing gift. Why would God place in me the ability to heal? Why would this gift be a blessing and a curse at the same time? Was this a big mistake?

Why would my prayers for others, tear at the very foundation of the reality I based my life on?

* * *

I hadn't seen Cyndy for a period of time when one day I received a phone call from her. "Shirley," she said hesitantly, "I know you don't like to answer questions that are of a psychic nature, but," Again she hesitated. "But do you think it's possible that I might be pregnant?"

I paused, took a deep breath then responded, "All I know is, whatever is happening to you, is a gift from God."

As I mentioned before, having children was one of Cyndy's great desires, perhaps even the greatest. But her doctor had said she would never be able to bear children because of her condition.

It turned out that she was indeed pregnant and seven months later she gave birth to a beautiful healthy child. Cyndy not only gave birth to one child but she was also able to conceive a second child who was also born healthy two years later.

Working as a partner in Cyndy's healing, my first inclination was to focus my thoughts on her hands and deformed fingers so she could utilize their full mobility to live more efficiently. But every time I would focus with this intent, my own hands would rebel and would move to other parts of her body, which I did not understand until her phone call telling me that she believed she was pregnant. I realized then how limited my expectations were for her, but God's expectations for her had clearly been so much greater in helping her realize that the power of healing was within her. By healing her body, she was able to give birth to two healthy children.

I had learned so much from being a part of Cyndy's healing; such as how we hold unresolved emotions and negative thoughts in our bodies that add to our susceptibility to illness; how we are the ones that must participate in our healing process and learn as much as possible about ourselves so our state of wellness can last a lifetime. It is vital that we participate in an empowered partnership where we both, as the patient or health provider, can work together, and honor each other's wisdom and intuition.

The most important realization for me was finding that there is a well of knowledge and wisdom within us. When I intently listened within myself, I was given insight to the place where I would find the answers I was searching for.

This was the beginning of my spiritual awakening that led to a spiritual practice. My daily practice included intentional prayer, listening to my inner senses and intuition, and making sure my logic was partnering with my new way of being. Logic was very important to me. It is the part of me that brings everything together to make sense.

Helping another brought great joy to me, and I became in awe of our potential as human beings. Something I had not planned for was happening in my life.

I knew I had to pay attention to these experiences and not dismiss the spiritual learning I was being given. My fears and concerns started to subside. I realized that being fully engaged in what I was doing had a positive impact on the negative obsessive thoughts that had plagued me for months. I realized I didn't have to work so hard on not having them because by focusing on the things that were important in my life, my fears had diminished. I also had a job I loved that paid me a good salary and I had time to take care of my children. I began to feel that my life was starting to come together. All my hard work was beginning to pay off.

I was always an early riser, waking up by four o'clock in the morning. I had decided that it was now time to set aside a time for prayer every day. If I prayed as soon as I woke up I still had time to finish household chores and make breakfast and help the girls get ready for school while waiting for Jake to come home from the night shift.

My prayers were the traditional prayers of my Christian faith and I soon began to add prayers for those who were sick and for those who had passed on, just like we did during Mass. I also began to add specific people in my prayers who I knew needed help. One day the thought of my mother came to mind. She had severe arthritis of the neck and was in constant pain because of it.

Since I was able to help others, then why couldn't I help those that were in my own family? I couldn't think of one person in the world that didn't have a family member or friend that didn't need help.

*   *   *

One morning during prayer time, a scent of roses filled the room. I could feel a presence that was familiar to me. It was my grandmother. "I know you're really here," I remember saying to her. I opened my eyes and saw my grandmother in a hue of bluish, white light. She seemed to be very far away, but I could make out that it was she in this light. Through thought alone, she began to tell me that my Aunt Mur had been hospitalized. She asked if I would go visit her. I told her I would, and with that, the vision of my grandmother disappeared, but the scent of roses lingered throughout the house. I called my mother, and without her knowing of my grandmother's visitation, she confirmed that my aunt was indeed in the hospital dealing with complications from the medications she took for her diabetes.

A couple of days later, on my day off from work, I drove to Worcester to visit my aunt. It was such a delight to see her again, despite the circumstance that led to her stay in the hospital. As we sat and talked about each other's lives, I began to feel my grandmother's presence around us. "Aunt Mur, would you be open to my placing my hands on you in hopes of a healing?" I asked.

To my surprise, she was delighted. As I laid my hands on her she told me how my grandmother healed the warts on the hands of the children in the neighborhood by making the sign of the cross with a common pin over their watts then burying the common pin in the ground. She also explained how debilitating it was to have warts on your hands, because they were painful and difficult to get rid of.

After our visit was over, I decided to stop by my parents' house to see if they were home. My mother was home alone and I had the opportunity to share with her my visit with my Aunt Mur whom was her sister. I didn't dare mention about my "Laying on of Hands" or our conversation about my grandmother's healing abilities.

Right before I left, I heard a voice from within me say, "Take your hand and place it on your mother's neck." My hands began to tingle. As I began to ask her if I could place my hands on her neck to help her pain, she suddenly shouted, "Shirley, you gave me a shock. That hurt!" My hands never even touched her. I was seated about two feet away from where she was sitting. I burst into tears.

"I'm so sorry, Mom!" I exclaimed. "I didn't mean to hurt you. I was only going to see if I could help relieve your neck pain."

"You can't," she stated. "Nothing has helped to get rid of this pain."

Later that month during one of our phone conversations, I asked how she was doing. She told me that her neck pain was gone. Not once was anything mentioned about the day she felt an unexplained electric shock from my presence.

I was delighted that my mother's pain was relieved. I truly believed that even though I hadn't touched my mother physically, the spark that she felt healed her. From this, I realized that the healing energy from within us surrounds us as well. That is when I began to discover books explaining energy fields that emanate from all living systems, sometimes referred to as auras. I believed this energy to be a living communications system that extends beyond our physical bodies. Just by my mother and I being in each other's energy space, a healing had occurred. If this is possible, then how might we affect each other on a daily basis just by being in the presence of one another?

Years later, only months before my mother passed away, while sitting together in her home, she asked me a question, "Shirley, do you remember that time you put your hands near my neck and healed me?"

Surprised, I turned to her and said, "Yes...I do."

She paused for a while then looked at me and asked, "Why me?"

I replied, "Because God loves you."

Then she asked, "Why you?"

And with a smile, I said, "Why not?"

Chapter 4

Awakenings

I soon began to build more confidence in helping others. One day, I received a call from Melanie, a young woman who was distraught over her career. The outcome from our session surprised me.

Melanie had recently graduated from college with a degree in elementary education and had been hired to teach fourth grade. But something unusual happened. Teaching, which she totally loved, began to turn into a nightmare. Instead of feeling confident and excited about her new career, she began to have episodes of anxiety.

My first logical thought was she was having this anxiety because it was her first time teaching students. But that wasn't the case.

We sat in my living room to discuss her anxiety. I explained to her that I was going to take a couple of minutes to quiet my mind. As I did, a vision came to me. I saw a little girl who loved to dance and sing. As a child, she would fantasize that she was a famous singer. When I shared this vision, Melanie said that she could relate to this story. When she was a child, she would make believe that she was standing in front of an audience singing. "Everyone loved to hear me sing." She said.

Then another vision came to my mind from another time in history: a young woman with red hair, wearing beautiful clothes who could sing like an angel. In this scene, stood a man, who I believed to be her father. He was well-known in his community, but, he did not like that his wife was a music teacher and had a beautiful singing voice. It seemed to anger him that she was given great accolades when she would sing at church and for community charity events.

When I finished telling her of my vision, Melanie gasped. "That reminds me of my father!" she exclaimed. "My father never wanted me to sing. In fact, when I wanted to take singing lessons as a child, he wouldn't hear of it."

"But, Melanie you don't need singing lessons," I told her. "You have a natural singing ability. This is a gift from your soul."

Melanie went on to explain how she loved children and that she wanted to teach them, but that her true love was singing. She couldn't understand why every time she began to sing, she found herself feeling reluctant and even shy.

"I've been asked to sing in a small quartet," she went on, "but I don't know if I can do this."

I then shared with Melanie flashes of another vision. It was of the same man yelling at this young woman until one day, her spirit became so suppressed by his power that she gave up singing and began teaching in the town's school.

"I don't know what to do with this." Melanie stated.

I went on to explain that her love for teaching children was still deeply a part of her, and as soon as she recognized the truth of how she was subconsciously suppressing her love for singing, her life would come together.

Could this have possibly been a past life memory I had tapped into? If so, were they held within this field of energy that comes from and emanates through and around us? Well, I had no factual evidence that proved this to be true. I did know, from reading about Edgar Cayce, that during many of his psychic readings, he would bring up past life events of his clients to help them understand their present life conditions. Because this was one of my first experiences with this, I had to trust that it helped Melanie, but I had no way of knowing whether or not it did.

While writing this book, more of my own past experiences began to surface. Max was the name of the boy I was dating at the time. We had so much fun together and loved many of the same things in life. One evening we went to the movies and saw a film from a historical event. We enjoyed the movie so much so, we saw it twice. I remember how much I loved the theme of the movie and, at times, when I looked at Max , I would see a different face overlaying his own.

During this same time, while I attended my history class, I would have similar challenges, Flashes of images that quickly moved through my mind caused such anxiety that I would have to leave the class just to catch my breath. Several months later, I stopped dating Max yet, the visions didn't stop.. A door had been opened within me, to where, I did not comprehend.

Because of my work with clients and their spiritual experiences, this gave me pause to think that what I had experienced may have been fragments of another time, a different lifetime. Our ability to understand experiences like these are understood more now because of the vast scientific research regarding past lives and the unique way we experience spirituality. Is it possible that we have been here before and the people in our lives, might we have been with them in other times?

* * *

Since then, because of my experiences with others, I have come to understand that in the matrix of our energy, we contain the wisdom that will assist us in becoming whole. Within this field of energy, memories from past lives are left as imprints to assist us in understanding soul consciousness. We are multidimensional beings.

* * *

Soon after, a man came to me with a condition that the medical profession could not resolve. He was a creative artist in music and dance. At the top of his career, he suddenly became afflicted with a severe limp in his right leg. This disabled him so severely that he could not teach dance, which limited him both professionally and financially.

As he began to explain this, I saw in front of me a young boy who was playing ball with another boy on a lawn in front of a house. His friend threw the ball to him, and when I described the scene to this man, he said, "To catch the ball, I had to back up into the street, where an oncoming car hit me." I then asked him what happened after the car struck him. He said, "My leg was injured in two places."

I then asked, "What was going on for you during that time in your life?"

He answered, "I was at the top of my class in sports as well as dance. After the accident, I lost my opportunity to pursue a career in sports. My rehabilitation took a long time, but brought me to a place of accomplishment by my being able to heal my leg through rigorous discipline and strength training. I became a successful dance instructor."

"Do you understand why the trauma from your past surfaced in your life at this time again?" I asked.

He took a moment to think and then responded, "Yes, I was fearful then and now that I'm getting older, I'm fearful again that I won't be able to stay at the top of my career."

I asked if he was open to a mind technique that would alter the way he was thinking about his situation using positive thoughts. He responded, "Yes." We worked for the rest of his session on his ability to see his leg completely healed. When a negative thought came up in his mind we talked through it to understand the thought and then transform it. By the end of the session, this man got up from the chair and walked out of my house, with no limp in his right leg.

* * *

I began to understand that the information I received while assisting my clients to heal came to me in many different ways. When my world and theirs came together, and I was in a clear, focused state of mind, the information would come to me. I used all of my senses and an aspect of myself I did not understand as of yet. These perceptions came to me as flashes of insights through my thoughts, sometimes seeing pictures, while at other times I saw sentences, as if I were reading a book. Most importantly was the understanding that the truth lies within each and every one of us.

This information was not related to me, yet it all came together as if I were watching a movie that was imprinted in their energy field. It was evident to me, after I would share these insights with my clients, how the information I gave helped to shift their perceptions and beliefs to a positive state of mind. Many would tell me that they felt a renewed sense of freedom from the burden they had been carrying for many years.

* * *

Integration of body, mind, and spirit became the foundation of my work. I began to understand that how we perceive our experiences and what emotions we suppress in our subconscious plays a vital role in how we deal with the challenges in our lives.

It was now time for me to find others like myself who were on the path of spiritual enlightenment. This led me to a bookstore that I had heard of at the Unity Church in Hyannis. There I found a treasure of information on new age and holistic healing. This was not as difficult as I thought. As soon as I gave myself permission to seek out what I was looking for, my instinctual compass directed me to find it.

At the Unity Church, I learned about a woman who lectured on an approach to healing through laughter and positive psychology. She lived a couple of towns west of Cape Cod, and when I called her and told her of my ability to assist others in healing, she invited me to a lecture she was giving to a national organization for nurses. There, she spoke of the healing ability of laughter. The audience loved her presentation.

At the lunch break, a physician who played in a musical quartet played for all of us. As I was sitting and talking to others a woman began to sing. I looked up from eating and to my surprise, there was Melanie singing solo. Now something in the air was definitely changing . . .or was it me?

These experiences came and went, and I began to realize that, in order for me to be happy and fulfilled, I needed to incorporate new ideas and concepts into my life. The knowledge that others shared through lectures and books sometimes fit and sometimes didn't, but I do know one thing, when I didn't trust my own intuition, I was in trouble.

* * *

Everything in my life felt like it was coming together more smoothly. The children were busy in school. We were excited about our plans for having their grandparents, aunts, uncles and cousins visit during the summer. Jake had a new love, solar energy that kept him active in the prospect of a lucrative business in natural resources. My family seemed to have a new comfort level with my job and my interest in healing. So seeing strangers come and go from our home became a normal event for them.

Meagan had heard about my ability from a friend who knew of Cyndy's life transformation. Meagan was in her early 30's with two small children, a good husband, and a life that she truly cherished. I had also come to find out that she had a heart of gold. Meagan was diagnosed with cancer, and even though she was following the doctors' advice to have chemotherapy treatments, she still thought it would be a good idea to meet with me.

During our first visit, Meagan shared the deep sadness she felt every day of her life. "No matter what I accomplish and feel good about," she said, "there is always something that comes along and destroys the good feelings I have about myself and all I have accomplished."

I sensed whatever this was that had a hold on Meagan, literally took her breath away.

I shared with her knowledge about the body's natural wisdom to heal and how our bodies hold onto unresolved emotional issues. This in turn may block the natural flow of energy that keeps us healthy and vibrant.

"So Meagan," I said, "if you allow me to, I would like to place my hands on you to see how I can assist you in your healing."

Meagan agreed. As I began to center myself I could immediately feel a resistance coming from her. It was as if she had an impermeable wall that she held close to her body. And I was not being given permission from her deeper self to enter her inner world.

I thought I might be wrong so I placed my hands on her anyway, but a massive force stopped me from going any further. She had created a powerful wall of energy to protect herself. Because of this healing and love that was in her life couldn't find a pathway through to affect her in a positive way.

It was then I realized that the emotions Meagan had suppressed, were blocking the pathways in her body. I believed her ability to embrace and understand her feelings, was the way to her healing. That is when I suggested she seek psychotherapy.

Meagan and I kept in touch with each other over the next several weeks. The psychotherapy sessions improved her outlook on life tremendously. She also shared that she was learning about her feelings. She was becoming more open in accepting people, as they are, therefore not allowing them to have a negative effect on her life. As her psychotherapist put it, "You are no longer a victim."

Then a phone call came from Meagan, "The doctor told me I am in remission."

"This is great news! I am so happy for you!" I responded.

Meagan went on to explain that she would continue with her psychotherapy sessions and use the tools she had learned to help her cope with life's challenges. She thanked me for the advice and support I had given to her at such a critical time in her life. Then, we said our good-byes.

After several months, I received another phone call from Meagan. But instead of hearing her happy, joyous voice, she sounded very different. This time it was very serious, and we made an appointment to meet.

"I don't want to live," she said, as we sat in my living room.

"What has happened to you?" I asked.

"I just can't be myself," she answered.

Here was the moment of truth that Meagan had hidden even from herself for a long time. As I mentioned before, her protective mechanism that guarded her from, what we had identified as being hurt by others or dealing with situations that she believed she had no control over, also unconsciously kept her from taking in the love and joy in her life.

Meagan began to tell me that even though she had come to accept this, people in her life, like her mother, fought her even more so. Meaghan had made the change but this change created a greater challenge for her.

I reached out to Meagan and held her hands. As she sobbed, I asked for guidance in helping her.

I went on to say, "Meagan, please think about staying in psychotherapy. You were doing so well when you were focused on yourself and how to deal with your emotions."

"No!" she stated emphatically. "It doesn't help. I just don't want to live anymore."

Meagan's pain was so deep, that it consumed her. She was exhausted. Going through chemotherapy treatments, having to keep up with her daily responsibilities as a wife and mother, and dealing with her emotional turmoil left little reserve for anything else.

I asked Meagan if she was receiving support from other family members and friends. She told me she was, but then she went on and said, "No one really knows how difficult the relationship with my mother is for me. It is difficult to let others know how this affects me."

"What would it be like for you to share your feelings with them?" I asked.

In response to my question, she just shook her head no.

I then asked her if she would approach her therapy to learn specifically how to deal with her feelings and challenge she had concerning her mother. That was a good option to her, and she told me she would consider it.

She thanked me, gave me a hug, and as she walked out the front door, she stopped, looked back at me and said, "Shirley, I truly will consider what you suggested."

Several months had past when I received another call. This time it was from Meagan's husband. She was in the hospital and had asked to see me.

I met him outside her hospital room the next day. "It happened so suddenly," he explained to me. "She was beginning to do better after she returned to therapy. But at her checkup, the doctors found the cancer had returned and had spread to other parts of her body."

I was stunned by this news. I put my hand on his shoulder to comfort him. Then I entered Meagan's room. I found her lying peacefully in bed, an oxygen mask over her face to help her breathe, and an intravenous drip by her side to ease her pain.

As I sat in the chair next to her, Meagan's eyes would briefly open and then shut again for long periods of time. The nurse in her room explained that this was because Meagan was drifting in and out of consciousness. If I spoke to her during one of her waking moments, the nurse felt for sure Meagan would be able to hear me. So I leaned in close and whispered, "Hi, Meagan. It's Shirley. I'm sitting in the chair next to your bed."

A subtle smile slowly emerged on Meagan's face.

"Meagan, I am sorry that you aren't feeling well. What can I do to help you feel better?" I asked.

Her body stirred as she willed herself to become more alert, and in a weak voice, she whispered, "Just love me." Then she closed her eyes again.

I bent over and placed my arms around her, as best I could, told her how much I loved her and that she was one of the most loving, kindest women I had ever met.

At that moment, the nurse came over and suggested it was probably best for me to leave. I left her room; stunned by the changes in her from the last time we saw one another. That was the last time I ever saw Meagan. She passed away that evening.

* * *

From years of experience, education, and self-study, I do know that a complex set of variables cause critical imbalances in our physiology, from one's constitution at birth to genetic influences, environmental stresses, and the power that we ourselves have over our thoughts, emotions, mental attitude, and the choices we make in our lives.

The life experiences of Cyndy and Meagan were very different and unique, which made a world of difference in the best way to assist their healing. Their attitudes were also totally different. Cyndy jumped right into creating her healing. Meagan had a challenging time dealing with suppressed emotions. These women, even though similar in some ways, had different life experiences and outcomes.

They were two very loving, intelligent women yet very different from one another. It is important to take the time to evaluate our personal needs in order to achieve health and happiness. We are unique individuals, therefore our challenges may be similar to each other in some aspects but may be very different in other ways. What are your specific challenges in life? What are your beliefs in overcoming them? Do you have support and understanding from others? These questions may be the most important questions to ask yourself: Are you empowered to make the decisions and changes needed to overcome any obstacle?

The reason why I emphasized this last question is because in some cases, drastic measures must be taken in order to heal. Here is just one situation where this had occurred.

* * *

This story is about a woman who also had cancer. Although she was not a client of mine, she told me the story of how she healed herself. (I will call her Claire.) Claire was very well-known in her community. She was a prominent leader in several local organizations. Organizing charities, volunteering at a well-known hospital and still making time for her children and husband. She would offer advice to those who asked and she felt she could conquer anything.

At her yearly checkup, Claire's doctor told her that she had cancer. I do not know what type of cancer or what stage. She told me she fell ill very suddenly after being given her diagnosis and became bed-ridden. During this time, she reviewed her life and decided that she was going to live and that if she had to redo her life over, she was going to do whatever it took to get well.

Now Claire didn't wait until she felt better to change her life. She began right away by letting everyone know that she needed time to heal and that she wanted peace and serenity in her life. In reviewing her life she asked the questions: What are the factors in my life that drain me of my energy; and what are the ones that give me energy or a sense of peace and flow in my life? She recognized that she needed to let go of some things in her life, including people. In order to do this she had to change what she thought as important that kept her from being happy and healthy.

She stepped down from the positions she held in the organizations she was dedicated to. She would only listen to friends when they were being positive and talking about good news. She began to read books on diet and health and made healthy lifestyle choices. Claire found her core issue was her compulsive drive to make sure people thought the best of her and that she shined in their lives. Now she didn't care what people thought of her because she found it was these thoughts and concerns of hers that were making her sick.

When I met Claire she had been cancer free for over seven years. She went back to school and is now a life coach doing what she loves to do in an empowering way.

* * *

We have a powerful impact on one another. Few of us know what to do for ourselves or how to help another, in situations such as this. We sometimes allow fear or helplessness to be the power, instead of having confidence in our abilities to make healthy choices. Choosing to take positive action, even though that may mean changing your lifestyle temporarily, will bring about positive results. Assessing your attitude is critical in developing positive thoughts that will lead you to boundless information in finding a solution to any circumstance.

*   *   *

In another situation, I knew of a man with a cancerous tumor. The man's son was a member of a prayer group that met weekly and prayed for those who requested prayers for healing. After a month of prayer, the man's CAT scan besides other laboratory reports showed that the tumor had disappeared. The rest of his family could not fathom this change and insisted that the doctor find this tumor, even though the same clinical tests showed the tumor was no longer present. The family members quarreled, stating that the son who belonged to the prayer group was giving false hope to their father. Others in the family believed this was a miracle.

Another month went by, and another CAT scan was taken. This time, a small tumor was found but not quite the size of the first one, in the same area. This led me to ask the question, do we ourselves reject the idea of the possibility for healing to occur and then do we re-create with our thoughts and beliefs the same disease to manifest again?

*   *   *

After Meaghan's death, I began to doubt myself as a healer. I then began to question myself even more: Who was I to help another person in their healing? Maybe these healings that I engaged in happened by some fleeting anomaly. Besides, I still didn't know how this all came about. Where is the scientific research to back up these experiences?

My logical mind finally took over and I decided I had to let go and get back to the "real" world. I gave up not only my healing work, but everything else that went along with it, including prayer. I had a good job with Dr. Siding, and was earning a good salary. I set my sights on saving a portion of my earnings every week until I had enough money to go back to school and finish earning my nursing degree. Once I had my degree in nursing, I would be in a profession that was accepted. Now that sounded more like a "real" plan.

*   *   *

I felt I had done well on my commitment to help grow Dr. Siding's business. My energy was focused on learning as much about the human body as Dr. Siding could teach me. I had established a strong rapport with our clients, who naturally shared their personal stories with me. I was a good listener and confidant, and my interactions helped to build healthy relationships for Dr. Siding. This contributed to a strong, positive reputation for giving excellent care. I had accomplished what I set out to do for Dr. Siding. Our patient numbers exceeded his goal to the maximum level he was capable of handling on his own, and he was now considering bringing another doctor into the practice. As for me, well, he had other plans.

One of Dr. Siding's clients invited me to a seminar on alternative healing, so I asked for the afternoon off to attend. I believed this seminar would help me to integrate what I had already learned in working toward my nursing degree. But Dr. Siding responded, "Shirley, your personal interest in healing is taking your focus away from the business."

I was shocked to hear this, because I had never allowed my healing work to interfere with my job. Besides, I had recently given it up entirely. So I replied, "But I'm not …"

"Your attention is not here," Dr. Siding interrupted. "I'm sorry, Shirley, but I have to let you go."

What was he talking about? I wondered. *Didn't he understand that taking this seminar on health would improve the work I could do with his patients and allow me to return to school for my nursing degree? Hadn't I worked diligently to help him build his practice?* But none of this mattered to him.

* * *

Did you ever feel like your whole world kept collapsing, and no matter what you did, nothing seemed to work out? That's what it felt like to me. It was "the domino effect." I had everything lined up in a row, and because one domino fell, all the rest came toppling down, as well.

* * *

Jake became more concerned over our finances with the loss of my job. He didn't say much, but the silence between us told me everything. I felt very distant from him and the children. They were still enjoying the summer activities with family and friends. I acted as joyful as possible throughout the summer, even though inside me I was wandering in a sea of emotions that now had become a tornado of confusion. I hid from everyone the battle that was going on within me. The conflict, the pain … when will it end? I was fighting desperately to get back to what was normal. I felt I had lost my place in the world.

Transition on Cape Cod from summer to winter can be challenging for those who live here. The fun and excitement of going to the beach everyday to picnics, concerts and participating in wildlife programs are mostly over by the end of the fall. The children transitioned back to school quite nicely but I felt myself closing down and pulling away from the outside world even more.

Jake and the children became my safe haven. Spending time with them got me out of my head and into life when I was with them. I realized my response to life had become much slower than my usual fireball self. Since the beginning of my paranormal experiences, tossing and turning in bed had become a ritual. As if on high alert, I would awaken to almost any sound. But now I was sleeping soundly.

What a luxury, a vacation from all the chaos and confusion surrounding my life. My dreams changed from the dreams when I felt I was out in the cosmos searching for answers, to dreaming about my teenage years.

There was though, one recurring dream that never ended well. In this dream, Max and I were sitting on the swings in one of our favorite parks, talking and laughing about, who knows what. During a certain part of the dream, I would begin to tell him something important but I could never finish because he would just disappear.

Then one evening I had another dream. I found myself once again in a sterile, white room, but this time, unlike my first dream, everything was stagnant. I had no direction, and like the particles outside this room, I was floating aimlessly in the dark.

"You can't stay here," I heard a voice say.

"But it's so peaceful here," I responded.

"You are always a part of here, and here is always a part of you." the voice echoed back.

"I don't want to leave here." I said.

"Then bring what you have found here into your waking world." the voice replied.

"What? Bring what into my what?"

And then I faintly heard the words, "Heaven on Earth."

* * *

I hadn't realized how much I had changed until one day when Jake, the girls, and I went shopping. A major turning point came about from an awareness that had occurred when we were in an electronics store.

I was in one part of the store while Jake was in the television aisle, looking at the rows of TV sets on display. When I went to join him, he noticed as I walked down the aisle toward him, that each television screen would suddenly turn fuzzy, and the crystal, clear sound became static. He took my arm and walked me down the rest of the aisles to see if the same thing would happen. It did. Jake and I just looked at each other, as if we were agreeing that this was just another unusual experience, and we then left the store.

From there, we stopped off at a drugstore. As I walked up to the register to pay for my purchases, the electronic cash register malfunctioned and became jammed. The clerk couldn't figure out what had gone wrong and could not fix the problem. He was getting both frustrated and irritated. All of a sudden, Jake silently gestured for me to move away from the cash register. As soon as I did, it started working properly.

After we left the store, Jake looked at me and said, "Shirl, I think you interfered with the electronic systems, in both places." He had no understanding of the paranormal; he didn't talk about it and had not read any about the books on it as I had. But his instincts and professional expertise with computers led him to this conclusion, because I seemed to be the only common factor between the two incidents.

We both stopped and stared at each other, and then we burst into laughter at the same time. His insight was so unbelievable that our laughter helped us to deal with the absurd.

Somehow, the laughter released me from the depressed state I was in. I remembered that my inner voice had recently said, "You are always a part of here, and here is always a part of you."

I needed to trust in whatever the meaning was behind the synchronicity of all these events and the voice from within.

Once I made this realization, I emerged from my peaceful inner state and became more aware of what was happening around me throughout the day. I came to the understanding that if I didn't integrate my new awareness into my life, I would stay in this peaceful floating state while I was somehow unconsciously creating havoc seen by the experience with the electronic systems in the stores we visited. I believed the voice in my dream was trying to wake me up to the importance of listening to the wisdom these experiences were giving me.

I began to recognize that while I was in my state of peaceful floating, the feelings about my waking world began to emerge from underneath my state of calm. Then finally, one night, they erupted.

Chapter 5

Point of No Return

One night, I was awakened by the sound of knocking . . . knocking as if doors were opening and closing. It was in the middle of the night, when the house was quiet, the girls were asleep, and Jake was working. After listening intently to this sound, I thought it was our new home settling, so I went back to sleep.

But the following night, it happened again. I again listened intently and sensed that the sound was coming from somewhere downstairs. I didn't want to deal with this, so I quickly pulled the covers over my head, and began praying for the sound to go away, but it never did.

This went on for two more nights, and on the fifth night, I heard, "*Mommmm!*" It was Melyssa.

I opened my eyes, and Melyssa was standing next to my bed.

"What's the matter, Sweetheart?" I asked.

"I hear a noise coming from downstairs." she responded.

"What do you mean?" I asked, hoping she wouldn't say . . .

"I hear something coming from the kitchen, like something is banging," she said in a sleepy voice.

I took a deep breath and sighed, "Okay. I am going to tuck you back into your bed, and then I will go downstairs to find out what it is."

I tucked Melyssa in her bed, gave her a kiss, and reassured her that everything was going to be okay. I then went into Krysie and Laurie's room, where I found them both sleeping peacefully. I could no longer hide under the bed covers and make the excuse that this was only an illusion. Melyssa's awareness wouldn't allow me to.

When I approached the top of the staircase, I paused to get a sense of what might be going on downstairs. The air was still, except for the subtle sound of knocking. My heart began to beat faster, and I could feel a rush of energy move through my entire body. There was no denying it. I was petrified!

As I slowly walked down each stair, I thought of keeping my children safe. My children have always given me the strength to confront any situation, and this was one of those times.

When I reached the bottom landing, I could see the faint moonlit shadows of the trees outside dancing on the living room walls. Then I heard a more distinct sound of knocking . . . knocking ever so lightly. It was clearly coming from the kitchen.

"Please, dear Lord, be with me, please dear Lord, be with me," I repeated over and over again as I approached the doorway to the kitchen. At that point, the knocking became louder and more distinct. As I looked around, I could see static electricity in the air, moving swiftly about like little particles of dust, colliding into each other. I felt as if I was in the eye of an electric tornado.

The force in the room became stronger; the cabinet doors opened and shut faster, making the knocking more dramatic than before. I could not move. There I was, standing in the middle of the kitchen, observing this phenomenon.

I cried out loud, "What is happening?"

Then I heard, "This is a gift. Use it wisely."

This voice penetrated the fabric of energy surrounding me. Then, like magic, all became still. Exhausted from the turmoil, I laid down on the cool kitchen floor and fell asleep.

I awoke around six o'clock to find myself still lying on the kitchen floor. The sun was coming up and touching the kitchen windows. All was calm.

I got up from the floor and went upstairs to check on the children. They were still sleeping soundly. Even Melyssa, who had heard the knocking, was sleeping peacefully.

When Jake arrived home, I told him what Melyssa and I had experienced during the middle of the night and what I had seen in the kitchen. We decided to call Reverend Harding right away. She was the only one we knew who could see the things I could see. She had helped us before, and we trusted her to be able to help us again in understanding what this paranormal event was about.

* * *

Reverend Harding came that day and walked through our home just as she had before, moving serenely from room to room, making her assessment until she wound up back in the kitchen. There, she sat down with Jake and me at the kitchen table.

"There is nothing here from the spirit world," she concluded, much to my surprise. "Amelia and others from the spirit realm are not present. Your house is clean." She paused, and I could feel my whole body tighten as she looked at me and said, "Shirley, I believe this phenomenon is being created by *you*."

I was astonished and gasped, "By me? How could I have created this?"

Jake turned to me and said, "Shirl, do you remember what happened at the electronics store and then at the drugstore a couple of weeks ago? Remember what I said to you?"

"Yes," I responded. I was now beginning to quiver.

Jake told Reverend Harding about the incidents and then looked back at me. "Maybe it's true. Maybe it is coming from you," he said.

At that moment, I felt completely disconnected from them both. Their voices seemed so far away, and I felt displaced again from my surroundings. It was as if putting myself in a different place could shield me from what they were saying.

Suddenly I felt a surge of energy rise up from my chest to my mind, and I heard a voice say, "Pay attention!"

"What?" I asked the voice.

"Don't forget your feelings."

My mind frantically traced the past month, and to my surprise, I realized I had been feeling angry and frustrated. I was in complete denial that these feelings even existed. I had detached once again from my feelings, allowing them, this time, to control me from an unconscious level. These feelings were still alive and powerful.

Then more thoughts came flooding through my mind bringing with them deeper feelings to my awareness. Laughter, fun, then fear turning into complete confusion in my mind. As soon as this door opened, it shut quickly, leaving only a hint of something. It felt like I was waking up to deeper feelings that I had suppressed.

As I became fully present again in the room, I heard Reverend Harding suggest that we attend a service at her church. "Maybe it would help you both to know there are others who have had similar experiences," she advised.

So that weekend, Jake, the children, and I drove to Plymouth to attend a service at the Spiritualist Church, which had been dedicated to healing since 1975. I was surprised when Reverend Harding explained that spiritualism is actually an ancient religion, not New Age. It recognizes God, as the Universal Source and teaches we are an integral part of God's power.

Over the next several weeks, we continued to go to their Sunday services as a family, while still attending Mass at our own church. I was also invited to attend their classes, where I met other people who had gifted abilities as well.

Reverend Harding's classes were an awakening for me, as I finally came to understand these unusual abilities I possessed were not so unusual after all. What I was experiencing was in fact a part of a natural life process called, spiritual awakening.

I had been blaming my "gifts" for my marital and other problems, including all the financial difficulties Jake and I had been going through. It was time to stop blaming this natural spiritual process and begin to understand how it was helping me in my life.

Yet still, the voice I heard that spoke to me that morning, came from outside of me. It was not an inner voice like I was used to hearing. This was a new phenomenon and a mystery.

* * *

As I worked with other clients who were becoming spiritually conscious, I found that we all experience unconscious feelings manifesting in a way that we may not want them to at times in our lives. Examples include compromising our physical health, wrongful actions, displaced emotions toward others, and misdirected guidance. We find ourselves acting out underlying impulses through behavior that we may find difficult to understand or explain.

Our feelings are what I call our emotional barometer of our heart's desire. They allow us to gauge right from wrong and to determine what our true desires are in what we want, compared to the current reality we are living. When we understand our feelings, where they come from, and the important role these feelings play in our lives, then the decisions we make and the actions we choose to take will be more in alignment to create what we want.

I was feeling more confident again, then came the time that I had feared the most about my Catholic upbringing.

* * *

Our community Catholic Church didn't engage in "laying on of hands." I found out that some of the other Catholic churches were doing it but not ours. One morning during mass, the priest told us about a young child in the parish that was sick and asked if anyone knew what to do for him. The medical profession could not find what the cause of his illness was, so as a Christian community we prayed with a special intention.

Jake and I decided to visit the priest and share with him the healing phenomenon that was occurring through me. His response to the healings was emphatic. "My dear, you cannot have the gift of healing . . . you're not a priest. And to this point I am saying only priests who have been specifically ordained to heal have this ability."

I understand now that the laying on of hands is an accepted form of healing in many Catholic churches as well as other Christian churches but during my awakening, this was not a part of my experience. What I knew from my own experiences is that we all have the gift of healing. This is natural to all of us especially when you have the desire to heal.

When I was a teenager, I attended St. Peter's Central Catholic High School in Worcester, Massachusetts. This was a very important time in my life, and it was there that I was taught the art of communication and dialogue. Our headmaster, Father Stearns, encouraged all students to passionately communicate with one another, while emphasizing the importance of respecting individual talents and abilities. He emphasized the means of dialogue to take the place of judgment.

So, regardless of this priest's dismissal of my gifted ability, I knew from what I had learned from Father Stearns was to believe in myself. I also learned from Reverend Harding to look upon this as a gifted ability of the spirit. The door to this new world of healing opened once again, and I chose to walk through it.

* * *

To avoid causing my energy to erupt as another poltergeist activity, I knew I had to learn how to consciously work with my energy flow instead of suppressing it or acting as if it didn't exist. So I set out to become conscious of my thoughts, the way I reacted to situations in my life, and to be conscious of the underlying feelings I had towards daily circumstances and interactions. This meant that I had to be mindful of my body as well as what I had been thinking that created the feeling. Being consciously present and aware was the path I chose to take. Prayer and self-inquiry were aspects of my life that I now knew were imperative for a safe experience through my spiritual awakening and transformation.

As I observed different experiences since my spiritual awakening, I highlighted different scenarios of events that I had been through. In every situation, there seemed to be a theme leading me to a deeper level closer to my heart. This was no easy task, since I was busy in my life, and my automatic pilot button seemed to be turned on more than it was off. But as you read on further, you'll see I hadn't yet understood the core of my mounting frustrations.

* * *

One day after the girls had finished eating their lunch, I asked them to go upstairs to the bathroom and brush their teeth. Instead, they continued joking with each other and playing at the table. I began to get upset so instead of yelling I repeated myself, more firmly this time.

"Girls, please go to the bathroom and brush your teeth." As I was speaking, I moved toward the kitchen table where they were seated to straighten out a chair. But before I could place my hands on the back of the chair, it leaped into the air and crashed into the wall, four feet from where it had been, leaving a gash in the wall.

All three of my daughters reacted with shock and then disbelief. I fell back against the countertop and burst into tears. Melyssa made a frantic call to Jake at work, asking him to come home right away.

That incident made me realize that as determined as I was to harness this energy inside me and to achieve self-awareness, I was not succeeding on my own. I also began to have burning sensations underneath my feet. They would come at very unusual times. It felt like I was a conduit for an electrical force, and my electrical wiring was short-circuiting. I remembered the voice I heard during the visit with Reverend Harding after the first poltergeist incident, which spoke about my feelings; I was suppressing, in my unconscious, feelings of anger and frustration. There were still roadblocks within me that were getting in the way from being happy, productive, and balanced in my life. I needed help.

* * *

I turned to psychotherapy as my next step for my personal healing. I called Dr. John, the professor who taught the psychology course I took while working toward my nursing degree. He was a well-respected professor who inspired his students. I felt comfortable enough with him to engage his services to help make sense of my experiences through psychoanalysis.

Our first psychotherapy session went very well. I was able to comfortably describe the phenomenon that had been happening around me since moving to Cape Cod. I told him of the healings I'd successfully helped with, as well as the failures, and described the poltergeist activity I had triggered on two separate occasions in the kitchen of our home. Dr. John listened with a focused observation. I believed I was in good hands. I left his office feeling that I was on my way to making progress. How could I go wrong? Dr. John had his Ph.D. in Psychology. He could help me figure out what I was repressing. Now, I was going to get somewhere.

The following week for me was busy and productive. Taking action to find the answers gave me strength and a healthier daily attitude. The children kept me busy with their extracurricular school activities, and I started to find friends and new interests in the community. Melyssa's best friend's mother invited me to play tennis, and I was delighted to be active in a sport that I loved.

Meanwhile, my second therapy session was approaching. As I thought back to my first session, I began to feel anxious. I had felt very comfortable in the doctor's presence that first time, and felt safe while sharing with him my experiences. But now, for some reason, I didn't feel that way. Something seemed very wrong to me.

The morning of my follow-up session with Dr. John, I became aware of how apprehensive I was feeling. When I arrived at his office, I hesitated to go inside. Fear and anxiety were touching me so deeply that I couldn't bring myself to even open the door. I stood there breathing in and out in a controlled manner until my anxiety calmed and I became relaxed. Then I began to see flashes of scenarios in my mind, disquieting images of Dr. John talking about me to someone, speaking judgmentally, and the two of them laughing afterward. I couldn't get a handle on what this all meant, but my inner voice kept urging me to pay attention to my feelings and to trust my instincts. I knew the truth behind those images lived in the space I was about to enter, and I needed to trust what was about to happen.

There was a small sitting area where Dr. John's patients would wait. As he opened the door his phone rang and he gestured for me to come in and have a seat in his office. Those few moments allowed me the time to allow my insights to come forward in my mind. My head cleared of the uncertainty, and in that moment, I felt solid and strong in my body.

After he finished his phone conversation, he reached out to shake my and for a second time gestured for me to sit down, but I could not. My energy was forcing me to stand and this is what I said, "Dr. John, I have been having an uncomfortable feeling since our initial visit."

With a warm smile, he replied, "Well, Shirley, that's not so unusual given all that you've been going through."

I swallowed hard then said, "No, it isn't because of that. It's because I know you spoke to a colleague of yours about me, and both of you have labeled me schizophrenic."

I paused a moment and then went on, "I also know that you've made jokes about me to your wife!"

Dr. John paused, stared at me for a few moments then, again gestured for me to sit down. Still questioning if what I said was true, I moved forward and took a seat.

Then he said in a serious tone, "Shirley, how do you know these things?"

I started to calm down and I replied, "I don't know how." I just do."

The rest of the session went unexpectedly well. Dr. John asked many questions about the paranormal and even hinted that he himself had experiences that he could not explain. Without him outwardly verifying the truth to what I accused him of, he was inadvertently admitting to its truth.

In light of this I returned for two more sessions only to find myself explaining my insights to the questions he had on paranormal experiences. I was the teacher and he was the student. I was paying him for a service I should have been paid for. It was time to end the sessions. After this realization, I never returned to his office.

I had gone to Dr. John expecting him to know why these things were happening to me. What I had perceived in my mind was this: because Dr. John had his Ph.D. in Psychology, he would be the one to help me find my answers. If I hadn't listened to my instincts, I might have been led down the wrong path. He might have prescribed medication to control my spiritual awakening.

The experience with Dr. John had empowered me to move forward in my life with a resilience that couldn't be broken. I now knew I could trust my intuition and the inner guidance it gave me. I was stronger in my body and in my mind. I was confident and capable to focus on the choices I would have to make to resolve the two most important issues still before me. First, I needed to be gainfully employed so that our family would have financial stability. Second, I wanted to take a more traditional approach to healing, which meant returning to college to finish my nursing degree when the funds became available. Great, I was all set now!

* * *

Later that week, I called a family meeting. I had thought long and hard about what I must do for the sake of my family and how difficult it was counteracting the resistance I was experiencing as a healer.

"What do you think about me giving up my healing work for a normal job?" I asked.

The kids started to clap, and Jake had a look of relief on his face. I actually could not believe the relief I felt as well from this decision. I instantly felt happy, upbeat, and ready to pursue other possibilities.

I heard about an opening at Falmouth Hospital. It was a secretarial position to the doctors and nurses on the floor. I would also be responsible to make sure the patients' charts were correctly maintained and easily accessible to the doctors, that the medical supplies were always well-stocked, and generally to manage the business aspects of the ward.

I applied for the position, believing I could channel my passion and desire to work in a healing environment, in such a way that the spiritual experiences would come to an end. Two interviews later, I was hired.

The town of Falmouth was a thirty-mile drive from where we lived in Sandwich. This meant a forty to fifty minute commute, each way, depending on the traffic. Since I was no longer working close to home, I would need someone to watch the children until I arrived home at the end of the day.

Diane and Mike had just recently moved into the house next door. They were a very pleasant couple with two children of their own around the ages of our two youngest. Diane and I quickly became friends, and their children and ours played well together. Since Diane and I often took turns babysitting for one another, Diane agreed to watch our children.

My first day at the hospital was exhausting, just trying to keep up with the hectic pace of the doctors and nurses. Yet despite my exhaustion, I felt a deep satisfaction in knowing that I was starting to make good on my two goals. I resolved not to repeat the mistake I had made with Dr. Siding, allowing my consuming interest in alternative methods of healing to interfere with my work. I would put that on the back burner for now and I would focus all my energies on my job.

On my way home, while I was driving the stretch of road on Route 6A, between the Bourne, and Sagamore bridges, my heart seemed to leap into my throat, and my mind was alerted to a horrific scene. I could see in my mind a blood- soaked towel wrapped around a child's hand.

As quickly as I had this vision, I looked over to the oncoming traffic and saw Diane driving past me in the opposite direction. I turned my car around and followed her, catching her attention to pull her car over.

There in the back seat of her car was Laurie, her hand wrapped in a towel that was drenched in blood. As we were placing Laurie in my car, Diane explained what had happened. Our garage door that had a sharp steel edge to it had severed off the tip of Laurie's baby finger. That was all I needed to hear.

While I was driving back toward the hospital, I remembered that the State Police barracks was a couple of miles up the road so I decided to stop there for help. Laurie was crying quietly in my arms as a state trooper drove us to the hospital. Carefully, I unwrapped the towel from around her hand so I could see her injured little finger. While looking at the wound, my heart started beating a mile a minute just as it had earlier when I'd experienced the vision. Then my hands began to tingle. I knew what this phenomenon meant. I began to breath calmly so I could stop the urge to heal.

Then I heard a voice within me say, "You are always a part of here, and here is always a part of you. Bring this into your waking world."

I placed my hand above her injured finger and visualized it being completely healed.

When we arrived at Falmouth Hospital, the emergency room was almost empty. One of the physicians on staff was able to take Laurie right away.

As I waited anxiously for the doctor to report back to me, the fire department arrived with the severed tip of Laurie's finger, and it was rushed into the examination room. A short while later, the doctor called me in. He asked me to sit down and he began to explain his prognosis.

"Mrs. Beauman, the fire department was able to retrieve the severed part of your daughter's finger," he said. "Under normal circumstances, I would say I would be successful in reattaching the severed part of Laurie's finger." He then took a breath and sighed. "But I've never seen anything like this before; your daughter has about several days worth of healing on her finger already."

Hearing this, Laurie chimed in with, "Well, my mom put her ..." I quickly gave Laurie a look that said, "Don't you dare say anything," so she didn't finish her sentence.

"Something tells me to just leave things alone," he added. "Let it heal as it's been doing, and I'll see Laurie in two weeks to check on her progress."

As the doctor left the emergency room, I went over to Laurie to comfort her. As I held her, I whispered in her ear, "I want you to remember one thing, no matter what anyone tells you, your finger will grow back!"

I never returned to work after that day. As Laurie's healing progressed, I re-established my practice of prayer. There was one unusual morning when, in prayer, I asked God to be with her in the healing of her finger. Out of the early morning hours I heard Laurie yell out, "Mom, stop! What you're doing to me!"

I was astonished. I stopped praying and went upstairs to Laurie's room. She was lying in bed, and I asked her, "What are you talking about?"

She replied, "You are healing my finger, I can feel it tingling."

"No, I'm not, Sweetheart," I said. "I asked God to heal your finger."

Her statement perplexed me. How is it possible that she could instantly receive healing from my prayer? How could God instantly awaken the healing power of Laurie's finger? Where was this energy coming from, and how did it reach her?

I was still struggling with my own beliefs when Laurie looked at me. "Mom, I want to do this myself. I want to heal my finger," she exclaimed.

* * *

Out of the mouths of babes! I thought. Laurie took to this idea like a fish does to water. The belief of my own child began to be my saving grace. Laurie cared for her severed finger daily. I watched as she cleaned the fingertip; she would tell everyone, even the priest at church that her finger was growing back. How excited she was. I remembered what the inner voice told me when I was grappling with helping Cyndy: "Belief." Laurie's belief was unstoppable.

Today, I know that we are all born with an innate knowing of the truth. This knowing is most keenly experienced in childhood, before we are taught to believe otherwise. But as we mature through childhood into adulthood, this awareness gradually slips away until we have blocked it out of our consciousness in some respect. Laurie was still open to this awareness.

* * *

A week after the accident, Laurie and I had a significant encounter. I had prayed for her healing two more times and had to cease immediately because of her outcries of feeling intense tingling in her little finger. I had to control my urge to pray for her to heal. Then one morning, I happened to walk into the bathroom and found her caring for her finger.

I was shocked to see how much healing had occurred. Her finger was almost completely healed. Yet on the very tip there was a mass of fleshy skin that concerned me. So my motherly instinct took over and I touched this piece of fleshy skin to see how securely it was fastened to her finger. Laurie pulled her finger back from my hold, and from this action, the fleshy substance came off. Laurie was horrified. I had interfered with Laurie's progress in her own healing. It was over.

If you looked at Laurie's finger today, you would see a slight indentation where the healing had ceased. I was the one who told Laurie to trust that her finger would heal completely, and yet, ironically, I put an end to her finger healing completely.

I can imagine what you might be thinking as you read this part of my story. I had experienced two healings, which one might call miracles. So why was I still struggling with the concept that we can heal ourselves? The answer to this is because there was a battle going on inside of me that I was not aware of. A deeper inner conflict from what I had been entrained through life to believe, compared to what God was trying to show me now. So from my unconscious level, I was, in fact, struggling with two opposing beliefs: (1) we have the power to heal, and (2) we do not have the healing power to manifest healings that are out of the norm.

After this experience, I realized that whatever was occurring in me had the potential to either heal . . . or harm.

Now, you might be thinking: this was an accident; you didn't mean to stop the healing.

You're right. Consciously, I didn't mean to stop the healing, but we often make decisions that if we gave more awareness to our thoughts and the truth about our feelings, we would have made a better choice and that would have created a better outcome.

My actions were destructive. Was it safer for me to believe, but not participate in this belief? I decided the answer was yes. I concluded that the energy that came from me to bring about healing was the same energy that had also produced the destructive poltergeist activity in the kitchen.

This indicated to me that whatever I might be thinking or feeling at any given time controls how this energy manifests itself, either for good or for ill, healing or the cessation of healing. In other words, it meant that I was an active participant in what had happened, and my subconscious impulses were part of creating what was manifesting. My logical thought process had gone to sleep, and I was letting those subconscious impulses rule the outcome in this situation. My conscious awareness was not in control: my subconscious impulses were.

Next question: How much of my world, meaning my life, was being shaped by my own thoughts, emotions, intuition, logic, determination, and subconscious impulses? And, subsequently, how much of this was impacting everyone else around me? These questions are the type of questions I would ask during my self-inquiry, bridging my consciousness to the power of my subconscious.

Laurie forgave me, and it was from her unconditional love that I became aware that even though I was the adult, the answers I sought were brought to me in many different ways, most importantly, through my own children.

* * *

This would be the beginning of many spiritual experiences that Laurie would have because of her own capabilities. Through my children I began to realize how we are connected in a fabric of energy glued together by the greatest emotion of all, love!

I began to pay attention to my daughters' experiences, that I may have dismissed as being unimportant...my children became my teachers.

For example, Melyssa had been attuned to the poltergeist activity I was creating in the kitchen and made simple yet profound statements filled with wisdom and knowledge beyond her age. She also had vivid dreams about an American Indian who would take her places while she slept. He would teach her about the vital importance and wisdom held in nature and its kingdom of animals and plants, before I even understood the concept of spiritual beings.

Krysie seemed to be the one that was more emotionally sensitive to the feelings of others. Even as a newborn, she was drawn to those who were more loving towards her. As a toddler, she was drawn to those whose presence she instinctively felt most comfortable, but she would immediately pull away from others who had a rougher exterior.

Laurie had a sense of knowing the unknown. She had a keen intuitive sense ever since she was very young. There was one situation that happened while she was in the third grade. One morning her teacher began yelling at the class for no apparent reason. Laurie raised her hand and when she was called on she said, "Mr. Longwood, you're not angry at us, you had a fight with your wife this morning before coming to school, and you're angry at her."

Well that didn't go over very well since I received a call from Laurie's guidance counselor. Mr. Longwood had spoken to her about Laurie's comment.

"There are teachers who are aware of the psychic abilities that some children have. Your daughter is one of them." She said. She went on to tell me that these children are very sensitive to their surroundings and that most of them are gifted in one way but may have challenges in other ways such as their intellectual capacity since they are more prone to intuiting information.

I was astonished. I asked myself, *is everyone born with this ability in what scientists now call our sixth sense? Can we access greater knowledge and wisdom directly? Do we lose touch with this aspect of ourselves as we become more intellectually developed and assimilated into our adult world?*

* * *

Four years after we had moved into our new home, Krysie had developed difficulty breathing. Jake and I had taken her to Children's Hospital in Boston, where she was diagnosed as having severe allergies. She was placed on a strict diet, and we changed our own diet to accommodate her needs. Even though I thought I was doing well by feeding the children more natural foods, we found that Krysie had allergies to several of them.

On a snowy, windy, winter night in, Krysie's ability to breathe worsened, and I became more concerned than usual. That night I sat in a rocking chair beside her bed, watching over her as her medication and vaporizer helped her to rest. I was scared. Jake was working the night shift and I planned, as soon as he came home, to bring her to Children's Hospital in Boston. I sat next to her bed and I fell asleep around four in the morning.

I awoke at seven o'clock. Krysie was not in her bed. Then I heard a rummaging sound coming from her closet. There she was, scrambling to find something to wear to school.

"Krysie, what are you doing?" I asked.

She looked at me as if nothing was wrong and replied, "Mom, I'm getting ready for school." She was smiling and looked the picture of health. She was no longer sick. So after breakfast, she went off to school, acting as cheerful as could be, leaving me amazed and completely baffled by the sudden transformation.

That evening as I was tucking her into bed, she seemed a little perplexed.

"What's wrong, Honey?" I asked.

"Mom," she replied, "I have something to tell you."

"Okay, what is it?" I asked.

"Mom, there was a lady in my room last night," she answered.

"There was?" I said. I then waited patiently for her to tell me the rest of her story.

"Yes. She was very pretty and she had stars all around her head. When I woke up, she was stroking my hair." Tears started to fill my eyes as Krysie went on with her story. "She told me not to worry, and that I should go back to sleep. She told me that I would be better in the morning." At this point I didn't know what to say to her. "Who is she, Mom?"

"I bet she is your guardian angel," I said.

"Yeah, I bet she is my guardian angel," Krysie agreed.

To this day I do not know for sure who the spiritual lady was, yet I believe that her presence and love healed Krysie that evening. Since that occurrence, throughout the rest of her childhood Krysie had minimal bouts of sickness.

Chapter 6

When One Door Closes

What had happened with my three children affected me deeply. Each of them brought my attention to the wisdom I kept trying to avoid. I could not escape the fact that all these spiritual events were natural parts of life and that I was becoming more conscious of them.

Jake's solar energy and building business began to become profitable. It did so well that he gave up his job at PAVE PAWS. Now that our money crunch began to lighten, we discussed what I should do next. Together, we decided I should fully commit to my healing ability.

We transformed our beautiful dining room into a healing room. It was not by word of mouth alone that people found me. Business cards were printed and I was interviewed by a reporter from our town paper for a special article on healing. Before long, people were showing up at our front door, asking for help. I charged for my spiritual counseling services, but I set aside Thursdays for hands-on healing, for which I did not charge a thing. Many people came with different ailments, both physical and emotional. When they asked what they could do to repay me, I asked them to do something for another person, unconditionally.

Lingering still was my desire to integrate and dedicate my new awareness into a mainstream profession. Being a spiritual counselor and healer was far from, being recognized as a mainstream career. Financially, I was not making a good living from my spiritual counseling services. I had to make a decision once and for all; either I must strive to find a second job to compensate for my not making a profit, or I must somehow find another way to create financial stability with my profession in healing.

I was so frustrated about this that one day I was standing in my living room and said out loud, "Okay, God, tell me what to do!" As I turned to walk into the kitchen, I heard the voice within me say, "Teach them how to do it themselves."

I was startled by this suggestion, because I simply had no idea how to go about teaching someone else the things I had learned and was still learning. The learning process helped me adapt to a greater spiritual consciousness and assisted me in thinking more openly about greater possibilities, but at times it was like putting on a new pair of shoes over and over again, trying to break them in.

With that thought, I decided I needed proof that this was the right direction to take. Again, I questioned the validity of what my intuition was telling me. So, I demanded to whomever, whatever, wherever God was to send Mary Anne Lucas to my door. Then, I would take this as a confirmation to believe the message. After that thought, I began laughing and asked myself, who am I to command God?

In fifteen minutes, there was a knock at my front door. I opened the door and there stood Mary Anne. She was well known in the Cape Cod region. She and I had met through another woman who had come to me for a healing. Mary Anne was an energetic woman, well versed in health, wellness, and spirituality.

"Mary Anne, I can't believe this." I said when I saw her standing at my front door.

"Shirley, I was having a cup of tea with a friend," she said, "when all of a sudden I thought of you, and I felt an immediate urge to come and see you right away."

When I explained what had just happened, we both laughed about the absurdity of it all.

After I told Mary Anne about my dilemma she responded, "You can give classes and maybe your counseling and educational classes can be given in other communities as well."

"How?" I asked.

She began to explain that she knew of many interested people who would love to take a class such as the one I was considering giving. Then, those taking the class will spread the word that you are working in an alternative field for healing. Many are seeking alternative means in finding the answers they are asking about the health and their lives."

I was amazed at what had just happened. Mary Anne was not only a very spiritual woman; she was an extremely competent businesswoman who was always on the lookout for ways to help others.

I began to understand how God works with all of us, helping us connect to the right people, at the right time, to assist one another in our life's purpose. That which I was lacking Mary Anne had. Her business acumen could create success around a very simple yet unorthodox idea. She researched how much to charge people for the classes as well as how to market to the right clientele.

I created a class using the steps I had followed in learning how to heal. These were, after all, some of the steps I had encouraged Cyndy to follow in order to assist her with her own healing. These steps have evolved over the years into the approach I take today in the field of human potential and spiritual consciousness.

* * *

During this same time, I had heard of the Interface Foundation, a holistic education center, in Newton, just west of Boston. The school offered degrees in holistic counseling and other degrees related to alternative concepts in healing. It was my belief that earning a degree in holistic counseling would bring me the academic credentials I needed to be accepted by other professionals.

After looking at the coursework, I realized my knowledge was well beyond the material that was being taught but I still chose to apply. I was accepted and I began focusing on my two year journey in studying an integrative approach to wellness. As the second half of the year was approaching, I was called into my advisor's office for a meeting about financial aid.

I needed to apply for financial aid to ease the burden for the rest of the course. Because there was not enough time to file, I was in a difficult position. We reviewed again my reason for wanting a degree, but until the next semester, I would have to take a break until my application was approved.

But he had an idea. He suggested that I speak to Joshua, one of the instructors at the foundation. He believed Joshua could help me open a satellite office and begin working with a group of established health practitioners.

Joshua had a Ph.D. in Psychology and was a practicing Psychotherapist at the Aqua Retreat Center in Brighton, Massachusetts. He arranged for me to meet the head of the center, and two weeks later I began working at the center as a healer. Another door had opened for me and I had to make the commitment to step through that door, and did. It was there that I felt at home with other health practitioners whom I could relate to as a professional.

There were over a dozen integrative practitioners that worked at the center ranging from nutritionists, psychotherapists, acupuncturists, and other integrative therapies. Many of the well-respected and from successful business and academic population would frequent there, using these alternative approaches to wellness.

* * *

My work at the center in Brighton was very rewarding. One day I received a call from a doctor who had a holistic practice in Newton Highlands.

"Shirley, I'm Dr. Aasen from Newton Highlands," the caller said. "You were recommended to me by a colleague of yours. She told me of your natural abilities in helping people heal and I want to know if you would be willing to meet with me at my office to discuss what you might be able to do to help one of my patients."

"I would love to," I said, and we arranged a day for us to meet.

Dr. Aasen was a very tall man with light, brown hair. He had an infectious smile. He believed that if patients had hope, he could help them find a way to accomplish balance and healing in their lives. Surprisingly, the patient he wanted me to see turned out to be his wife. Her name was Adya; she had been stricken by what the medical professionals believed was a virus that had left her with substantial hearing loss.

Adya was tall, like her husband, and quite beautiful, with very dark hair and deep brown eyes. She had come to the United States from her native country, India to attend college. While she was finishing her business degree, she met Dr. Aasen. She remained in the United States after graduating, and they married. They now had two young children, one a newborn, who were, along with her husband, the entire focus of Adya's life.

During our initial discussion, Adya did not say much that would help me assist her in her healing process. With little to go on, I explained to Adya the importance of knowing her "truth." I said I would help her in bridging her awareness to her feelings and thoughts. At the end of our discussion, I laid my hands on her, but I felt nothing except for stillness.

Her second session was basically the same. Very little was shared from our conversation, but this time when I placed my hands on her, I began to hear a subtle sound, but I couldn't interpret the vibration into information. It was as if Adya and I were on different planets. Our worlds were not in communion. *This was not going to be easy*, I thought.

Patience was not one of my strengths, but patience is what I needed to have while working with this healing process. As I placed my hands over her heart, the distant sound became clearer. It sounded as if she was screaming inside, and no one could hear her, not even herself.

After this session, Adya's internal energy block began to free up, and a more synergistic flow of energy began to occur. That is when I sat down with her for our first honest conversation.

"Adya, what is it about your life here that is uncomfortable for you?" She seemed shocked at my straightforward approach.

"I don't know," she answered.

"Well, what are some of the discussions you remember from the past month that you find difficult to understand?" I asked.

She bowed her head for a moment, sighed, looked back up at me, and said, "I can't even tell you because I would be disrespecting the sacredness of conversations I've had with others."

I paused for a moment and then asked, "How would you be disrespectful if you told me?"

A subtle smile came across her face and she said, "I would be disrespecting the way I was taught to respect my personal values and how I was brought up. I was taught that personal information is sacred and should only be shared with family members and close friends."

I felt like I was walking in a field of energy constricted by how unique the importance of cultural morals and values were to Adya.

I realized then that in order for me to work with Adya I would need to become her trusted friend first. So I did. We spoke about my life, my children, and what it must be like for her to have a newborn with her parents and family living so far away in India. This was a delightful session. It was more like having tea with a girlfriend.

Adya began to share more about herself during our sessions. She told me she felt like she was living two lives. One was with her husband and friends, and the other was with her family, who had their own traditions and cultural beliefs. She explained that she knew the importance of the differences between the two cultures, but her husband, friends, and family did not understand how the two cultures were so different from one another and the impact this had on her.

I asked, "Then what would it be like for you to explain to them what it is like for you to be living in America and having a different experience than what they are having?"

"I don't know how that would feel," she stated.

I decided to gently take Adya through a guided visualization for her to see her future without her pain and her self-inflicted submission to ideals that did not fit her own beliefs. Tears began to run down her face as she told me the story of respect and honor she had for her family. Even though she found happiness in her new life in America, she also found that freedom didn't necessarily mean happiness; for her, it meant evaluating her choices. She also told me that the key to her personal happiness was in how she upheld her values and beliefs in her life. We finished her session and decided to meet again the following week.

During our next session, Adya began the conversation.

"Shirley, something happened to me this week that changed my hearing," she said.

I was surprised at this, because I was thinking that I might not be able to help her.

"Adya, what happened?" I asked.

She shyly smiled and said, "After our last session on Wednesday, I cried for two days." She paused and then went on, "At some point during the day on Saturday, I felt something pop inside my head, near my left ear, and I began to hear tones that I haven't been able to hear in a long time."

She went on to explain how difficult it was for her to communicate some of her new choices to her family because of how much she respected them. At times, it was difficult for her to explain to her husband and friends that she could not participate in certain conversations since she believed some of their discussions devalued another person.

This conversation opened another door for me to explore with her. I shared with her that I believed one aspect of her hearing loss was related to an unconscious emotional perception she held from all the difficulties she was trying to adjust to. It may have been a way of shutting out all the external conflicts in her life. As she became more aware of her truth, she began to release some of the energetic blocks that were hindering her hearing. I agreed with her that crying for a couple of days helped to release those emotional blocks, and that's when her ear popped.

At her next session, Adya told me that in the days that followed, she found herself being more honest when discussing her feelings with her husband. Feelings that she had suppressed out of fear that she would not be understood. This allowed him to better understand and help her, both as a husband and doctor. Adya's attitude improved dramatically, and she was now ready to work with a psychotherapist. This was her last session with me.

* * *

Adya was the first of many people I would meet who came to live here from other countries to find themselves searching for some common ground between maintaining respect for their cultural values and embracing their new American home. This experience showed me just how important it was to understand and embrace cultural diversity.

I have also found that those of us who are born in America have the same challenges when we embrace the differences we encounter from one generation to another and the diversity of family values and ideals in a community.

When we are at odds with the importance of diversity, our behaviors may project attitudes such as bigotry, prejudices, and conflict between generations, races, age or sexual discrimination. Adya taught me so much about the importance of understanding diversity and the importance of respecting another's culture and heritage. We all feel more comfortable being with people and situations that are familiar to us, but when we are brought together in a diverse group with the same purpose, that is when we have a greater capacity to grow and learn.

Dr. Aasen was so pleased with his wife's progress that he asked if I would be open to see another patient of his and I agreed.

* * *

I believed people held their stories in many different places in their bodies. I had often found that disease did not come from their behaviors alone, but also from the stories that were never told. These stories were embedded deep within them in the fabric of subtle sound and vibrational energy. And because these stories were never expressed and healed, they began to manifest as physical ailments.

* * *

During my teenage years when I was so confused, illness came over me. I thought for sure I had pneumonia but the doctor told my mother that he could not find any reason for my depression and shortness of breath. That is when the laughter, fun and fear turned into numbness.

Ann was a young woman who had been seeing Dr. Aasen for only a short period of time. She owned a home on the outskirts of Boston, where she and her husband lived and practiced a holistic lifestyle.

Ann was a believer in the macrobiotic philosophy, which maintains that all of us are the product of and are continually being influenced by our *total* environment: the foods we consume, the geographical location and climate we live in, and our social interactions. She loved to cook and always prepared meals for her family and guests from fresh, all-natural ingredients, including whole grains, beans, vegetables, and fruit.

So it came as quite a surprise to Ann when her doctors diagnosed the pain she was having in her abdomen as a tumor in her uterus. Because of the complication in how it was attached to her uterus, the doctors recommended removing her uterus.

Ann was devastated by this news. She subscribed to the belief that every aspect of the physical body plays a vital role in how we function as a whole being. So having surgery to remove a tumor was not an option for her. Worse, the prospect of undergoing surgery absolutely terrified her. There had to be an alternative.

She decided to go with her beliefs and do everything possible to heal herself naturally, which was how she had come to consult with Dr. Aasen, and why he now turned to me for assistance.

As Ann and I sat and talked, I told her there was a reason why this was happening to her and, that I would help her to discover what that reason was, by accessing her energy and helping her to understand her present situation.

"Let me explain what happens," I said. "Our body is constantly giving us information. When our physical body is in pain or suffers, it's an indication that we have missed what our intuition and instincts have been trying to tell us. Specifically, direct guidance and logical ability to make healthy choices. When we heed these stages of guidance to find the cause and correct it, our life force can then flow freely, the way it is intended to."

"People call me a healer, yet all that I'm doing is listening to your body and then sharing with you what is happening in your energy field. It's your own life force and your own beliefs that bring about the actual healing. We can all learn to heal ourselves and our lives."

"Okay," she said. "How do we begin?"

After praying the Lord's Prayer in silence, I placed my hands on certain parts of her small frame until my intuition guided me to focus more deeply on her back and then on her abdomen. As this was happening, Ann said she experienced a pleasant tingling sensation throughout her body and felt a strong sense of calm.

The minutes went by as the vibration of her field went from a chaotic expression of energy to that of latticework, like that found in patterns of fine lace. A beautiful soft light was now emanating from her body. I then had the urge to place my hands over the area of distress in her abdomen. Suddenly, I could feel the distention in her abdomen recede, and Ann could feel it too.

I never try to anticipate what the healing response will be. I want to keep my mind clear to discern what should happen next in the person's healing process. I had worked enough with healing to know that everyone's healing process is unique; all I had to do is be aware of my intuitive guidance in the moment. I was assisting, and her life force was doing the healing.

Overjoyed by our success in this session, Ann scheduled several more sessions with me. And each time, the tumor would shrink a little more, until finally her abdomen returned to its normal size.

As these sessions progressed and her energy field grew stronger, I began to see the difference in the mass of energy that was out of sync with the rest of her field. This fabric of energy looked as if it was an entangled ball of fine threads that was enmeshed in it, choking off the flow of her life force through her uterus.

Contrary to the opinion of her doctors, I believed she did not need her uterus removed to heal her.

We had come quite far in healing. Although the size of the tumor had been reduced by the alignment of her energy field, there was still the issue of the core of the tumor. As I tapped into the energy of the core of the tumor I felt there was great fear that she was not aware of. Ann wasn't making a full recovery, I realized, because something in her unconscious was holding her hostage and I believed it was about a childhood memory.

I took a break from the hands on part of the healing session and sat down to talk with her.

"Ann, do you have a fear of hospitals?" I asked.

"Yes," she replied.

"Do you remember when this fear began?" I asked.

Ann paused as if searching through her mind for the answer.

"Since my brother died, when I was a child," she responded.

"Do you remember what the circumstances were of his death?" I asked.

Ann gasped and began to cry. "Yes, he went into the hospital to have his tonsils removed. But he never returned home." She sobbed. "I was three years old at the time. I remember how confused I was. My mother, father, brother, and sisters were all crying, and every time I would ask where Teddy was, they just told me he had to go on a long trip. Later, when I was older, my mother told me he had died from a complication during surgery."

Ann's eyes filled with tears as she relived the loss of her brother, a memory that had lived within her all these years, tucked away in her subconscious until this very moment. The more we delved into her memories, the more Ann came to realize how overwhelming the impact of losing her brother was in her life. It was why she had chosen to live her life in the healthiest way possible. This experience set in motion her passionate interest in diet and health, which had become her life's work. Yet she had not realized that this trauma left her with unresolved feelings, which covered up her fear that she may someday lose her health. And even greater, she wanted to always stay healthy because she thought if she ever had to go into the hospital, she may never come out alive.

All of this knowledge lay nestled in the unconscious regions of her mind and in her body, waiting to be dealt with. Now Ann realized why she had such an incredible aversion to hospitals: "People could go into them for the littlest things and might never come out." She explained. Until she recognized this, she was in conflict within herself about hospitals and surgery. This was a powerful moment of awareness for her.

We then revisited the issue of surgery. I reassured her that I truly believed her uterus would not have to be removed, because I had seen another option.

"None of my doctors will believe that," she insisted.

"Then keep looking for one who does," I countered.

But she wouldn't have anything to do with my suggestion. Emotionally, the cure was worse to her than the disease. For the moment, it was preferable to do nothing.

*　*　*

Several weeks later, I heard from Ann again; she sounded so uplifted and happy.

"Shirley, I've found the answer to my dilemma," she said over the phone.

"How exciting, Ann, what is it?" I asked.

"I've found the man that is going to heal me," she exclaimed.

"Ann, you found a surgeon who can remove the tumor without taking your uterus? That's great," I replied.

"No," she said, her tone dropping several octaves. "I found a psychic surgeon."

Having no idea what a "psychic surgeon" was, I didn't know what to say to this. Ann then explained how she had heard about this man in the Philippines who had successfully operated on people without the use of any surgical instruments.

"He just uses the energy in his hands to root out the sickness," she said with excitement. "Come with me, Shirley. I don't want to go alone."

Again, I didn't know how to respond or even how I felt about all this. Seconds passed in silence until Ann said, "Shirley, let me send you the brochure on this man. Then give me a call to let me know how you feel about going with me after you've read about him."

That seemed reasonable enough. "Okay," I replied. In the back of my mind, I was thinking of how much Jake and the children had been through with me already, what would they think now of my traveling to the Philippines to visit a psychic surgeon?

Ann had assured me that the psychic surgeon only took donations for his healing work. That made me feel more comfortable, since Edgar Cayce only took donations, and to me this felt fitting for such a gift to be used for good.

A couple of days later, the brochure arrived in the mail. I remember sitting down with Jake at the kitchen table to discuss the material in the brochure. I was excited about having the opportunity to learn from this authentic healer, and besides, we would only be gone for five days. Jake read the brochure and then looked up at me.

After taking a long deep breath, he said, "Shirl, this is not a good time to be traveling clear across the world. I can't believe this would be a good thing, especially since their country is in so much turmoil right now."

He then went on. "Besides, you don't even have a passport or your immunizations to travel. Ann will be leaving in less than a week."

Jake was right. It seemed impossible for this to happen for me. But then Jake shared another thought he had. "I can't tell you not to go if you truly feel you are meant to. I've seen too many positive experiences happen from your healing work. I will help you in any way I can."

Now it was my turn to be hesitant. There seemed to be no logic to this hesitancy, other than Jake's comment about the political chaos in the Philippines. Still, according to the brochure, many people were traveling there to meet with this psychic surgeon all the time, and their safety had apparently never been in jeopardy. So that wasn't the reason for my hesitation. But I had to make a choice: go with Ann and seize the opportunity to meet this man and see him work, or stay home. Right then and there, I chose to go.

I would have to move quickly to get my passport. But how hard could that be? All we had to do was go to the passport office in Boston.

We drove to Boston that afternoon. The official who took my application said, "I'm sorry, miss, you've got all the necessary information you need for your application, but I can't say for sure when you will receive your passport. It usually takes up to three weeks for the process to be completed. Even if you have your airline tickets and a departure date, we need at least a week to complete your application."

For some reason, I was relieved to hear this, and then he stated, "You can use your birth certificate and driver's license if you don't have a passport." With that statement, I began to feel uneasy again. Both Jake and I thanked the man and drove back home.

The next afternoon I was in the kitchen when Jake came through the front door, yelling my name, "Shirl. Shirley."

"I'm in the kitchen." I yelled back.

As he approached me, I noticed he was holding the mail.

"Open this," he said as he held out an envelope.

"Okay," I said with a curious look.

As I began to open the envelope, I realized what it was.

"My passport!" I shouted. Then, in total amazement, I said, "But how could this be possible?"

"You're asking me?" Jake replied with a surprised tone in his voice.

We both just stood there, staring at each other in amazement.

Finally, Jake broke the silence. "I guess you're supposed to go."

Now, you might think I would be excited about this, but I wasn't. In fact, I wasn't feeling good about this at all. Don't get me wrong, I'd seen with my own eyes incredible spontaneous healings, but with my passport arriving less than twenty-four hours in the mail. Ahhh, I just couldn't wrap my head around this one.

Chapter 7

On a Wing and a Prayer

Ann and I made plans to leave for the Philippines from Logan Airport in Boston.

At the airport I met Ann's family for the first time. Her husband and two children looked very concerned about her leaving but I assured them I would watch over her. It seemed so much more relevant than before to help Ann after meeting her family. This will not only help Ann but will help her husband who looked so concerned about his wife.

After saying good-bye to my children and Jake, I boarded the plane. Ann was so happy that I was with her. She had such unbelievable faith that this newfound psychic surgeon would heal her. On the other hand, I still had an uncomfortable feeling.

The trip was long, and our only stop was in Japan. As we waited in the airport, I was still in a funk. Ann sat next to me, very involved in what she was reading. Right before we boarded our next plane, I saw something that grabbed my attention. There were several women between the ages of twenty and forty exiting a plane, one after another, holding small infants and toddlers all under the age of two years old.

Something clicked inside of me, and I suddenly came out of my funk. These beautiful little children were wrapped in blankets and wearing little caps on top of their heads. One woman gestured for another woman to take the infant she was holding, and as she started across the way, I asked her where all the children came from.

"Why, these children are being adopted by families all over the world," she said.

Her smile was gentle as she gestured at all the women she was traveling with.

"We work for an adoption organization that ensures the safety of these children while moving them from one country to another. And, hopefully, they will have more of a fulfilling life than they would have, if left in the impoverished situation, they had come from."

"God bless you," I responded. For the first time, I realized how limited my knowledge was about others in the world. It is one thing to read or see situations such as these on the news; it's another thing to experience it in your life.

* * *

It was late morning when we landed in Manila. As soon as our feet hit the ground, Ann started to have misgivings. "I don't feel good about this," she said suddenly.

"Why?" I asked.

"Something isn't right," she answered vaguely.

"Ann, we just got here," I said. "You're the one that wanted to do this." I paused and then said, "It'll be okay."

All of my doubt had faded away after seeing the women and children in Japan. My soul had been deeply touched by them. This had somehow transformed me, and I was ready to learn things that I could not have learned if I hadn't been on this trip. Now Ann was the one who was questioning her choice to come.

We emerged from the terminal into the oppressive heat and humidity and saw a taxi driver holding a sign with Ann's name on it. He greeted us without words being exchanged and without even a smile.

Ann was very quiet as we sat in the backseat of the taxi. I had many questions to ask the taxi driver as we made our way over rugged roads, passing peasants and farmers with chickens scattering in front of the cab. I posed one question after another, yet the driver responded to none of them. I assumed he spoke no English, so I gave up asking. Ann and I then spent the rest of the drive to our hotel gazing out at the war-torn streets in silence.

When we checked into the hotel, the desk clerk asked us to surrender our passports. "I'll put them in the safe," he said. "The city is crawling with thieves," he cautioned, "and there are men with guns everywhere."

I had never been out of my own country before, so I naturally found it comforting to know that the hotel we were staying at would watch over us. So I gave him my passport. But Ann refused. In fact, she was angry.

Her look was fixed on the clerk, and she asked, "Why do I need to give you my passport?"

The clerk sighed and repeated, "For security purposes, ma'am."

I looked at Ann and realized that she was very uncomfortable. "Ann, what do you want to do?" I asked.

She looked me straight in my eyes and said, "I'm not giving him my passport."

"Okay," I responded. "Okay, don't."

The clerk just looked at both of us, shrugged his shoulders and walked away.

Our room was pleasant and looked out over the city. As I looked down at the city, I could see many cardboard boxes lined up in a row directly in front of the hotel gate. At first, I thought they hadn't picked up the trash, and then my vision focused on something more. I had to go downstairs to the street to see what it was.

As I exited the hotel, one of the attendants who worked there stopped me and asked if I wanted a taxi. "No," I said.

"Miss, where are you going?" he asked.

I told him I was going to take a walk, and he told me to be very careful if I went beyond the gates of the hotel. I thanked him and went on my way.

I know it is one thing to see impoverished circumstances on the news, but to walk the streets where they exist, made a profound impact on me. I saw poor people living in the cardboard boxes that were lined up right outside the wall of this plush hotel. This city was a mixture of the greatest wealth and the most abject poverty.

Little children appeared from everywhere, running toward me with beautiful smiles. All of them stopped about two feet in front of me and respectfully held out their hands, asking silently for anything I could give them. These children were frail and malnourished, and underneath their smiling faces, was a deep sense of needs. I had nothing to offer them.

I was touched deeply. I thought of my own children and how much I wanted them to have every opportunity they could in life to be happy and healthy. I promised myself that someday, somehow I would do something for children. As I walked back toward the hotel with my eyes fixed to the ground, all I could think to do for these children was to pray for them, and so I did.

I know that there is poverty and sickness everywhere in the world, even in our own country, but until I experienced it close up, I hadn't realized how fortunate I was to live in our free country with all the opportunities we have.

*   *   *

Ann and I had an early dinner that evening. We wanted to get a good night's sleep in preparation for our meeting with the psychic surgeon early the next morning.

The next day started out sunny and hot. After eating a continental breakfast in the main dining room, Ann and I waited in the hotel lobby for our ride to the surgeon's home. We were both dressed comfortably and were prepared for the hot day, but Ann still wasn't feeling good about being in the Philippines.

I was looking forward to experiencing another healer's abilities, and especially excited about meeting a person who performed psychic surgery.

Psychic surgeons had the ability to perform surgery without using any instruments. They would make an incision just by using the energy from their hands. Once a physical opening was created, they would then remove the diseased tissue, again, only with their hands.

The Philippine psychic that Ann had chosen was highly recommended by close personal friends of hers. My ability as a healer was in understanding people's energy and the importance of the integration of their field, which would then allow them to heal. Psychic surgery was beyond my knowledge of energy.

The taxi arrived, and Ann and I were driven from the safety of our hotel and the city to a more remote part of the country. We drove through increasingly poorer areas of Manila to the outskirts of the city. There, the road, which was roughly paved to begin with, turned to a mass of ruts, like a trail cut through the jungle. As we drove, the roads became narrow and the vegetation became increasingly dense. The brush was so dense that it brushed against the sides of the cab.

Out of nowhere, we came upon a clearing, and there stood one of the most beautiful houses I had seen since we arrived. This house looked like one of those restored mansions you see in the South, like Tara in *Gone with the Wind*. It had a beautiful, rap around porch surrounding the front, with rounded white pillars that braced an overhanging ceiling. The house was painted white and the front door was ornately exquisite.

I noticed many people waiting to enter the psychic surgeon's house. These natives seemed to be undernourished, enough that their bones seemed to protrude from under their flesh. Some of them carried live chickens, and others balanced baskets of vegetables and fruit. Later I learned that this was their fee for their appointments with the psychic surgeon.

Visitors that came from other countries, including Ann and myself, were allowed in the doors before the others. We were then escorted to a fine sitting room. An assistant explained to us in detail how the psychic surgeon would work on us. We were to stand close to the front of the room, where he would have an easier time addressing his foreign guests. Then we followed our guide into another part of the house.

The room where the psychic surgeon would perform his surgery was the largest room on the first floor. The air that filled the room was hot and humid. The only piece of furniture was a long wooden table that stood at the furthest end of the room. As I looked at the bare essentials in the room, I just could not fathom how this man was going to heal Ann and these people under such unsterilized conditions. Ann and I both stood there in silence.

From outside the mansion, drums began to beat, and I could feel my heart jump as I tried to stay calm. The others began to enter the room and push against us; there was not enough space to accommodate the crowd. All of us stood there waiting patiently for the healing to begin.

Ann turned to me and grabbed my arm. "Let's leave," she said in a stern voice.

"What are you talking about?" I asked.

"I want to get out of here!" she insisted.

"And do what?" I replied. "Walk back to the hotel through the jungle?"

"None of this feels right, Shirl," she exclaimed. "None of this is right. Even the feeling of spirit in the room is not the same as when you are healing."

"Ann, this man is famous for his work," I said. "This is a wonderful opportunity for you to be healed by a practitioner who's famous for performing psychic surgery. We should feel privileged in having this opportunity to meet with him," I said.

As if on cue, a door opened, and a tall large man entered the room, followed by a small, dark-skinned man. My first assumption was that the tall man was the psychic surgeon, but the small man stood behind the table in preparation for the healing to begin. He was dressed all in white: white shoes, white pants, white shirt, and even a white sports jacket. I surmised the tall man was his bodyguard. The bodyguard stood in the front corner of the room watching over the audience.

The psychic surgeon leaned over, placed his hands on the table, and bowed his head. "See," I said to Ann, "he's praying! Can't you feel the energy shift in the room?"

Ann paused for a moment as if she was trying to take in the feeling.

"Yes," she replied, "but I'm still uncomfortable."

As I glanced back to the front of the room, the psychic surgeon's eyes shifted from one person to the next, almost in preparation for how to proceed. At this point, I was calm and thought that he seemed like a holy man, very devoted to his cause of helping others. On the other hand, Ann was not buying any of it. "What have I gotten us into?" she exclaimed under her breath.

The psychic surgeon then pointed to a native man, who came forward and lay on the table. During my clinical days as a student nurse, I would become squeamish at the very thought of surgery, so I began to pray even more for all to go well.

Suddenly the psychic surgeon stopped what he was doing to the man and looked around the room. He paused and began to open up the man's stomach energetically. I was so grateful to be a part of such an incredible experience that I again began to pray silently. The psychic surgeon, with a gesture of dissatisfaction, quickly raised his head and walked around to the front of the table, looking at his audience; his patient remained on the table.

"He is looking for something," said Ann.

"Like what?" I asked her in a whisper.

"I don't know but the energy in this room sure has changed."

Then the psychic surgeon's eyes met mine, and as I felt him glare deeply into me, I became faint.

"Ann. Ann!" That was all I could say before I collapsed to the ground.

The next thing I knew, Ann and I were being escorted out of the large room into a small waiting area. The tall bodyguard offered me a glass of water, and as we sat there, the psychic surgeon entered the room.

Ann was quiet and observant at this time. He shook both of our hands and sat in a chair behind a desk. I was shocked when he began to speak. "How are you feeling?" he asked.

He can speak English, I thought to myself. "Better," I replied.

"The energy can do funny things to you sometimes," he responded.

Ann started to squirm in her seat. As I gazed from him to Ann, I could tell that she wasn't buying into any of this.

"So you are from America?" he stated with a smile as we both nodded. "Well, why are you here?" he asked.

Though his manner was friendly and not at all offensive, Ann stiffened and refused to answer. I was excited to be able to speak to this man one-on-one, so I jumped in to answer. I explained that Ann wanted to be healed and that I had traveled with her so she would not be alone in a strange country. Then I added, "I'm very interested in your work."

Suddenly, the air changed in the room. It was so thick it felt like you could cut it with a knife. His dark brown eyes seemed to turn black as he focused on me. I could hardly catch my breath.

Then the psychic surgeon said, "You cannot stay here."

I was shocked but collected myself. "Why not?" I asked. "My friend needs your help, and I'd like to learn how you work."

He shook his head. "No. It would be better if I did my work with her individually," he said. "I will help your friend, but not here." He then stood up and left the room. The meeting was over.

His bodyguard returned and told us that the surgeon would meet us later that evening in the travel agency's office located inside our hotel. Because of the extreme heat, he would be performing Ann's surgery in a cooler environment. We were then escorted to an awaiting taxi, the same one that had brought us, and we were driven back to the hotel.

On the drive back, Ann began to talk again about her concerns. "Shirley, there is something very wrong."

"What do you mean?" I replied.

As she turned to look at me more directly, I caught a glimpse of the taxicab driver, who seemed to perk up as we continued our discussion. "I still don't get a good feeling about being here," she replied.

I paused for a moment and then replied, "Okay, I'm paying attention, so what do you want to do?"

Ann sat back, pondering the situation, and said, "Since we came all this way, I will meet with him tonight and then decide if I want to go through with this healing." We were both silent for the rest of the ride back to our hotel.

That evening Ann and I ate in the hotel's dining room, and then prepared for our meeting with the psychic surgeon. As we entered the waiting room at the travel agency there were several other tourists from the morning healing session who were waiting there as well. Ann was not surprised to see the rest of the tourists also there for private sessions.

Ann was finally called into the healing room, and as we approached the door, all of a sudden, I was told that I could not go into the room. The door was closed quickly behind Ann. As I sat down to wait, I began to wonder what had just happened. Before I knew it, the psychic surgeon opened the door and invited me into the room.

Ann was lying on a table in what seemed to be an incoherent state. My focus swiftly turned to the psychic surgeon, who was holding up a large mass of what I assumed was human tissue. "See?" he exclaimed. "This is what I took out of her."

I then focused on Ann, who was being helped off the table by one of the psychic surgeon's assistants. She looked glassy-eyed and out of it.

"I've got to call home," she said sluggishly.

"What for?" I asked.

"More money," she answered.

"Why?" I asked. I thought about how Ann had not felt good about being there. I knew to pay attention to what I was hearing from her now, especially since I hadn't been allowed to enter the room where the psychic surgery was performed.

"To pay for more surgery," she responded.

"How much more?" I asked.

"Three thousand dollars," she replied.

"No, Ann, you can't do that," I said firmly.

I turned to the surgeon and asked, "What is she talking about?"

Ann responded, "Shirley, we will have to stay here longer, and I need that money to be completely healed."

I turned back toward the psychic surgeon again and asked, "I thought your brochure stated that you took donations only."

The psychic surgeon quickly left the room without another word. I led Ann back to our room, where I helped her into bed to sleep off whatever happened to her while having psychic surgery.

I felt imprisoned. I began to pray, "Dear God, help us!" A thought came to me before I was even finished with my prayer. We were scheduled to return to the States in three days, yet I was guided not to wait.

"Get out of here as soon as possible," I heard a voice say.

As Ann slept, I decided to go downstairs to see if we could leave earlier. The man at the front desk was very kind to me. "There is no one at the reservation desk to change your travel plans, right now," he said. "Come back tomorrow morning and I will try again for you. That is the best I can do."

As I turned to leave the front desk, I remembered that they were holding my passport.

I turned back to the clerk and said, "You are holding my passport in your safe. I would like to retrieve it please."

He gently bowed and went to the room behind the desk. All of a sudden, I didn't feel very well. When he came out of the back room, I could see that something was wrong.

"I am sorry miss," he replied. "The travel agency that booked your tickets has your passport."

"What do you mean, you don't have my passport?" I replied. "I gave it to you for safekeeping, not the travel agency."

"I know," he said. "But someone from the travel agency took it a little while ago."

"Oh, no!" I exclaimed.

I was in shock. What is this? I thought. How could the desk clerk give my passport to a person from the travel agency?

I rushed to the travel agency. There were still patients waiting to see the psychic surgeon as I entered the travel agency's waiting room. The waiting room was full, so I said to the man at the desk, "My name is Shirley Beauman and I am here to pick up my passport."

"Of course," he said with a pleasant smile. I was relieved to hear that I could retrieve it without any more problems.

He then opened up a filing cabinet and took out a folder. As he pulled out an envelope, the psychic surgeon's assistant came through the door and asked me what I was doing there.

"I came to pick up my passport," I commented.

"We do not have your passport," he said in a stern voice.

The man who was at the desk put the folder back into the filing cabinet.

"But I was told that …" I began to say when I was interrupted.

"You will have to come back tomorrow morning, and we will help you then," he commanded.

"But I …"

"I'm sorry," he interrupted gruffly. "Come back tomorrow." I glared at him, and with that, he escorted me out the door.

I could not believe what was happening. As I ran up the stairs to our room, I could feel the anxiety rise up in my chest. My hands were red and sweaty, which was very unusual for me, and as soon as I stepped into the room, I locked the door. Trembling from the experience, I tried to arouse Ann from her deep sleep.

"Ann, Ann, wake up, wake up!"

Finally Ann opened her eyes. She appeared to be coherent, which was totally different from the mesmerized state she was left in from her psychic healing. "What? What?" she asked. I took a deep breath and explained to her what had just happened.

Ann threw the covers off her and jumped to her feet. "I told you so," she stammered. "What did I tell you?"

I could only look at her. Ann was weak and still could not get her bearings as she tried to maneuver around the room. Finally, I was able to help her back into bed and quieted her enough so she could fall back to sleep.

I paced the floor frantically. Thoughts kept running through my mind of what might happen to us. First, I believed we would be stranded until Ann came up with the extra money. Then I had a great idea: we would go to the authorities and tell our story. Oh, but who would ever believe that we were telling the truth. Mmm. Especially in a foreign country. Not a good idea.

"God, please help us. What should I do?" I asked the voice. I was so shaken that I could not calm down.

I then felt a change in the air around me, similar to when the cabinets in the kitchen were shaking.

"Listen carefully," the voice said. "This is a gift. Use it wisely."

This voice was not the voice from within me, but it resonated within my field yet further away than my physical reality. I waited patiently, but nothing else came. *Great,* I thought to myself. *Now I'm on my own again.*

As I sat there, thoughts about Cyndy's healing came to mind, reminding me how centered and clear I was when my focus was on her wellbeing. The steps I took that allowed me to understand that there was a core of wisdom within us also ran through my mind.

Of course, this makes sense now, I said to myself. *Safety.* I once again began to pray, but this time I was more specific. I prayed for the return of my passport and our safe return to the United States. The confusion dissipated, it was clear in my mind what I had to accomplish. My whole body was fused with energy. Then there was a cool sensation that I felt. And there it was, a humming sound that emanated the life force from within me to expand. I knew clearly what was in front of me to do. My fears disappeared, and I envisioned Ann and me safely home!

It was 2:15 a.m., when I knew I had to go downstairs to the lobby of the hotel. Without hesitation, I awakened Ann.

"Ann, Ann, wake up!" I said. "We have to get downstairs, right away."

"What time is it?" she asked.

"It's about 2:20 a.m.," I said. As she slowly sat up, she began to realize the importance of our day.

"Why do we have to go downstairs so early?" she asked.

I was so exhausted from being up all night that I could hardly speak. "I don't know, I just know we have to go downstairs now."

Still groggy from her experience the evening before, she replied, "You go ahead, and I will meet you down there in a while. I need to take a shower and try to wake up."

"Okay," I exclaimed as I gathered my belongings. It was probably better that I went alone, because I didn't fully understand why I had to be in the lobby so early.

The lobby was deserted. I went to the front desk and said out loud, "Hello, hello, is anyone here?" No response.

Then my focus went to the door of the travel agency. As I moved toward the middle of the lobby, I knew to sit in a particular chair in the middle of the foyer, where I could see all the doors leading to the different shops and the dining area of the hotel.

"This is starting to feel a little crazy, even by my standards, and believe me I have experienced a lot of unusual things." I said out loud. "What do I do now?"

I waited for some thought about a direction to take, only to find myself feeling small in the stillness of the early morning hours. No thoughts, no voice, just stillness.

A clock hung over the entrance to the dining room. The time was 3:05 a.m.

Then the time was 3:43 a.m. Still nothing happened.

Ann came down the stairs, carrying her luggage and she still looked as if she wasn't fully awake. By this time, it was 4:27 a.m.

"What are you waiting for?" she asked.

"I really don't know," I said. "Maybe for the travel agency to open."

"Shirley, it is 4:30 in the morning." she replied.

"Oh, well." I said with a questioning look on my face.

The seconds that ticked by seemed like minutes, the minutes like hours. I looked at the clock hanging over the front desk. It was 4:50 a.m.

Just then, a small woman entered the lobby from the front door, carrying a bucket and a mop. She stopped in front of the travel agency, put down her mop and bucket, reached in her pocket, and pulled out some keys. She opened the door to the travel agency. "Bingo!" I said softly.

Still exhausted and shaken, I gestured to Ann to be quiet as I made my way across the lobby to the now opened door to the travel agency. I went through the door, still not clear as to what I was going to do.

"Excuse me, excuse me, Miss." I said. The small-framed woman began to speak in her native language, and, of course I couldn't understand a word of what she was saying, but it was clear to me that she was upset by my presence.

As I moved toward the filing cabinet, I said calmly, "I'm here to pick up my passport. You see, I wouldn't normally do something like this, but in these circumstances, I have no other choice. You understand, don't you? I'm sure if you were in my position, you would do the same thing, so I'm sorry to interrupt your morning, but I have to get my passport so I can leave here as soon as possible."

I knew she didn't understand a word I said, but it was best to be honest and hope that somehow she understood me. As I pulled on the cabinet drawer, it opened. I prayed that my hand would grab the folder where my passport was kept.

I proceeded to pull out the first folder I placed my hands on. I opened it, and no passport.

I took a deep breath and pulled out a second folder. I opened this one, and no passport.

Then I knew I had to focus and visualize in my mind that I had my passport already in my hands, and with that thought, I pulled out another folder. In it was a white envelope with my name printed on the front of it. I tore it open, and there was my passport.

I was so relieved that I felt like hugging the cleaning lady. Instead, as I clutched my passport, I anxiously apologized for the intrusion as I backed out of the door of the travel agency.

Ann could see the smile on my face as I hurriedly walked toward her. "Let's go!" I said. With luggage in hand, we hurried out the front door and out of the front gates to find a taxicab. There was one cab sitting on the side of the road.

I could see that the cab driver was resting with his eyes closed, but as soon as we were several feet from him, he opened his eyes and went into action. As I handed our bags to him, I noticed that he was the same driver that had picked us up at the airport and had driven us to the psychic surgeon's house and back.

"Please hurry!" I said. "We have to get to the airport as quickly as possible!"

The cab driver stopped and looked deeply into my eyes. Then a look came over his face as if he understood what had happened to Ann and me.

Once we were seated in the backseat of the taxicab, he took off with great speed down the pitch-black road to the airport. Ann and I were tossed and bounced from one side to the other as the cab made its way down the dark, bumpy road. A flock of chickens rose up in front of the headlights; the driver hit the horn to warn them to get out of the way, leaving them squawking and flapping their wings to get out of the way.

I turned to Ann to see how she was doing. She seemed to have finally shaken off the effects of whatever she experienced from the psychic surgery. "Boy, there is nothing like a mad dash along a bumpy road in a foreign country in the early hours of the morning to get the adrenaline flowing." I said, trying to lighten up the moment. And that it did, believe me, for all three of us.

We finally reached the airport. Ann and I jumped out of the cab as the driver retrieved our bags. I dug into my purse for the fare, plus a big tip for being our guardian angel, but when I tried giving him the cash, he just waved it off and blurted out an urgent, "Go, go, go!"

"May God bless you," I shouted back to him as we ran for the airport doors.

Once inside the terminal, we headed straight for the TWA ticket counter, where I asked for the next flight to the United States.

A 6:00 a.m. flight for the United States was already boarding, and the plane was about to close its doors for takeoff.

The ticket representative made a call to the gate, asking the attendant to hold the doors open for two more passengers. We paid the exchange fee and rushed to board the plane.

Minutes later, we were in the air.

I could breathe again. I pushed the button on the armrest and melted into the seat as it reclined. I looked over at Ann, who had her eyes closed and was trying to calm herself down.

As the plane began to ascend, I thought of what had just transpired. I then heard a voice say, "Job well done."

* * *

I thought back to Cyndy's healing and knew that having a clear focus was what helped me to listen to my own intuition and inner direction. And what would have been the odds that I could have retrieved my passport if, during the night before, I hadn't seen the assistant place it back in the file cabinet? Yet still confusing to me was the voice that had no face, no name, and no point of origin. This was still a mystery to me.

After our trip, Ann and I lost touch. Maybe what we had gone through was too much to think of once she returned to her family and busy life. She had believed this psychic surgeon would heal her, and that wasn't what had happened. As for myself, I didn't know what to think except that we had an incredible experience in a foreign country and we returned home, safely.

* * *

Early one evening, about six months later, I was preparing dinner when the phone rang. It was Ann.

"Shirley, I had to call you," she said. I was a little taken aback, not knowing what to expect, since we hadn't spoken since our trip to the Philippines.

"How have you been?" I asked.

"Actually, that is why I'm calling you. I wanted you to know that I'm completely healed," she replied.

"What do you mean, Ann?" I asked. "Did the Philippine surgeon actually heal you?"

Ann laughed at my question. "No, I had the surgery, Shirl. I found a doctor who was open to hear what I had to say about my healing, and we worked together as a team.

"And, you were right. He was able to remove it without taking my uterus."

I was thrilled for Ann. All of what we went through had significance for her. The experiences she chose were perfect for her healing: her belief in God, her trust in me, her belief in others to heal, and for the courage and strength she had to keep searching for a physician who would listen to her. After a devastating event, she could have become discouraged but Ann continued her search for healing. This left me with a great sense of gratitude.

Later on, I realized that this conversation with Ann had stirred up unresolved feelings I had about our trip to the Philippines.

* * *

Thank God one of the quantum leaps I made was to realize that my feelings made me aware of my hidden, "unfinished business" I held about people and situations in my life. You know how it is. You think that you're done with something, only to have a similar situation happen again, and there you are, feeling the same way you had before.

So I knew the frustration I was feeling about the trip was telling me: "Pay attention. You have more work to do." Since then, my conversations with God have been more honest, yet honest doesn't necessarily mean nice.

Honesty makes room for us to be authentic and allows emotions to surface so we can understand every aspect of ourselves as we really are. Hiding truths in some deep place inside us may cause illness as well as the potential for us to project these emotions into other situations, inappropriately and impulsively. Instead of acting on my impulsive feelings, I had learned that I could go to a place within myself and have a conversation with God. I also knew not to let my ego overshadow my true feelings when it came to these reflective moments. Being honest takes courage.

* * *

So, I was angry. I couldn't understand what I needed to learn from the experience in the Philippines. The voice that had no face, no form, and no point of origin perplexed me. It was easy for me to see spirit when this source was around others, but this voice held no specific place of origin.

Is it possible to find solutions while under severe circumstances? Was this voice trying to help me until I realized that when I learned how to stay calm, I could tap into a reservoir of information as close as my breath? Well, at least one thing had improved with me: no more poltergeist activity.

But what is wrong with this? I thought. I still wasn't open to learn about the belief systems of others and how they received divine guidance. I began to realize that I would always seek ideals and beliefs that were similar to my own. I still relied on the comfort of these beliefs, as my guide but I was still closed down to anything that didn't resonate to my way of thinking! It was safe, I understood it, but it wasn't necessarily helping me evolve spiritually.

Why was it that I chose to stay closed to the beliefs and ideas of others? Why was I afraid to open up and learn something different from someone else, who might have different beliefs from my own? Why wasn't I striving to understand the diverse ways in how others experience life? *The final decision is mine to make,* I thought. *I'm the one who decides what I believe in and what I choose not to believe so why not try to understand the many ways by which the answers come?*

When I completed my personal inquisition, I decided to open my heart and mind to engage in trying to understand what others believe, even if this meant going outside of my own comfort zone. I knew by doing research on spiritual healing and religious beliefs, this would help me understand why the Philippine psychic surgeon and I clashed the way we did. So when I began my search, I read about a priest with the gift of healing from Fitchburg, Massachusetts, who was ordained on May 9, 1976. Father Ralph A. DiOrio, Jr., travels around the world in his healing ministry. This was comforting to me because of my belief in Jesus Christ and the teachings of the Catholic Church.

By researching spiritual healing in third world countries, I found that in many cultures that have limited medical technology the community of those cultures rely strongly on what has been passed down to them from their ancestors to restore health and well-being. I began to relate to our own history in the western world. We too had to rely on the wisdom of the elders in our communities before modern medical practices and procedures evolved.

I found the psychic surgeon and I had something in common when I researched my own family history. My grandmother used prayer and believed that by making the sign of the cross with a common pin over the warts of the neighborhood children, they would be healed. And they were! Now I was starting to wake up!

So what did I learn from experiencing a different culture and a different way of healing than my own? It was this: The cultures and the people that I read about all had their own unique way of healing, yet the common thread between them all was they believed in a power greater than themselves.

I also learned that greed is one of the factors that can take such great wisdom and change it into something less than what it was meant to be. Just like the psychic surgeon, who chose to request a greater fee, we are all fallible in making choices such as this.

But what was more important to me was I needed to make a choice in order to help others heal. I wasn't a doctor. I still didn't even have my nursing degree.

I then heard a voice say, "The Healer Within."

Chapter 8

Inside Heaven's Door

One morning, I had an appointment to see Reverend Harding from the Spiritualist Church. It was going to be a catch-up visit, since my profession as a healer had blossomed. I remember thinking how much I was looking forward to seeing her again as I drove onto the ramp to Route 6 that headed off Cape Cod. Then, there it was, smack in the middle of my mind. I saw in a flash a car accident, and I would be in the middle of it unless I took quick action. I had been warned by my precognitive abilities to get out of harm's way.

I pulled my car off to the side of the road as two cars crashed in front of me. I had pulled away from the accident just in the nick of time. I breathed a sigh of relief when out of nowhere, another car slammed into the collided cars in front of me, turning one of the cars around and directing it toward me, hitting the back side of my car and turning me out toward the road again. I stepped onto the gas pedal to try to move my car forward out of the way, but it was too late.

After my car had been hit, it careened back onto the road and crossed over the median and I found myself heading directly into oncoming traffic. I was on the wrong side of the road! I could do nothing about it. I was dazed. What happened next, seemed surreal.

A peaceful feeling came over me. My mind instantly became clear. I was alert and ready to take action, but not from my own direction. I was in touch with something greater than myself. I was encased in light and it was then that I heard a voice. It was the voice of my Uncle Eddie, who had passed away just a few years before. I saw his face appear from within the same light that encased me. His voice then penetrated my thoughts: "Shirley, take your foot off the gas, put it on the brake, and pull the steering wheel to the right. Now!"

I took my right foot off the gas pedal, placed it on the brakes, and pulled the steering wheel to the right. The oncoming traffic disappeared from my sight and my car crashed into a scrawny pine tree in the middle of the median. My life was saved.

As I became aware of my surroundings, I knew someone was in great need. At a distance was a car that had turned upside down. I leaped out of my car and ran to see if anyone was still in it. I found a woman strapped in her seat belt, sitting upside down in her car. I lay on the ground and reached into her car to place my hands on her for support.

"You're going to be okay," I said. "The police are on the way. I can hear the sirens."

I stayed with her until the police arrived, and then I went directly home.

I walked away from the accident unharmed, and there it was again: that place where there was no point of origin, but this time my Uncle Eddie was there. Somehow I was connected to something greater that was watching over me.

I will never forget that experience. There was something happening here. My spiritual awakening was beginning to expand. I was inside heaven's door.

* * *

It felt so good to know about this energy of light and the protection it gave me during the accident. I now understood this energy protects and surrounds me all the time.

As days passed, I realized this energy allowed me to keep a feeling of peace. I no longer reacted to stressful situations in the same way. My body felt healthier and my mind stayed clearer throughout the day. I began to integrate this connection into my daily prayers, allowing myself to sit quietly for longer periods of time, just bathing in this light with my focus on a peaceful mind and a healthy body. This was a very simple yet profound experience.

* * *

During one of these moments I had an unusual experience. A man, in spirit, appeared to me in my mind. He had an illuminating light emanating from his body, and I could feel rays of energy touch just the perimeter of the white light I was encased in. Through his light, I could see that his skin was dark, and his clothing looked like those worn by the Indian cultures from the East. It was as though we were communicating by a slight touch of each other's energy, and then he disappeared from my sight.

That afternoon, I was preparing the children for their yearly dentist checkup. As I stood in the hallway, calling for the girls to brush their teeth, I thought of the man that had visited me during my morning prayers. Then I had a thought, but I knew the thought wasn't mine. The thought was that I should call a woman by the name of Elaine, who I had met briefly when I worked for Dr. Siding. Elaine was an artist and her husband was a screenwriter. As I began to dismiss the thought to call her, the impulse to contact her became stronger.

"Now?" I asked out loud. "Can't I call her later?" "Now," I heard a voice reply. Still standing in the hallway, I looked behind me to see my three children, looking at me as if they were saying, "Who are you talking to Mom?" I gave them a smile and sent them off to play outside until we left for the dentist's office.

I anticipated that I would have incredible anxiety, as I usually did when I was about to do something out of the ordinary, but I had none. I looked up Elaine's number, and called her.

"Hi, Elaine," I said. "I don't know if you remember me, but I'm Shirley Beauman."

"Oh, of course I remember you, how are you?" she replied.

"I'm fine." I hesitated but then went on to say, "I know you might think this call to be a little unusual, but I'm calling you because there was a man who appeared to me this morning after my prayer work, and he wanted me to call you."

There was a long pause on the other end of the phone. "What do you mean, Shirley?" My mind at this point was still very clear, and I felt calm and peaceful. "Did you have a guru or teacher that used to live in India?" I asked.

"Oh, my!" she exclaimed. "Yes!"

"Well, he wanted me to tell you that he gave you your spiritual name, so you would know it was him, and that he is in a place where he cannot be reached at this time."

"Oh, Shirley, he still is my spiritual teacher. He lives in India," Elaine replied.

I was a little confused by what she said. Then she went on, "I was meditating when you called. I never let anything interrupt my meditation time, but I knew to come out of meditation to answer your phone call."

"I don't understand," I remarked.

Elaine laughed slightly and went on with her explanation. "He must be on his spiritual retreat. I have been trying to get in touch with him for a couple of months." I still didn't understand what she was saying. I was confused. *Could it be possible that Elaine was able to communicate with her deceased spiritual teacher?*

So many thoughts were running through my mind. Why was it that I was not able to hear Jesus but Elaine could communicate with her spiritual teacher?

Then I heard Elaine's voice break into my thoughts. "Shirley, you are in touch with my spiritual teacher, who is alive!" she explained.

"He's not dead?" I asked.

"No," she said with a slight laugh again. "No, he's alive."

At this point in our conversation, I was very confused.

Elaine laughed again. "Your vibration is attuned on levels of consciousness that allows you to communicate spiritually," she explained.

I was astonished. So many thoughts were running through my mind.

"Elaine, I still don't understand." I said. Then I remembered the children and their dentist appointments. "Oh, Elaine, I have to go," I said. "Can I call you later?"

Elaine and I decided we should meet and discuss what had happened. The day we met was the beginning of my introduction to Eastern spiritual beliefs and meditation. As we became friends and shared more about our beliefs, we found that they were quite similar.

Elaine now became my mentor in helping me to understand spiritual consciousness from an Eastern perspective. She had explained how our bodies were our temples of God and that within us was the divine connection to the source we call God, Source, or Divine Light. Her guru was her spiritual teacher in the understanding of her own self-realization. Elaine understood that the teaching of Christ consciousness was everyone's divine right. Jesus the Christ was one of the first souls whom evolved in enlightenment to a God being.

That which was similar was that I believed that Jesus the Christ was both human and Godly. Where we differed was that I believe this great being came into our humanly experience to set us free from bondage that kept us in pain and suffering. To me he is my redeemer. There are many paths that lead us back home, Christianity was the path that I was brought up in.

Elaine's husband Zach was a skeptic when it came to spiritual concepts. But because of their respect for each other, Elaine could engage in meditation and travel to India yearly to visit with her guru without creating any conflicts between them.

With Elaine's help, I now understood what I was doing by sitting still at the end of my prayer work. I was utilizing an aspect of meditation. I was listening to God's divine response to my prayers. On another occasion, in the quiet of my prayer work, I heard a voice from deep within me say, "Be still and you will know me."

There are many forms of prayer and meditation. The information is so vast that I chose not to place them in this book. But just as healing can occur in many ways, the use of prayer and meditation can be practiced in many ways as well. As I have shared with you before, I'm a Catholic girl, and just recently, I found several articles written by Catholic priests who teach how prayer and meditation work together in Christianity. The voice I heard said, "Be still and you will know me." The verse in the Bible reads: "Be still and know that I am God."

My choice of contemplation in God is through Christ consciousness. During my research, I found the acknowledgment and understanding of Christ consciousness in all the great religions. Even if a person has no belief this consciousness exists, it is a state of being that is within all of us. It is in this state of being Christ-like in our thoughts, actions, and the way we live our lives that we become like him. Buddha, Krishna, and other spiritual teachers, have also exemplified Christ consciousness as well.

* * *

Sitting quietly and focusing on God in meditation can be a challenge. But with consistency and repetition, balance and clarity of mind can be achieved. So I chose to be a mind-full participant in my spiritual awakening. I created a discipline that worked for me and incorporated it into my life. Instead of being unaware of the many ways in which God was responding to my needs, I chose to be awakened, not to the process but to what my prayers and quiet time brought to me from within. I was beginning to understand that these experiences brought a positive change to my life.

* * *

One morning while I was in the quiet part of my prayer work, I became aware of a cluster of light beams. I knew nothing about these little beams of light, but what I did know was that I was being asked to relay a message to a well-known actress. I will call her Suzanne Langely.

In order to get the message to her, I decided to ask Elaine's husband, Zach, to help me.

As I mentioned earlier in this chapter, Zach was a skeptic. I had no idea how he was going to respond to my request. But I knew the universe was asking me to bring a message to someone who had a very important decision to make in her life.

I called Elaine and explained why I needed to meet with Zach. She responded, "Shirley, I would love for you to talk with Zach, but I cannot tell you how he will react. He may think you're crazy!"

"I guess I'm willing to take that chance," I said.

"Okay," she responded. "I'll ask if he will meet with you."

It was only a few days before I was standing in front of Zach. His tall stance seemed stiff and inflexible as he looked down at me with sharp piercing eyes. Even though I was feeling intimidated I, in response, looked directly into his eyes then launched into the purpose of our meeting.

"Would you be open to helping me get a message to Suzanne Langely?" I asked.

Just as Elaine had warned, Zach responded, "Are you f*!^ing nuts?"

I took a deep breath, "This request does not come from me, but from a higher level of consciousness, from those that know she is about to make a choice that will change the way people view reality."

Zach's demeanor changed right in front of my eyes.

"I don't know why," he said, "but I believe you."

Zach and I sat down and talked for what seemed hours about spiritual consciousness. At the end of our discussion, he asked me a question that related to his work.

"I've been contracted by Universal Studios to write a screenplay about a young man who dies and tries to find his way to heaven. Would you be interested in helping me understand what you and others see in those invisible realms?" I accepted.

* * *

There is one more experience I would like to add to this chapter, even though it happened about one year later. I was traveling back and forth between Boston and Cape Cod to see clients. My friend Mary Anne Lucas had opened a bookstore called Angel Work Metaphysical Bookstore where I would often meet with clients. After finishing with my last my last session, I told Mary Anne that I had to leave right away. I was already late for my next client's appointment, a cancer patient who lived in East Sandwich.

Mary Anne took one look at me and said, "Shirley, I'm concerned about you. You have been running around meeting with clients, and you haven't once stopped to eat." Mary Anne was always helping others in their lives, and I told her I would be just fine. But, before I knew it, she took a small trinket out of her pocket that looked like a ring holder and said, "Shirley, open your mouth and stick out your tongue."

As I did, she sprinkled a little bit of an ash like substance on my tongue. The material dissolved instantly without my even swallowing.

"Now," she said, "I feel much better."

"Why do you feel better?" I asked.

"Because I know you will be safe and cared for through your hectic schedule." She said.

I began to laugh. It was so much like MaryAnn to say something in that way. Her intuition was telling her something about my situation and when she felt better she knew she had found the right remedy for me!

"What is that substance?" I asked.

"This is from a man known as the 'guru of gurus,'" she said. "I brought this back from my trip to India where I went to visit him. It is called Vibhuti."

Mary Anne was always trying something new, and because she had such a great capacity to nurture and love, I just trusted her implicitly. I gave her a hug then hurried out the door.

I stopped at a small convenience store and bought a chocolate wafer bar to eat on my way to my new client's home. While I was driving, a long thin piece of the chocolate wafer dropped onto my lap. I happened to have been wearing a white dress that day. It was very hot, and I did not have the air conditioning on in my car. My windows were down so I could feel the salt air from the Cape's ocean. I kept trying to pick up the fallen piece of chocolate from my lap, but it began to melt into the material of my dress.

I knew that I could not meet a new client wearing a chocolate-stained dress! Trying to clean my dress, I took my eyes off the road twice, once almost hitting another car and the second time almost completely driving off the road while the chocolate melted, staining my dress.

"Oh, no!" I said out loud. As I drove further down the road I noticed an image in the sky. This image was of a man in spirit who gestured for me to look down at my soiled dress, and before my eyes, the chocolate disappeared, leaving no evidence that it had ever been there. I was astonished!

Later that evening, I called Mary Anne and shared with her what had happened. She asked me what the man in spirit looked like. I explained to her that he was of Eastern descent, with dark skin and dark bushy hair, wearing a bright colored garment. Mary Anne in awe replied, "Shirley! That was Sai Baba!"

She went on to explain that Sai Baba, an Eastern Indian guru, who was still in body at the time of this experience, gave Vibhuti, a sacred ash, to his devotees for safety and protection. Mary Anne, out of love and her spiritual guidance thought it would help me, and it did. This was not unlike what my own faith teaches about the blessed sacraments. Each sacrament is a blessing directly from Jesus Christ. The Vibhuti was a blessing directly from Sai Baba.

After these experiences, I realized how important it is to know and understand that we are all connected through this divine energy. We are all equally important in the heart of God. No matter what our spiritual beliefs are.

I consciously experienced this universal energy first hand in the Philippines, when the voice helped me until I could connect to my own knowing, then during the car accident through my deceased uncle, and then by the divine power of Sai Baba, a well-admired Eastern guru. Our spiritual natures are in communion with those that have passed on; yet still exist on another plane of consciousness, and this same spiritual nature is so powerful that we can connect to those who live clear across the other side of the world. The lesson? There are no boundaries when it comes to God and divine love.

I believed that by opening myself to go beyond my comfort zone, I came to the understanding that there are various ways we can experience God's blessings.

* * *

Christ Consciousness exists within all of us. Before this, I wasn't aware of these greater levels and how we, through our beliefs and daily actions, are building up a life of goodness while breaking down the old paradigms of limitation, prejudice, cultural differences and more.

I began to integrate this essential knowledge into my life by assisting others in understanding levels of their unique spiritual conscience, and the importance of how these dimensions are aspects of us and how they play a vital role in our lives. There are many paths that lead to the same source.

Chapter 9

Reaching Through Time

One day, Mrs. Morgan, an elderly woman who lived in the town of Dennisport, called me for help. "Something is happening in my house," she said. "During the night, I wake up because my bed is shaking, and I hear sounds like someone is knocking on the walls."

After taking a deep breath, she went on, "My children want me to go into the hospital for testing. They think something is wrong with me. The only saving grace I have is my sister, who came to stay with me for a couple of days. She also heard a knocking noise."

I told Mrs. Morgan that I would be happy to come out and visit with her at her home. I drove out to her house the next day.

While I was driving, I had a wonderful spiritual experience. Beautiful ethereal flowers appeared all around me. I could visibly see and smell these beautiful flowers.

To give you a more detailed understanding, they seemed to fill the car, right up through the roof but I could see through them. They did not disturb my normal vision I could see the outlines of the flowers more vividly than their inner structures and I could smell only sweetness in the air.

As I kept driving, I looked at the paper where I had written Mrs. Morgan's address, the sweet aroma of flowers grew even stronger. I looked up from the paper and my head instinctively turned toward her home. Along the front lawn of this small house were rows of flowers. The street number on the house verified that, in fact, this was Mrs. Morgan's house. As I stepped out of my car, I had a sense of peace and thanked the spirit for sending me the ethereal flowers and guidance to her home. I then walked up to the house and knocked on the front door.

An elderly woman opened the front door. "Hi, Mrs. Morgan? I'm Shirley." I said.

Mrs. Morgan, who was in her mid-eighties, greeted me with a warm smile and a gentle handshake. As I walked into her living room, I noticed the spirit of a medium built elderly man who looked like he had been physically active until the time of his death. This spirit stood behind the sofa as if he had done this a million times before, standing right behind where Mrs. Morgan sat. She began to tell me about the paranormal events that were happening when I bluntly interrupted her because the man in spirit started to communicate with me.

"Mrs. Morgan, has anyone in your family passed away recently?" I asked.

"Why, yes, my husband passed away a couple of months ago. He was a good man. All of the flowers in front of our home are his work of art."

I couldn't help but smile as the spirit of Mr. Morgan continued communicating with me.

"Mrs. Morgan did you and your husband have disagreements around spiritual beliefs?" I asked.

"Why, yes," she replied.

Mr. Morgan began explaining to me how their disagreements would go.

"Let me just share with you what I sense," I said.

"Of course!" she replied.

"You would both be in bed reading books that you enjoyed. You would be reading a book on spirituality and your husband would either be reading his golf magazines or, a book on gardening. Is that accurate?" I asked.

"Why, yes, that is exactly what we would do before going to sleep."

Mrs. Morgan seemed a little surprised at the detailed information I was able to give her.

"Yet when you shared with him that you believed in life after death, he didn't agree with you."

"Yes," she said sadly. "Herbert and I always agreed on everything, yet he just couldn't understand the concept of there being a heaven."

Mrs. Morgan looked down at her wedding ring.

"Well, your husband's spirit is here with you now, and he is telling me that you two made a pact that the one who passed away first would come back and tell the other if there was life after death."

Mrs. Morgan looked up at me with her eyes glistening as I spoke. With great excitement she responded, "Yes, yes that is true." Then I shared with her what Mr. Morgan was saying ...

This was quite an exciting moment. Of course, in my mind, I was waiting for him to tell her how much he loved her and that he would be there waiting for her, but none of that occurred.

I just heard him say, "Yup, you're right, Martha." As soon as I shared this with Mrs. Morgan, he was gone. I felt a need to apologize to her. "I am so sorry, Mrs. Morgan. That is all he said, and now his presence has left."

"Oh, no, my dear," she replied. "Don't be sorry! That is how my husband is, a man of few words and very direct. That's my Herbert."

I was quite relieved to hear that Mr. Morgan was still the same as he was when he was alive. I explained to her that the knocking sound from the walls, she heard, would cease. Since her husband had now made contact with her, he was ready to go beyond this dimension.

A week later, I called to check in on Mrs. Morgan. She informed me that after she shared with her children what had happened during my visit, they finally stopped talking about her needing a psychological examination. The shaking of her bed and the knocking on the walls ceased. Confusion was transformed into peace and love, which now permeated her home.

As I was writing this I recalled more of what had happened to me as a teenager. At one point during my junior year I thought I felt something around me. This feeling came and went. This something was unknown to me, leaving me with feelings of extreme fear.

Then a day came when my classmate Linda and I were working on costumes for our high school musical. At one point, Linda stopped what she was doing, looked at me and out of nowhere said, "Shirley, do you believe in ghosts? I was shocked. Could this be what was happening to me?

That day, on my way home from school as I walked up the stairs to my parent's house, I found myself saying out loud, "What do you want from me? What are you trying to tell me?" My father, who had been standing at the door, overheard me and asked, "Shirley, who are you talking to?"

As I quickly moved past him and began to run up the stairs to my bedroom, I responded, "No one Dad!" I was terrified. But was I terrified of this presence or was I more terrified of what others may think of me if they knew!

Because of the unusual nature of paranormal events, people often question the validity of their experiences. Many are left confused, and unable to regain their focus and presence back into their lives. That is why it is important if you have experienced a paranormal event seek out a reliable expert in the field to assist you.

* * *

I received a call from a colleague, who worked for the State Police Missing Bureau Investigations Unit asking if I would be open to speak to a woman who was in great distress. She lived in the Midwest. Her husband had been missing for several days, leaving his family and business with no indication of his whereabouts.

The woman's husband, whom I will call Evan, had been working in his father's business for most of his professional life. He was in his forties at the time of his disappearance. His wife explained that she felt he had become depressed from the stresses of the business.

I felt there was more to it than what she had told me, so I asked if I could speak to his father. That evening, Evan's father called, and we had a lengthy discussion about the family business and what might have caused Evan to just pack up and leave. I asked Evan's father this question: "Outside of the business, what kind of relationship do you have with your son?"

He responded, "What do you mean? There's nothing but the business."

My next question was, "Do you have a loving relationship with your son?"

"Of course I do. I've given him a good job and a way to have the type of lifestyle others can only dream about." At that point, Evan's father started to break down. "Evan is the type of man who can express his feelings, and I have a difficult time doing this."

"Okay, then would you be willing to think of Evan every day for a period of time and tell him through your thoughts how much you love him and that you're sorry if you have hurt him in any way?" I asked.

With a deep sigh he said, "Yes, I will."

My next question was, "Do you believe in prayer?"

"Yes, my family is Christian," he said.

"It would be helpful for you to pray for his safe return home," I said. Evan's father agreed.

Five days had passed when I received another call from Evan's wife. "Shirley, Evan has called and he's coming home!" she said.

"This is great news." I responded.

She went on to explain what had happened to Evan following the conversation I had with his father. She said that Evan, while driving to work began to feel the same panic and thought if he just took a longer drive that it would calm him down but it never did. He ended up driving to Las Vegas. He booked a hotel room and stayed in the room the whole time he was there. Every time he thought of returning home, he became confused, angry and frustrated. Not knowing what to do he began to drink which made matters worse.

"I feel like I'm in a cage and I can't get out," he explained to his wife. "My life is passing me by, and all I do is work!"

Then his wife went on to explain what gave him the courage to face this situation. "He began to hear in his mind what he believed to be angels asking him to call home. There were no words that he heard, just the deep feeling of a presence of angelic forces and the feeling that he needed to call home. Through this spiritual experience, he knew everything would be okay. He also sensed that his father was in deep remorse over what was happening to him. A feeling he had never had of him before."

I sensed a great positive change was about to occur if only Evan had the strength to tell his father how he truly felt.

Evan told his wife, "I need to come home and deal with my relationship with my father."

* * *

Prayer is not only for christians. Even a thought with great intentions can be called a form of prayer. I have learned that whatever your intentions are and however you choose to speak these intentions to the universe, God or whomever you choose, you are emitting a vibration to bring about your request. We are very powerful human beings.

I was introduced to Julie through another client of mine, whom I will call Lynn. Julie was excited about preparing herself for the next phase of her life, a plan for her retirement to enjoy life on her own terms. She was a vivacious woman who had just celebrated her fiftieth birthday. Since her boys were both out of college, she and her husband were looking forward to enjoying the home they had built on a scenic lake and to do the things they both enjoyed.

When I met with Julie, her session went well; she had a good solid plan to initiate what she wanted to accomplish. She scheduled minor elective surgery to ensure that she would look and be in the best shape possible. I met with her only this once.

The following year, I received a phone call from Lynn stating that Julie was told she had cancer. She wanted to know if there was anything that I might be able to do for Julie. I told Lynn that I would visit Julie to assess what I might be able to offer her. That one visit turned into many visits because of her desire to heal.

At times during her sessions, Julie's husband would come downstairs, to the sitting room in their home where we would meet. I didn't understand these interruptions until one day Julie said, "He doesn't believe in what you do, so he feels uncomfortable when you are in our home."

"Well, should I speak with him and explain my work?" I asked.

"No, that won't help. I think he's just having a difficult time with my being ill. I'm learning so much about myself and the spiritual world, and this is so comforting to me," she replied.

Julie focused all her energy on the potential of getting well until her doctor told her that her cancer had advanced and the treatment she was on was not helping her. Julie became more obsessed and fearful about dying. One day while I was visiting her, I noticed a little black dog from the spiritual dimension jumping up and down in front of her. "Julie, did you have a little black dog that used to jump up on you for attention?" I asked.

"Oh, yes," she said. "That's Titan, the family dog. Titan lived for 18 years, until I went off to college."

"Well, he is here right now, and there is a medium built man, with gray hair and a rounded face, with him," I said.

"Oh my God, Shirley, that's my father!" Julie exclaimed, and with that, the man from spirit bent down and kissed her on her forehead.

"Your father has come to tell you not to be afraid of dying because dying is a part of living," I said to her. "Do you know what he means?"

"Yes I do," Julie said. "My father was not one to waste time in worrying about things that you couldn't do anything about."

We sat there in silence as she took her time with the awareness her father brought to her.

"Would you ask him something for me?" she asked.

"Julie, you can ask your dad yourself," I said, "because he can communicate with you directly and he feels everything that you are feeling. In fact, you won't need me at all if you could only open yourself up and believe you still have a heart connection to him."

"I don't think I can," she replied.

"Yes, you can, all you have to do is think of the love you have for your dad and just listen to your feelings in your heart. He will feel and hear what you want to say, even if you can't see him," I replied.

I then had a feeling that this was a good time to ask my next question.

"So how do you want to leave the earth when you are ready to enter heaven?" I asked.

"What do you mean?" she asked.

"Well," I replied, "I know exactly how I want to leave when it's my time; I believe we can choose how we would like that to be for ourselves."

I was surprised how easily Julie responded to this concept of creating her own reality, even about her death.

"I would like to have my family and closest friends around my bed, and I would like to go in the early morning hours," she explained.

"Who do you want to come for you from heaven?" I asked.

"You can ask for someone to come?" she asked, surprised.

"Yes, the souls that have been in our lives that have passed before us will come to greet us and help us in our transition into heaven," I replied.

Julie's father's spirit was still present as she stated emphatically, "I want my father to come for me." A smile came over his face, and he then disappeared.

Everything changed for Julie in the following weeks. She planned a great celebration for the fourth of July with all her family and friends. I was invited, and it was a wonderful celebration. Julie was radiant, and I could tell she was having the time of her life.

A couple of months after her party, Julie passed away. Lynn called and shared with me how Julie's wishes came true.

"She was in her bed when her family and friends were called that evening. Everyone was there, and she still wasn't letting go," she said. "Her husband, not knowing what to do, got up from sitting next to her on the bed and went downstairs to the room where you and Julie met for her sessions. After a while, he returned to her side, picked her up in his arms, and whispered in her ear, 'Julie, your father has come for you.' At that moment Julie took one last deep breath and passed away."

After the funeral, Lynn spoke to Julie's husband and asked him if Julie had told him how she wanted to die. When he remarked that she hadn't, Lynn then proceeded to share with him what Julie had told her about how she wanted her life to end. Surprised at what Lynn had told him, he then said that he couldn't understand what possessed him to go downstairs to her sitting room. He also went on to share with her how he began to pray, which he hadn't done for years, and the thought of her father waiting for her came into his mind. That is when he knew he had to tell her that her father had come for her.

This was a peaceful ending of Julie's life here, with her family and friends surrounding her while her father and others in the spiritual realm greeted her to her new home.

It still amazes me how on one level we can be shut down from the spiritual world, yet on a deeper level we are still intertwined through love that keeps us connected to others that have passed on.

* * *

I have had numerous experiences with clients where the preparation for death, such as what happened with Julie, opens up a whole new world of realization, which may not have been recognized throughout a person's life. A person may have never thought of their spiritual beliefs, yet may still experience a presence, a thought, or a knowing that a divine presence was with them.

Those who are caregivers (personally or professionally) to people who are preparing to pass on can extend their love and support, while those in the heavenly dimension extends their love downward to greet them.

* * *

I was called to work with a real estate company that had their office in a newly built building in Mashpee, Massachusetts. Mashpee is a town nestled between the towns of Sandwich and Falmouth on the upper end of Cape Cod. The building was a simple structure that held several offices for various businesses.

As I sat down with the owners to discuss their concerns, I noticed that their energy fields held murky colors that were similar, as if they were experiencing the same physical ailment.

Mr. Johnson, a manager of the real estate company that leased two of the offices, was the first person to speak out. "Mrs. Beauman," he said, "the reason why we have asked you to meet with us is because we have heard that you are the best professional in the area to help us understand paranormal events.

"Everyone in this building has come down with the same physiological symptoms - a harsh cough, dizziness and an inability to work because of mental confusion." He sighed then continued. "When we leave the building, the symptoms cease to exist. My physician can't figure it out except to say there might be toxic elements in our building that are making us ill. We had the building tested for toxic materials but there were no positive findings. Still our symptoms persist."

I paused for a moment, and then responded, "Hmmm. Except there are two people in the building that have not been affected. Is that correct, Mr. Johnson?"

"Well, yes! That is true," he exclaimed. "The chiropractor that has an office at the end of this corridor and his receptionist, have not been affected."

With that information, I asked if I could walk through the building. As I did, I came to a door in the hallway and asked where the door led.

"The basement," Mr. Johnson said.

"I need to go into the basement," I told him.

"I will have to get the key," he responded as he coughed uncontrollably.

I noticed his uncontrollable cough began when we stood in front of the door that led to the basement. I thought there had to be toxins that the environmental tests might have missed. But when I walked down the steps, it wasn't toxins that I found.

As I approached the third to the last step before placing my feet on the ground, I sensed not to move any farther.

At the bottom of the steps a small light appeared that expanded until I could see the spirit of an American Indian dressed in ceremonial clothing. He wore a beautiful headdress that flowed to the ground. Everything that he had on was white except for the beading that covered his chest.

"You are on sacred ground," the Indian man said to me, telepathically.

"What do you mean, sacred ground?" I asked out loud.

Mind to mind he began to tell me a story of how the land and building in question, was a part of many acres that the Mashpee Indians called sacred land. The great white spirit was well known to this tribe and guided and protected the Indians to live in peace. By living in respect to the land all their needs would be fulfilled. He wanted me to tell the others that they had built their offices on sacred ground.

At first I thought this pertained to a sacred burial ground but in fact, I was wrong. I went on to receive thoughts about the natural vibration, given off from the earth in this particular spot was very high in energy. He went on to explain that the earth has its own vibration from its core, which emanates differently in places all over the world.

I asked the spirit of this Indian man why these people were ill. He went on and explained that the elements that our human bodies are made of come from the earth and the stars and our bodies resonate to these elements. The energy is helping them to heal but they may not be aware that what they think and do may suppress the alignment with this healing force. Their bodies were reacting to their inner spirit that is naturally connected to the earth. I was astounded by what I heard.

What I understood him to say was that the people from the past who existed there lived in such a way that was peaceful and respectful. Mr. Johnson and his employees had become ill because they somehow came into conflict with these natural laws. The Indian in spirit understood these natural laws and was there to pass this wisdom on to those living and working on these sacred grounds. It was later confirmed, by the Mashpee Wampanoag Tribe's Historical Preservation Officer, that the regalia of the Indian spirit I encountered is not one an Eastern Woodlands Indian would wear. However, in their history, there was a known local medicine man who was often found wearing the white regalia of the West which was consistent with the spirit of the Indian man I encountered.

I realized it was going to be challenging to speak to these people in a way so they would understand what was happening. So I decided to ask them a question. I joined the rest of the group that was waiting for my return in their main meeting room. I sat down and began, without knowing what I was going to say.

"Do any of you know how your ailment might have to do with this land and building?"

"That's easy," said a woman sitting next to Mr. Johnson. "The history of this town is enmeshed in a legal dispute over the rights of the Mashpee Wampanoag Tribe whom has fought unsuccessfully to reclaim lands it held years ago in this area. Because of this, it has been difficult for many to purchase property, and to build since the ownership of the land has been in question."

"So what does this have to do with us all getting sick?" Mr. Johnson asked.

"I don't believe this has anything to do with you being ill. I do believe that this beautiful Indian spirit come to you to help you. He wants to assist you in understanding the natural vibration from the earth in this area. He spoke how we have fallen asleep from understanding what will keep us well and prosperous. The spirit of this Indian was part of the spiritual vibration here, to preserve the laws of the Great White Spirit. We coexist with spirit, and the natural forces. How we live our lives in helping each other is imperative to survival."

I thought Mr. Johnson would have the greatest challenge believing in the truth of what I was saying, but I was wrong. "Shirley, I believe I know what you are talking about," he said. "When I was a child I had an experience of a spirit in the house that my family lived in, and I have that same feeling here as I did when I was a child. I felt protected by this spirit when I was a child. From my Christian beliefs I would say the spirit of this Indian man is a guardian angel to us."

I began to breathe a little easier at this point in our discussion.

Mr. Johnson then went on to say, "I have had many business dealings in our community and I can speak as a representative of our real estate company that the Wampanoag Indians are our friends. We may have our differences at times but all in all we have created a beautiful community together."

Then he asked, "What do you recommend we do?"

I paused for a moment and then answered, "The chiropractor can assist you, since he and his employee have been able to uphold the synergy between themselves and the energy of this sacred ground. He will be able to help you understand how he has been working here with these influences."

Mr. Johnson spoke of how they might be able to participate in one of the Indian ceremonies to give thanks to the great white spirit and the land's guardian angels. Everyone thought that was a good idea and with that, our meeting was over.

A very important note about this story came about in 2007 when the Mashpee Wampanoag Indians, were officially recognized by our federal government as a tribe. This was a battle that took over 30 years to win. The history of this Native community is worth looking up and reading the details of their struggle and their triumph.

This is an exceptional story truly about the heritage of North America's true ancestors, their spiritual beliefs and their wisdom that has been passed down from generation to generation of the sacred earth and the Great White Spirit.

I had moved away from Cape Cod since this spiritual experience, but as spirit would have it, several years later, the woman whom introduced me to the realtor I happened to have noticed her name on Linkedin. I called Terry and while we were talking I asked her what happened to the realtor, the bizarre illness and the Indian spirit.

This is what she said." Oh Shirley you wouldn't believe what happened to them. They created the Indian ceremony, which they believe healed the energy in the building. But also there were three employees of the realty company whom were going thru divorce proceedings at this time and all three ended up reconciling with their partners." And even though they felt very guided by the spirit of the indian, they never felt him again, after the building was healed.

*   *   *

We live in a fast paced technological world. Our stressors on our bodies are created from a combination of life situations. The least understood yet no less important is the invisible world of energy from our technology and the natural energy of our earth. This story happened about 5 years after the major events took place, which are in this book I chose to share this story because of the phone calls I receive from people having unusual symptoms that the medical and health profession could not find the cause. After I assessed their situations, I found environmental factors to be one of the main causes of their mental, emotional or physiological illness. Here is one of those true stories.

The first time I had heard of Karen Mileson was through Dr. B., a dentist whom I met at a lecture I gave for the American Dental Holistic Association. Karen was stricken with an ailment, which the medical and dental profession were having a difficult time finding the source of the multiple problems this woman was having.

Her symptoms ran the gamut from sudden poor eyesight to twitching in her face and other parts of her body. Other symptoms included muscle weakness, chills, tightness in the throat, and extreme fatigue. For a period of time, Karen was confined to a wheelchair.

One day, I had unexpectedly dropped by Dr. B.'s office, Karen had called in for her next appointment. I was standing at the front desk when Dr. B's wife Judy, answered the phone and told me there was someone on the phone that needed to talk with me. It was Karen. I made an appointment to speak with Karen that evening. From our conversation I believed her situation could be fatal so I made an appointment to visit with her the following day.

Karen is a kind and intelligent woman, and by the time I spoke with her, she was already exhausted from her symptoms and her search in trying to understand her illness and how to heal. She had worked with many beneficial medical and alternative therapies but her health was still in question. Because of this I wasn't sure if I would have a positive impact in this case.

As I was driving to her home, a very caring and loving spirit came into my awareness. I knew right away that this spirit was Karen's deceased husband, Don. He told me how much she had gone through and asked if he could help. During her session that day, I told Karen about her husband's spiritual visitation. She asked questions that only her husband could answer. He answered them all for her. This helped to reassure her that I just might be able to help her find her answers to her debilitating problem.

During my assessment, I realized that her energy was blocked in certain parts of her body. But most importantly I found that there was something wrong with the energy in her home. Karen was a health practitioner and had been a research assistant for a prominent physician who practiced in Washington D.C. She also studied with experts from all over the world pertaining to energetic health and healing, so what I told her made sense and proved to be very beneficial.

Her home was what some specialists call a "sick house." Because of the advancements made in communication technology, the invisible radio waves have created new stressors in our environment; Geopathic stress and electrical pollution, just to name a few. These environmental toxins can go unnoticed in our homes and can lead to illness. These stressors were adding to Karen's inability to heal.

The only way to help her heal was to heal her house. As I assessed her home energetically, I found an area where there seemed to be, what is called dirty electricity coming in from the roof of her home. I then decided to check the top of the roof. After assessing the Internet cable lines and dish technology, I found it was the Lightning Protection System and its lead wire that was drawing an abundance of radiation into their home. Ironically the lead wire ran down the wall beside their bed. It was in this area that her husband Don laid for several months after injuring his leg in a skiing accident, which never healed.

Karen tested this system many times and it always tested positive for toxic energies coming into the house from the LPS. But she never thought that this would lead to their horrific health problems! Karen and her husband lived in their home for almost 15 years and she had never been healthy there. Because of this she made an appointment with a practitioner who had recommended a homeopathic remedy for Phosphorous, which is used for radiation toxicity. Because of the other health considerations she did not make the correlation to the LPS and the radiation it continually drew into their home.

*   *   *

My spiritual experience with the Indian from spirit taught me the importance of the earth and that which surrounds the earth dwells in the life force of God. This led me to be aware that in Karen's case, her home was affected by the earth's energy as well as our modern-day technology. We must be aware of these invisible forces, including those from chemicals and toxins that dwell in and around our environments.

Karen worked with me for an extended time through her recovery, and I began teaching her about energy and how she could help assist her body in getting well. Karen became the expert. Karen can now ski, play tennis, roller blade, hike, and enjoy kayaking. We are the only ones who can detect how we feel in our environments. Now what about you?

Chapter 10

No Man's Land

Sara was a medium built woman with dirty, blonde hair in her twenties. She was a new client with a delightful, positive way about her, but what I didn't know was that her childhood, up to her late teen years, was filled with abuse that left her traumatized. When I asked why she didn't seek out a good therapist, she replied, "I have been in therapy for the past several years. It was my therapist who recommended that I come see you. She heard of your work and the results others have received." I didn't know her therapist, but other professionals had been recommending me to their clients, especially clients who were experiencing unusual symptoms and challenges.

Sara and I wasted no time delving into her situation. She shared with me what had happened during her childhood. Her family was involved in a cult where she, other children, and family members had been tormented physically, emotionally, mentally, and sexually. When Sara was seventeen, her mother somehow broke free from the cult with her children. Sara was then able to go to school and begin a life of freedom, except for the memories she carried within.

I asked Sara if she would be open to working with me on retrieving her power from the memories that she still held from these traumas. She accepted.

Sara and I began by making ourselves comfortable in my healing room. I took her hands and prayed silently, as I did with everyone, to align the energy of my heart and my mind with the divine source within me. I invited her to close her eyes and ask all those that she still had nightmares about to come forward in her mind.

"I have them now in my thoughts," she said.

"Okay Sara, what is the one thing that will finally free you of these experiences from your past?" I asked.

Sara thought for a moment and then responded, "I need to tell them something."

"Would it be good for you to bridge your heart to your thoughts as you are telling them?"

"Yes," she replied.

Sara began. She went to each one of them in her mind and spoke. As soon as she was done with one person, she would go to the next.

Most of Sara's conversations with these people were not what you would have expected from a heart-centered focus. Usually people think of heart as being about love, appreciation, caring, and other feelings of this nature. But her conversations were just as much heartfelt as those that I just mentioned but hers were about honesty, self-worth, and the right to be free to make her own choices.

After Sara finished I then invited her to visualize taking back those parts of her she had left with them. I call this integrating the fragmented self. Each aspect of her was different; one aspect represented her sexuality, another aspect represented her self-esteem, another represented her beauty, and, finally, the last represented her intelligence.

Depending on what her interaction had been with each person, Sara began to establish her personal identity again as whole. In her first session, her energy field looked torn apart with gaps and holes. Now it was more cohesive and integrated. Her energy field became illuminated.

* * *

Loving one's self and having healthy boundaries is a powerful, vital, aspect for survival, independence and a healthy life.

Sara was strong enough to be honest and placed herself as the important one in her life. When using a technique like this, I always make sure my clients align themselves to the power of love, within themselves, so their experience will create only positive outcomes that will help to shift their outlook, behaviors, and attitude toward life. At times we all have feelings of anger or sadness, but in the presence of love, the wisdom to understand assists in the transformation.

I also include an anchoring technique from the divine energy within them. This divine spark is the door that bridges us to the all knowing. From my experience, calling upon this energy gives the power, knowledge, and actions needed to deal with any given situation. This divine energy of love protects us, keeps our minds alert and clear, and gives us direction toward healthier and more productive experiences.

Sara finally had her say where it counted the most: consciously with herself. At the following session, she explained how the voices she heard in her head had disappeared. She now knew her past was no longer a threat to her existence. She knew what she would allow in her life, what she wouldn't allow in her life, and no matter what, she would never let anyone abuse her again.

* * *

I was beginning to feel more part of our community since there seemed to be an invisible acceptance from some health professionals that my work did have a place in the healing community. The validation came from the clients sent to me by other professionals in the area. I began to feel a sense of peace and calm from my own surroundings. My confidence as not only a healer but as an energy practitioner, I felt there might be a possibility that some day this type of alternative methods would be better received internationally by main stream professionals.

* * *

In our quaint town of Sandwich, there was a very special restaurant that Jake, the girls, and I would frequent for our Saturday morning breakfast. We always felt we were part of a large family there. Many times than none, it was difficult to find an available table, but everyone would make sure they did not linger if another family was waiting to eat. One morning when it seemed to be more crowded than ever, Sara and a gentleman walked into the restaurant as we were having our breakfast.

"Shirley!" she yelled out with excitement. "I am so happy to see you." Sara walked over and placed her arms around me as she introduced herself to the rest of my family. Behind her stood a medium built man with sandy colored hair. As I glanced at him, Sara turned around to pull him close to her.

"Honey, this is Shirley, the woman who healed me!" As her husband shook my hand, the conversations in the restaurant ceased. Even Sara and her husband noticed the silence in the room. She turned around and noticed everyone looking at her, so she exclaimed with enthusiasm, "This lady healed me! I am so grateful to her!"

The people in the restaurant looked very confused as to what she meant. My children were noticeably embarrassed, and it was obvious that her comment made everyone curious yet uncomfortable at the same time.

When we arrived home, Krysie asked a very important question. "Mom, why can't you be a school bus driver like my friend Jessica's mother?" I stopped for a moment and looked directly at the girls.

What am I doing to them? I thought.

Then I asked, "Okay, girls, my being known as a healer: what is it like for you with the unusual way I can help people?"

"Hurtful," Laurie said, as she looked down at her little finger to inspect it. "The doctor couldn't even put my fingertip back on my finger because of what you did, Mom."

I then looked at Melyssa. She just stood in silence.

Jake finally chimed in. "It's less unusual for us now because we are beginning to understand spiritually what is happening in our life, yet other people can't even fathom something like a miracle happening to them."

I just nodded my head in agreement, gave everyone their chores to do, and walked toward the pile of clothes that were waiting to be folded.

*   *   *

My career was demanding more of my time. A month later, Jake and I began to argue openly about the changes in his schedule that were needed in order for me to keep up with these demands. Then, finally, the day of truth came.

"I can't take this any longer!" Jake exclaimed. "I'm not happy."

"What do you mean?" I asked.

Don't you know what is being said about the work you're doing?"

"No," I answered.

Shirley, people are saying that this is the work of the devil, and that is why we are having all these hardships!"

"How can you of all people believe what they're saying? You've seen yourself what has happened for people through my spiritual work."

Jake responded very quickly. "I can't handle coming home to our house not knowing what paranormal event will happen next or if I will find that my children have experienced events that an average child isn't even aware of! And on top of it all, I can't handle not being able to focus on my own business without my day being disrupted by you or someone who questions me about your work!"

"You said it yourself, Jake, they just don't understand." I retaliated.

"I mean it. I want our lives to be normal!" Jake shouted back.

My thoughts ran rapid. How could I have missed how Jake was feeling and what some people in town were saying and believing about me? People were always kind to me. Many of them had found their way to our front door for healing. *Were they mirroring my own hidden fear and ignorance of these spiritual experiences?* I thought.

Jake just looked at me with such pain in his eyes. Then I exploded.

"I'll tell you what the work of the devil is," I said. "Evil comes from our own thoughts and actions. Evil is when people judge others unfairly. Evil is when we as a community smile and act nice toward one another, yet behind each other's back we put one another down and create separation from being good neighbors and friends to one another. Evil is created from our fear of the unknown and our own ignorance." Even though I was strong in my convictions, my heart was breaking inside.

God, how much more do I have to deal with? I thought. How often had I said there are places, I dare not tread. The people Jake spoke of were people that chose not to embrace the goodness in these healings. I had to take a stance. Too many positive experiences had already occurred. I knew there was no turning back.

After we both calmed down, Jake and I took a long walk and talked about how our plans for a life together had changed. He still wanted to share his life on Cape Cod with someone who wanted to go sailing, and after retiring, live on a sailboat. And until that time, he wanted to enjoy his weekends having fun exploring the other islands that were near Cape Cod. As for myself, I wanted to live in the city, where the children could be exposed to different cultures and opportunities.

We ended up talking about this for days, and as much as we tried, we could not agree on a common direction. Neither of us brought up the subject of my healing again, or what some of the community residents believed about my work.

*   *   *

Change had occurred. I was no longer the woman that he had married. Jake and I talked about how this was affecting the children. It was obvious that we both wanted the best for them, their upbringing, and their future, but we could not stay together. We finally came to the conclusion that we needed to separate.

I constantly questioned our decision, until one day Melyssa, seeing the pain we were both in, made a profound statement: "Mom, how am I going to find me if you don't find you?"

The look in my daughter's eyes and the sincerity in her voice told me it was time to stop putting my children through my confusion and get myself straightened out. I was awakening to the fact that Jake and I hadn't been happy together for quite a while, and this was the culmination of all of our suppressed emotions, which we still hadn't dealt with.

Jake and I agreed, since I was the one that was traveling for work and his business was now housed in the large garage on our property, that during the separation, he would stay in our home with the children, and I would rent a house just a few miles away. This decision forced us to work together in a different way. We needed to take into consideration many factors like scheduling my caring for our children, working with their after school schedule, his work schedule and my travel time.

Jake and I worked very well together during the separation. I stayed at our house during the times I took care of our children, helping them with their homework, making dinner and then leaving for the evening. The flip side of the smoothness of the transition, like anyone else who goes through change, my heart was breaking into pieces.

Some people have a path they follow, and everything in their lives seems to work out wonderfully. I felt like my life was like a jigsaw puzzle, and even though I was able to put many of the pieces together, there were other pieces, I couldn't for the life of me, understand how they fit. In a pragmatic way, this was all about choices.

Choices at times are difficult to make. I had counseled many others on what they valued the most in their lives and how those values direct the actions they take. Sometimes the importance of what we strive for outweighs the importance of other things in our lives. I was confused. Being a mom and wanting my children with me was an easy decision, but the pain Jake and I had inflicted on each other, was too much to bear.

All of our arguments and lovemaking in between as we strived to find our way back to one another showed me how much we truly cared for each another. If not we might have just walked away more easily. But then it was over. No more lovemaking, no more passionate arguments. Everything we had to express as a couple was finished. I was now alone for the very first time in my life.

Every night before bed I would walk around the open empty, house that I was renting. There was no familiarity around me. I had taken only my clothes and toiletries so as not to disrupt the children's sense of security. Everything was kept the same in our home.

One morning as I was preparing to take the children to the beach, I could not find my bathing suit. Now, how could I not find a bathing suit among the small amount of clothing that filled only two dresser drawers? The bedroom I used was located at the top of the stairs.

The more I searched for my bathing suit the angrier I got! Finally, I took all my clothes and threw them down the stairs then I burst into tears. There I sat on the top step for the longest time until I realized there was nothing for me to hold onto. Every morning I would drag myself out of bed barely making it to the top stair only to sit there for the longest time, looking down into a stranger's living room.

I finally succumbed to being ill. I had been in bed for several days with a fever that wouldn't break. I don't recall why, but one evening I decided to go for a drive. It was raining that evening, and a half hour into the drive, the rain turned into a severe storm. The wind blew intensely as the rain pounded down on my car, making it impossible to see even two feet in front of me, so I pulled the car off to the side of the road.

As I sat there, I burst into tears. I realized the rainstorm had somehow invoked my deepest feelings. I was alone. I had nowhere to go and no one to count on. All that I had built in my life was gone.

Flashes of my parents, my brother and sisters, my children and Jake came rushing through my mind. How difficult this gift of mine must be for them. "My God, I know I can't keep Jake's last name nor go back to my maiden name." I said aloud. I sobbed deeply. Then out of nowhere, a powerful yet gentle presence surrounded me. I then heard a voice.

"You may use my name," the voice said.

"Oh great," I said sarcastically. "What is your name?"

The voice replied, "Michael."

"Why should I use your name?" I asked.

"I have been your protector since the beginning of time." He replied.

Again through my tears I replied, "Let me see, Shirley Michael, hmmm, Shirley Michaels. Ah, no thanks!"

In seconds, the voice and presence of this spirit's energy disappeared, and the rainstorm was over.

*   *   *

The next morning, I sat on the top step of the staircase. The pain I felt in my chest was intense. So there I sat in the early hours of the morning, looking down into a stranger's living room, not being able to move. Sitting on the top step that morning was like hesitating to step down into life.

Where was that place of peace that I could go to where the voice said, "You are always a part of here and here is always a part of you," I forgot where that place exists.

"God, please help me with this pain." No change.

"Why isn't this working out in an easier way?" No answer.

"Why did I have to go through all these experiences? . . . Uh."

I was so desperate that I tried to make a deal with God. "I will follow the rules of living a normal life if you will just take away my pain." I pleaded out load. Still there was no change.

It seemed like every manipulative aspect of my personality was engaged in trying to find my way out of the hold this pain had on me.

Then suddenly rapid flashes of bits and pieces of memories came rushing through my mind. Memories of the times I hurt others; memories of the times others hurt me. Each memory bringing with it greater physical pain until the accumulation built up to such intensity that my breath was almost completely taken away. I felt as if I was having a heart attack! With tears streaming down my face, I was able to shout out one more time, "God, help me!"

Finally something shattered the wrenching feeling I felt from deep within. The constriction around my heart began to free up. I instantly felt lighter. If I were to give you a healer's senses of this, it felt like tiny illumined particles began to spin more rapidly without any harming me. Instantly my body cooled down from the fever I had had for days. The pressure in my head that I felt for months disappeared. The air surrounding me was like the air in my dream: the purest air I had ever breathed. Then came quiet, calm, and finally, peace. The storm inside of me was over.

*   *   *

During the days following this experience, I found myself looking at my situation in a different way. Even my body was different. My breathing was deeper, my posture was more erect, and my eyesight was the clearest it had ever been. There were no past events floating through my mind, just a sense of thankfulness and wonderment for everything life had brought me. I was forever changed.

I had gone through some sort of transformation. But what was it? I was compelled to try to understand what had happened. Mary Anne Lucas had suggested that I purchase the book *A Course in Miracles*. In the days after this enlightening experience, I sat and read the inspiring words of wisdom it carried. I was so immersed in the teachings that I decided to join a study group in a nearby town. I received such great support there. These women and men knew nothing of my personal situation, yet each of them listened to each other's exploration of what truths we had found by reading the same book.

The uniqueness of this book was in the way it incorporated the teachings of Jesus with our modern understanding of psychology and the ancient wisdom of Eastern philosophy. Forgiveness and giving are what stood out the most in my mind. I was coming home to a different home than something physical. I was coming home to a spiritual place.

I could now understand what had happened to me from the perspective of how emotions work in our consciousness. But, I still could not understand the physical changes I had gone through. The healings that had occurred to Cyndy and others didn't seem to fit my understanding of what had happened to me. So I decided to find the answer to these questions: If God is the one that brought this healing to me, why was it physically painful and how did my body transform?

I began to attend workshops and lectures given by people who channeled guidance and wisdom from spiritual sources. I started to research and came across a book by Anodea Judith called *Wheels of Life*. I perceived the concepts presented in her book to be a simple guide in understanding how the Eastern practice of yoga works with our consciousness.

Judith also explained there are many similar concepts of spiritual consciousness in other cultures. These similar teachings are found in cultures from Tibet, China, and India to our American Hopi Indians. Similarities of spiritual consciousness can be found in world religions such as Christianity, Judaism, and Theosophy, to name a few.

It took more research for me to finally answer the question, what caused the changes in my physiology? Just recently I found a simplistic statement in which this was explained, on the website of Deepak Chopra, the respected leader in the field of mind-body medicine. He commented in one of his blogs that it only makes sense that our physiology would need to go through a transformation to support our new states of spiritual consciousness. There it was: the evolution of our body and mind to embrace our spiritual energy, the new paradigm shift found within our own physiology.

The universe was responding to all of my heart's desires and needs, and I was finally open to the many ways in which the answers came. I was very comfortable with this. Finding my answers in other belief systems didn't make me any less of a good Catholic and Christian. In fact, it made me a better one.

The spiritual direction I now began to understand was an evolutionary process built upon many levels of consciousness, each level assisting and integrating with the other. My body, emotions, and mind, were illuminated by my pure spirit within. At times I would hear a voice. Other times I could feel energy moving throughout my body. Still other times I would just know. These levels of consciousness were like a symphony of subtle waves of frequencies harmonizing to bring the knowledge and guidance I was asking for, to my waking self.

I then realized that what I had gone through was, in fact, similar to what Cyndy and others had experienced in their healings. Now I was the one being healed by becoming aligned to the divine light within me.

There was still the dreams of Max to unfold. The last vivid dream I had about Max was, once again, talking to him while we sat on the swings in one of our favorite parks. I remember saying to him, "Max, I have to tell you something." As soon as I said this, his brother Luke, came running towards us.

"Hey Max, we've got to get home." As Max began to run towards his brother, he looked back and waved goodbye. That was the last dream I had of Max leaving me with a very unsettled feeling.

* * *

After this realization, I began to work with a transpersonal psychotherapist, who helped to expand my understanding of spiritual consciousness. I will call him Dr. Charles. From the first time we met, I knew he was the perfect therapist to help me understand and thrive on my spiritual path. The most important aspect that I learned in working with him was how the divine spark of light that resides at the very core of my being, is my direct connection to God. My Catholic belief that Christ is my savior allowed me to know that I was never alone, that Christ was an aspect that resided within me even though my Lord Jesus, hadn't appeared to me, like other spiritual beings had. The phrase "the kingdom within" kept coming into my mind, so I looked it up in the King James' version of The Bible. Jesus's teachings:

> And when he was demanded of the Pharisees, when the kingdom of God should come, he answered them, and said, "The kingdom of God cometh not with observation: Neither shall they say, lo here! Or, lo there! For, behold, the kingdom of God is within you" (Luke 17:20–21, King James Version).

This was a profound truth to me. I realized I had a personal experience of this truth. These moments of realization would come and go. Normalcy would once again be my reality yet I tried ever so intently to cherish them all.

I still didn't understand why I had to go through so much to attain this understanding until one day Dr. Charles asked me if I wanted to work with quieting my mind to find the answer to this question. I agreed.

Dr. Charles and I prepared for the transpersonal session by sitting quietly, and out of respect for my beliefs, we said the Lord's Prayer. Then he said, "Shirley, explain to me what happened during your car accident. Go back in time and allow the experience to come up in your consciousness as if it is happening now, and observe everything that is happening, using all your senses consciously. You are only an observer right now, allowing only love to gently guide you through each step."

As I focused on my breath, I felt like everything had slowed down to such a degree that my mind was looking at this event from a different perspective, one picture frame at a time.

The first thing I felt was a sensation of anxiety warning me of the impending car accident. Then there was a rush of energy flowing through my body, which carried with it impulses to steer my car off the road. I then noticed a car, which passed by me and hit the car that pulled out in front of him in the passing lane. I then realized I was observing the accident from a deeper place inside myself, as if I was in a tube of light. Yet the information I was receiving was coming from the energy emanating from around my body that extended beyond my car.

"Ah," I sighed. "I am still on the side of the road out of harm's way."

Then I felt a jolt of anxiety again, warning me of something else that was going to happen.

"I see a third car crash into the first two cars and begin to spin in a 180 degree turn being directed towards me then hitting the back left side of my car."

I took a deeper breath in. Then something different happened in my experience.

"Dr. Charles, the light around me is expanding beyond the accident."

I paused for a moment while I directed my emotions to move back into a place of calm.

"My car is now moving across the highway, onto the median and into the oncoming traffic," I said. "Again, I'm contracted into my body more than ever, but the light from this tube of energy within me is still expanded out even further from my car."

I wanted to stop the process at this point, but I knew I had to go on and finish with this increased awareness.

"I now see within this expanded energy that there are points of illuminated light everywhere." Then I recognized that the vision of my uncle came from one of these illuminations, and his voice echoed throughout the field of energy that now encompassed the entire scene of the accident.

That was as far as I could take the session. I told Dr. Charles that I needed to stop, and he agreed. I was now back in the present moment and very relaxed.

"Shirley, why did you need to stop the session when you did?" he asked.

I paused for a moment while my mind searched for the answer. "Because I not only saw my uncle and heard his voice," I said, "I also saw that everyone involved in the accident had a similar experience as well."

That surprised me. Even the people in oncoming traffic that I was about to collide with had light expanding from them that bridged into a field of light that created a web of energy. This webbing acted like a transmitter to receive information and give information, allowing a connection to each other, which is greater than us. I believe this web of light informed others of the potential danger ahead.

His next question surprised me. "Do you feel the other people knew about this web of light that was connecting all of you and connecting you to something greater than yourselves?"

I sighed and said, "No, not consciously. But on some level I believe they did, and they also were aware that we were all being safely guided by the same source."

Dr. Charles smiled as he said to me, "You have been able to quiet your mind enough in this session so you could integrate how spiritual consciousness was working in your life and the lives of others at the scene of the accident. How do you feel about your experience now?"

"I'm in awe," I said. "I'm incredibly grateful. I'm amazed how connected we are to the same fabric of spiritual energy."

Dr. Charles and I sat there for quite some time, and then it was time to close the session. Slowing down my mind allowed me to expand my consciousness. I was able to use my physical senses to see what was happening beyond my waking conscious level of awareness.

I'll never forget the power in quieting my mind so the details of the car accident could emerge from my subconscious. Bringing greater spiritual awareness into my life. I was inside a divine tube of light. I was this tiny spark of energy observing everything that was happening to me.

As I thought about the session on my drive home, I heard a voice say, "There is an invisible web of divine love that penetrates this world and everything in it. Sometimes space and distance is created, allowing opportunities for the right people and experiences to come together to bring the wisdom needed to assist in life."

This made sense to me since I had asked this question many times: why was I in the accident when my insights made me aware of the event just in time to get out of harm's way?

The answer was obvious. During my session, my mind was calm and not reactive to my memories. That is why I could be more aware of higher states of consciousness that held a greater knowledge. I also realized that working on my own transformation and finding my own divine conscience allowed me to understand my life experiences.

I could have perceived this differently if I had chosen not to see the gift in this experience. I thought of all the scenarios of possibilities of how I could have reacted to the accident. I could have just allowed myself to be traumatized, and that could have created a fear of ever driving again, which would have created an unconscious negative reaction, leading to stress that may have eventually led to illness. As a dear friend just recently said to me, "Sometimes, when the glass seems half empty, it's really half full."

* * *

The way we choose to perceive the truth either allows us to "Dare to Love" in a greater way or it becomes like a shadow that lingers, which may take from us the very breath that this divine source has given us for life.

I had been at the stage of giving up. My negative beliefs of myself became part of the shadow surrounding me, which could have taken my breath away. But my persistence in talking to God transformed the self-inflicted pain I was feeling. I had finally come through the darkest time of my life, and from it, I found a spark of God within myself.

This helped me understand why Jake and I chose to separate. We needed space and distance from one another so we could identify and clarify what it was that we each wanted as individuals and to give ourselves the opportunity for our own personal growth. Jake had been focused on my spiritual path long enough. It was time for him to focus on what he wanted for his life before his pain became a shadow that lingered as well.

* * *

Four months went by and my client load had diminished around the Cape Cod area. I realized I was going through another transition, so I had to be conscious and diligent about keeping my focus and momentum on my work, yet nothing I did seemed to matter.

I finally went to see a woman I will call Diana, a very gifted psychic I had met throughout my search. I knew she could help me decide what I needed to do next.

Diana began my session by talking about choices. She said, "These choices are a matter of two people - meaning Jake and you – who wanted their dreams to come true yet are not necessarily on the same path.

Sometimes we come together for certain parts of the journey to help one another, and then we separate and move on when we no longer can achieve happiness and fulfillment together."

I thanked Diana for the spiritual insight and began to get ready to leave when she said, "Wait, Shirley, there is one more thing. You will be changing your last name. There are five letters in the first part and seven letters in the second part of the name you will take. This is a gift from spirit given to you by a presence that has been watching over you since you were a child. This has been a desperate time for you and you have called out for protection and guidance."

"Yes," I said, nodding. "Yes, that is true but I won't be changing my last name."

Diana took my hands and looked at me and sighed. "This is not just for you but to release all others that do not want to be associated with your healing abilities."

Finally, that made sense to me. Jake and the children deserved a normal life and didn't need to be associated with what I had chosen to do as a professional, especially since it was far from being socially accepted. Now I understood.

* * *

Do you ever question if there are angels watching over you? Well, when I received an unexpected call from a woman named Carol Mann, who had taken a couple of my courses that past summer, I knew there had to be divine intervention working in my life.

"Shirley, I know you are having a rough time," she said, "and I was told by spirit to give you a call." I was amazed by her awareness. "You must come and stay with me for a while here in Boston. I want to help you expand your business." The invisible web of divine love was working in my life. I knew to take her up on her generous offer.

Carol was a well-respected counselor, and astrologer in Boston. She opened up her heart and her home to me and introduced me to both business and academic professionals whom believed in the importance of personal and spiritual development. After a few months, it was clear that in order to be in a community where I could also prosper, Boston was the place where I would live.

Growing further apart, Jake and I finally decided to divorce. I moved to Boston, agreeing that the children should stay in Sandwich, where they had established a healthy environment of stability and structure.

Chapter 11

The Heart that Heals

Carol and I became great friends. We had a wonderful time sharing her office and enjoying a tremendous partnership. She kept me very busy in those early months by introducing me to new people whom I would eventually counsel.

I will never forget this one man she introduced me to. He was a well-known television personality whom I will call Sam. He and Carol had been working together on projects in the Boston community, giving their time and celebrity status to greater causes for children.

I was in awe when I met Sam. He was a tall, lean, handsome man who had a heart of gold and a pristine reputation. He was known for television and broadcasting work he had done in Boston as well as other cities. He was most famous for a television show for children, which had been on the air for twenty years. I knew that everything about this man was good and giving.

Sam decided to book an appointment with me. When I opened the door to greet him, I could sense that his energy was severely constricted around his heart. I went straight to work and placed my hand over Sam's heart. A surge of energy went through him from my hand.

After this experience, he sat down to catch his breath. Sam then looked at me astonished and asked, "How did you know I was having severe chest pain?"

"I could feel what was happening with you as soon as you entered the room," I said.

Sam was thankful for the healing and as time passed we became good friends. He began introducing me to other professionals in the Boston area. One of these men, (I will call Dr. Evan), was the director of a center for autistic children. When Sam told Dr. Evan about my ability to interpret the human energy field, he was open to meet with me to explore alternatives to help improve the quality of care for the children at his center.

The center was housed in a small building on a busy street in downtown Boston. After Sam and I walked into the office we were greeted by Dr. Evan. Without wasting any time, Dr. Evan escorted us directly into an observation room, where we could watch the practitioners while they worked with the children.

"So let me first give you a medical description of autism," Dr. Evan said. "Autism is a disorder of neural development characterized by impaired social interaction and communication, and by restricted and repetitive behavior. It affects information processing in the brain by altering how nerve cells and their synapses connect and organize. In other words, these children are challenged with their ability to bridge themselves to others and their surroundings."

Dr. Evan explained that we could observe the practitioners and the children through a one-way mirror. The mirror gives the staff an opportunity to observe the children without creating more disturbances in the room where the children and the practitioners are working. He then explained that the children we would be observing had different levels of autism. He had set up three clinical routines for us to observe.

"The first child, whom we will be observing, is four years old and her name is Maggie. We have been assessing her over the last week. Her levels were found to be in the mid-range of the autism spectrum, which is an indication that we will be able to help her," said Dr. Evan. "I thought it would be interesting if you could give me your assessment on what you call her 'energy field,' before we bring the other students and practitioners in the room." I agreed.

Maggie walked into the room and stood in the middle, looking away from us. I was standing in between Sam and Dr. Evan at the time, when suddenly Maggie turned around and seemed to be looking right through the one-way mirror.

"Shirley," Sam said, "She's looking right at you!"

It did look that way to both Dr. Evan and me as well. After Sam's comment, Maggie walked over to the mirror, and placed her hand on it, right in front of me. I placed my hand over Maggie's from the other side. She smiled then walked away.

Dr. Evan was amazed by what he had seen. "Could you explain to me what just happened?" he asked.

"Yes," I replied, "but I would like to observe the practitioners and the other children first and then give you my full assessment at the end of my observations."

Several children entered the playroom together, and again I observed their behavior. Most of them were quite skilled on jungle gyms, using their feet to direct and guide them. I had noticed with all of my clients that we have an energy field that emanates from within us and surrounds our physical bodies, but in these children the energy field was more pronounced around and above their heads. The field around the lower part of their bodies was denser and closer to them. I presented, that, even though they were labeled as having autism, these children had greater capacities beyond our understanding.

Next, the working practitioners entered the room one at a time, and I observed how the children reacted to them. The practitioners were more involved mentally in working with the children, and because these children were challenged with their minds, they had a difficult time connecting to them. Even when the practitioners engaged a child in a task, it was still difficult for the child to respond, so the practitioner had to touch the child gently to get their attention.

While I was observing these interactions, a medium built woman with brown short hair entered the room where the children were playing. Dr. Evan did not explain to us who she was, as he was preoccupied in observing the practitioners while I explained to him what was happening. As we were talking, an odd thing happened. The children eventually looked up, stopped in the activities they were participating in and started to walk towards her.

"Dr. Evan, who is the lady who just walked into the room?" I asked.

"Why, she's my wife," he said. "She works in the office."

"Did you ever notice how the children are drawn to her?" I asked.

Dr. Evan looked both at Sam and me and said, "I can see that now, but I never noticed it before."

I stopped the director and explained the difference between his wife's energy field and the other practitioners. I explained to him that her field was more pronounced from the region of her heart, while the others were more pronounced from the region of their heads. I went on to explain that his wife was communicating with the children on the subtle level of energy created from her heart. This created a coherent communication system through her field to their field.

This experience helped me to realize the healing potential that we all have when we engage in our lives from our hearts. I then explained to him that Maggie was drawn to the mirror and placed her hand over it where I was standing because she could feel the energy emanating from my heart. We all have a heart that heals.

* * *

My learning developed and evolved into a more complex healing system by working with other children in one-to-one sessions in my office. Communication, learning, and behavioral issues are only a few of the challenges these sensitive children experience. And because of this, their frustrations build and their pent up energy eventually can do more harm than the disability itself. All children have these sensitivities, and it would be helpful for their health and happiness, if we chose to help them learn skill sets to understand what emotions are.

This is why it is important to understand that our emotions, thoughts and actions create energy that emanates from our bodies, and communicates information on a subtle level. Our fields of energy are merging and sending out messages to one another in ways that we are now just beginning to understand through evidence based scientific research. I believe these highly intelligent children utilize this field more than their physical senses.

* * *

Tyler was ten years old when I first met him. He was a special needs child, challenged with learning and communicating. His mother told me that he was not doing well in school because his behavior had become uncontrollable. She and Tyler's teachers and counselor could not get a handle on how to help him with this challenge. His diet, supplements, and medications were watched carefully, so Tyler's team decided to look into alternative practices to help him. Marcy, a mother of two boys that I had worked with, told Tyler's mother about the successful change in her sons while working with me. So Tyler's mother wanted to see what I could do for her son.

The first time I met with Tyler, I was surprised to find that his intuitive abilities were similar to my own. The first thing Tyler did was to walk around the counseling room in my office, pointing to figurines that I had displayed on tables. He accurately described them from a historical point of view and told me what they were made out of.

As Tyler walked over to the table with the figurines on it, he said, "Angel—plaster -- Spain."

I looked at Tyler and nodded yes. Then Tyler focused on the next figurine on the table. "Crystal -- Brazil." Then the next, "Buddha -- China."

I was astonished to his accuracy. Tyler also placed his hands around my head and moved his hands around the emanation of my energy field like he was pushing a puffy cloud, then smiled. It was clear that Tyler's inner world was definitely similar to my own!

During his second session, we established a stronger bond through our hearts, by just sitting together. Tyler and I began to breath to the same rhythm. One inhale, one exhale, calming and with ease. Through our energy fields, we were getting to know one another.

By the third session, Tyler was comfortable enough to express his feelings in a way that I could not have expected. We were sitting in the counseling room when I pointed to my chest and asked Tyler what he felt in his heart. All of a sudden, he became frustrated. To calm his emotions I asked him to take a walk around the office with me. I knew walking and breathing would help bring him back to balance.

We entered another room in my office where I had a full-scale storyboard on the wall. Drawings of children and posted manuscripts were plastered everywhere. I was creating a children's book series, and at first glance, I thought Tyler enjoyed looking at the pictures. As soon as Tyler gazed at the last story frame, he became enraged. He proceeded to tear down all the pictures and ripped them up into tiny pieces. As I watched him, I knew the feelings that Tyler was suppressing were becoming unleashed.

Then there was a knock on the office door. It was Tyler's mother. I decided not to disturb Tyler's process, so I asked her if she could please wait outside until the session was over.

After I shut the door, I looked back to find Tyler pushing all of my belongings off my desk. He stopped suddenly and ran to me, grabbing me around my waist and bursting into tears.

I let his mother into the office as Tyler continued to sob. She was astounded.

"Tyler never cries!" she said.

I remarked, "He needs to learn how to cry, and he needs to know it's okay."

I have to admit, after Tyler's mother saw what he had done to the children's project and my desk, I had some quick explaining to do as to why I didn't stop him. To say the least, she wasn't very happy about my unorthodox method on how to unleash pent up emotions. I didn't hear from Tyler's mother again after that session.

About a year later when I was visiting with Marcy she brought up how she had bumped into Tyler's mother. "Shirley, it was the oddest coincidence. She explained how she stopped bringing Tyler to you over a year ago and didn't realize it until a few months later that Tyler's behavior had changed. He was calmer and could concentrate better in school. What she said was that she had come to believe, whatever therapy you had used on her son, may have played a role in the change that had occurred with him." I was grateful to hear what Tyler's mother believed to be true about Tyler's improvement.

* * *

Children, whether they have challenges like Tyler or not, need to understand their emotions so they may navigate through life in a calmer more confident way. Even to teach children the simple tool on how to breathe when feeling anxious and to be in the present moment works wonders for a child's health and intelligence.

There were many children that I have worked with that, when taught simple tools, took to them like fish to water but trying to introduce new ideas to adults, was more of a challenge.

* * *

It was a rainy day when Carol drove me out to see one of her clients who had cancer. Susan was in her mid-forties and lived in a beautiful, large home right on the ocean. She was in Stage-4 and was not expected to live much longer. I had no clue as to what I could do for her. As I sat next to her bed, she told me that her husband had left her and began seeing another woman during her illness. He had just recently moved completely out of their home and was now trying to take their two children with him, since she was unable to care for them in her condition.

This was very difficult to hear, and yet I had to find a way to help her out of her emotional pain. I asked her what she wanted to happen in her situation. She said, "I want for my husband and me to heal our relationship so that I can leave here with peace and dignity."

As soon as I heard this, I asked for his phone number and I called him directly. Being that there was not much time, I asked if he would be open to meet with his wife and me as soon as possible. He declined, and I responded that her time was short and this was very important to do. He agreed that he would meet with her alone the following day, so Susan and I made another appointment the following week.

As I was leaving, Susan began to cry. Her emotional pain was greater than her physical pain, and I wanted to do something for her. The only thing I could think to do was to hold her; because she was too weak to sit up in her bed, I chose to lie down next to her and hold her until she fell asleep.

The following week when I returned, I couldn't believe the difference in Susan's condition. She was sitting up in bed, eating lunch when I arrived. She and her husband had made amends and were planning how they could make the best of the situation in a loving way. During their discussions, he explained to her how much pain he was in, especially because there was nothing he could do to stop her eventual death. The hidden truth of his deep love for her had been revealed.

*   *   *

Sometimes our actions are the complete opposite of what we are truly feeling, masking the pain of the truth that we will have to face such as what happened in the situation with Susan's husband. Susan passed away the following month, but I was told that she was at peace with her husband and her children.

The healer's heart of those in the health and healing professions emanated more healing energy than in any other profession that I had worked with. I believe this was because of the purpose and intent their profession is founded upon, that of healing and wellness. They manifest this alignment on a conscious and unconscious level, but I would soon learn that great compassion, heart, and healing also reside in the world of checks and balances.

Chapter 12

The World of Checks and Balances

My career was going exceedingly well, yet I was still trying to balance it with the nurturing and supportive time I needed to give to my children. This was an ongoing challenge because of the distance between us. Every chance I had, I would drive from Boston to Cape Cod, which was a 90 mile drive each way, even if I could only see my children for just a brief moment.

Melyssa and Krysie were at the age where they were busy with their friends and their extracurricular activities, so it never seemed to bother them not to see me every day. They were content as long as we had our nightly talks on the phone.

Laurie, though, would take long drives in the car with me while I listened to her talk about her school day and the fun things she found important in her life. Before I would head back to Boston, Laurie and I would hold hands and I would ask her, "Where am I?" And she would say, "You're in my heart!" And then I would ask, "And where are you?" And she would respond, "I'm in your heart!" And I would respond, "Always."

She never complained that I wasn't there enough for her, but she would always ask, "When will I see you again, Mom?" That question wasn't just a question. It was always the trigger to a bigger question. Is this the way I want to live my life? That was the real question, and it weighed heavily in my heart and on my mind.

There was still more for me to learn about myself. It was as if each client's courage to overcome their weaknesses and make changes to create the life they wanted helped me to become more courageous and honest with myself.

*   *   *

Back in Boston, Carol Mann was making sure I had everything I needed to feel comfortable and happy in my new community. She was always there for me to discuss how I felt about not being with my children full time and how I could make it better. Carol's door was never shut to anyone. I had total support from this loving woman, who believed in my work and the good that all like-minded people could create in the world.

The complex situations of my clients in the corporate world were new to me. I was surprised at my intuitive abilities to accurately give insights into strategic thinking and outcomes for ongoing business development, yet I still incorporated my ability as a healer to find the cause as to why many still felt unfulfilled in their work and personal lives.

I had only worked with a couple of executives when I received a very special phone call. The secretary for a well-known health institute located in Boston, called to make an appointment for the institute's founder, who was an internationally known figure in the new age health field. I will call her Grace.

Grace was the first business client who would teach me that businesses, like people, needed healing. Grace shared the following:

"Every business has a soul, created by the collective consciousness of the people that are united in a shared purpose. It has a personality created by the philosophy, values, and ethics everyone upholds in the business. It has a physical presence created by the products and service it gives that meets their clients' needs and enhances the welfare of life."

She talked about the importance of the earth and how we should each be in partnership to do our best to take care of it. She talked about caring for ourselves both physically and spiritually and said that we should find something that we have passion about and give our love and attention to it.

Then she talked about the opportunities in helping the planet evolve by creating a business that upholds spiritual attributes such as values, respect for all, accountability, and responsibility to meet purposeful goals, all done for the common good.

I was quite fond of Grace because of her spiritual presence and the integrated way she lived her life. This was evident in the books she wrote and the lectures she gave. Grace lived what she taught.

Grace had come to me with a very specific agenda. Her new partners disagreed with her about important guidelines that she wanted the business to abide by, that which she just could not live without professionally. Her partners refused to listen to her. As they perceived it, she was the creator; but they were the business aspect of the partnership. Her soul was aching because she was legally bound by a contract that she could not get out of, and she was trying to find a healthy solution.

Her attorneys felt that if an agreement could not be reached between her and her partners, she would have to separate herself from the present company and start up a new business of her own. This was devastating since she had placed all of her life's work into this organization. Grace finally decided to separate from her partners. She finally decided that she could live without the organization that she had worked so passionately to build, but she could not live without integrating the values and ethics that helped her achieve global recognition.

What Grace was talking about was the foundation in which she chose to live both her professional and personal life, one of truth, respect, and solid moral and ethical values. I did not give Grace any recommendations; in fact, all I did was listen to her and ask some questions to assist her in finding her answers; she came to her own truth. I was grateful in having the experience of being a consultant to Grace. It gave me the understanding of how important the integration of spiritual consciousness could benefit the world of checks and balances.

Meeting Grace helped me choose a greater spiritual consciousness in my own work. Little did I know how this chance meeting gave me the wisdom I needed for my next corporate client challenge.

* * *

Carol received a phone call from one of her clients, asking if she would be interested in a consulting job with his company. Because her schedule was already filled for the next three months, she asked me if I would be interested in meeting with him and I agreed. Mr. Kinsley was the CEO of a Fortune 500 software company on the outskirts of Boston. I was to meet with him in his office to discuss a consulting opportunity.

After I had entered the building of their main corporate headquarters, I was then escorted through three locked doors, which led to a luxurious office suite, where I finally met Mr. Kinsley.

As he stood up to greet me, he thanked my escort and asked me to sit down at an oblong table in the corner of his office. Mr. Kinsley was a tall, robust man who wore the presence of authority very well. But, instead of having the normal "get to business" attitude, he asked me questions like how I became a healer and intuitive consultant and what type of clients had I helped in the past.

After we spoke for a half hour, he leaned back in his chair and said, "I am quite impressed with what you have been able to accomplish. How would you feel if I hired you to train a team of my managers to become psychic?"

I paused for a moment, looking straight ahead at the fixtures on the wall. Then instead of answering his question, I chose to ask one myself: "May I ask why you want a whole team to be trained to be psychic?"

"Well," he said, pausing for a moment, "to be quite frank I want my team to learn how to do what you do so we can have a greater leverage on our competition. You know, tap into what our competition is working on, things like that."

I was shocked by the transparency of this man! "Mr. Kinsley, I am not the woman you want to hire to do something of this type of nature,"

I said. "My philosophy as a professional does not allow me to spy, let alone teach someone else how to spy on others. We all have the ability and we use this ability in subtle ways naturally so I would be more than happy to educate your group in how to explore their consciousness to access this energy.

This will assist you in knowing the right person to hire for your company and make appropriate decisions for your company's success, but not to spy on your competitors. Also, you will be able to resonate to the greatest value you can give in your industry, which will naturally bring you financial reward and leadership in the world."

I paused for a moment, and then added, "There are spiritual laws in the use of psychic abilities, just as there are manmade laws in how our nation is governed."

Mr. Kinsley's look became very intense, and he leaned forward as if he wanted to make his point very clear. "Then what do you think you are doing when you give someone a psychic reading?" he asked.

"I have the person's permission to engage in a relationship with them to assist them in their needs," I said. "As far as answering questions about other people, I still only engage with the person's energy, their vision and the outcome that they expect or want to achieve. This allows me to work only from their field of consciousness and the potentials that may occur."

I then said, "There is much more to it than just what you suggested. By my teaching you how to implement your own spiritual consciousness, you will enable yourself to know the directions you need to take to ensure success for your company."

"I still don't understand why a person cannot use their psychic abilities to find out what their competition is doing!" he exclaimed.

"Mr. Kinsley, I'm sure there are talented psychics that can do this, but I believe focusing on your competition in that way limits your ability to succeed in your own right. You have the knowledge and wisdom to make the right decisions for your business as well as in other areas of your life. If you need to be guided or cautioned about a competitor that also will come to you but from an inner knowing rather than external knowing. Now aren't you more interested in this, than in your team learning how to tune into your competition?"

Mr. Kinsley never answered my question. He just said that he had another meeting, told me he would have his assistant walk me out of the building, and then left the room. Needless to say, Mr. Kinsley and I never met again.

I recently explained to a colleague that thieves and child molesters also use their intuition and psychic abilities to get what they want, an innocent child to molest. So what makes the difference in how we use these gifted abilities? It is our true intention that fuels our purpose. So what are the ground rules? It is our personal moral and ethical standards that keep us to the highest standard in how we use this gift of intuition that guides us in our lives and helps us to manage our professional relationships.

We vote every day by how we use our consciousness in our lives. If we steal ideas from others and choose to live without respect, honesty, and truth, then we are voting for disloyalty and encouraging deception and failure to reign in our own lives. We all have these abilities to some degree so the importance is not what abilities we have, but how we use these abilities and our consciousness in our lives every day.

I was amazed by Mr. Kingsley's request. Yet it left me with a greater question to answer. How do I uphold my integrity and values in my personal and professional life? Just as organizations have rules of ethics and values I would have to be aware of upholding my ethics and integrity in my profession as a healer and spiritual consultant.

* * *

From discussions that I've had over the years with other healers, intuitive consultants and psychics, I have realized that we all have access to planes of consciousness that guide us to the answers we are searching for. I have never met anyone who does not uphold some standards of ethics when they use their abilities in their profession. I believe it to be rare when someone consciously is trying to use their gifts to the degree to spy or steal from others.

* * *

Rita, whom was now married to my brother, introduced me to a group of executives who were collaborating in developing a training program in leadership for Fortune 500 companies. For the first agenda item, we would discuss what makes a great leader in business. Even though I had met with corporate people individually, this was my first invitation to be a part of a corporate team.

This team was made up of professionals from different companies. We discussed higher levels of consciousness and how these spiritual concepts could assist executives and their employees to achieve greater ethical and leadership standards, which would create healthier and more productive corporate environments. Because Rita was able to integrate her own spiritual knowledge into her profession as well as her personal life, she invited me to explain concepts of spiritual consciousness to the group.

We held our meetings at a company's headquarters in Waltham, Massachusetts owned by a businessman, whom I would come to know very well. There were eight of us on the team, three woman and five men. Everyone introduced himself but when it came time for my introduction, I immediately froze. This was the first time that I had to introduce myself to a group of professionals who didn't already know my expertise.

I cleared my throat and began. "My name is Shirley Beauman, and I am an intuitive spiritual consultant."

I could feel the energy in the room shift as if others were trying to grasp what that meant; I imagined they wondered why I would be invited to join a leadership dialogue with executives who were clearly more astute in the challenges of the corporate world than I was.

Rita was an incredible facilitator and realized right away that she needed to explain why I was invited to be a part of the team. She explained that with many assembled talents of diversity, we would gain greater understanding of how to expand global thinking through personal and spiritual development. Her explanation seemed to calm their concerns.

This was only the beginning of my experience facilitating spiritual consciousness and transformation in corporate meetings and executive retreats, which in the world of checks and balances presents itself in how our personal morals, ethical values as well as corporate philosophies affect the outcome of our goals and aspirations.

The man that I felt a compelling force from was Doug Gorman. I didn't know, until he booked a session with me, that his opinion of me was questionable. Here are notes from Doug's actual diary of his recollections of meeting me:

I met Shirley when brought into a project for a Fortune 500 company. My company's expertise was in training and information development. Shirley's sister in law, Rita contacted me and since she was familiar with my company, we met at our corporate headquarters in Waltham and Shirley was at the meeting.

I couldn't understand what she was bringing to the project. She talked about "energy" and had no formal business training or experience. The main client contact had a human resources background and was more comfortable than I was with soft skills. The plan was to work as a team to develop a personal empowerment program that we called "You Inc." There was some friction between Shirley and me, for our worlds were totally different. In the interest of the project and a better team, Shirley and I decided to meet separately.

In my professional dealings there are business norms to be followed. Keep schedules, do what you say, follow through on your commitments. The greater business environment was new to Shirley, and I tried to help her get more grounded in understanding the business world while she helped me get a firmer footing in the spiritual world.

Here's where I was coming from: I was agnostic. I grew up in a small Republican town, and I was raised Protestant, but I saw tremendous hypocrisy in the church. The church did not speak out against war. I saw people in church who I knew were not living positive lives, but I assumed they thought they were doing so because they went to church every week. One church member was selling cars and I knew he was lying about where they came from and rolling back the mileage, another was hitting on my sister's friends, and I knew that a few of them cheated in golf, in the church golf league no less!

So my working assumptions were that God was made up and maybe I might make up God when I get older, but the miracles and even Jesus' existence were highly suspect in my mind.

Somehow, I had always known right from wrong, not that I never did things that were wrong, but I knew when I did them and had some amount of guilt that always seemed to outweigh the gain in any given situation, so I rarely repeated a wrong. My parents lived by right and wrong, and I certainly picked some of that up from them. I believe they went to church more out of a sense of duty and commitment to community rather than out of a search for God or Jesus.

Important filters for my world were business, technology, and education, and I saw Shirley as having none of those. I have a BA in psychology from a liberal arts school and a Master of Science in management from MIT. I thought psychics were quacks, making things up or responding to subtle cues with trickery and deceit. I thought science ruled all, yet I was intrigued with what Shirley was saying, and so I decided to meet with her for a private session. At this point, I was intrigued with Shirley, but not trusting.

My father had experienced heart problems followed by stroke and then cancer, starting before he was fifty. Every doctor's appointment we were told he would live for perhaps six months, but he lived for more than a dozen years, and I was wondering why.

When I met with her, she obviously knew things about me and had insights that on the surface were impossible to know. However, with my technology and analytical background I wanted to understand where this information was coming from. I was dealing with two life issues related to family and vocation.

I had a series of jobs with different companies and I was questioning whether I belonged in business. It seemed like every organization I was with had people who would lie and cheat and steal, in some sense, for personal gain. In my most recent job, I had been fired after refusing a venture capitalist's demand to do something I considered immoral, if not illegal. I had put all my liquid cash into a company and with a severance payment of three weeks and no access to money and with my first child due shortly and no resources, life looked pretty bleak. I had only been with my current company, where I met Shirley, for a few months.

Shirley was able to help me understand these issues in a way that my analytical mind could not. She taught me about the human energy system that was about body and soul. There was something there, but I still did not know what. Over the next few months there were three experiences that proved to me that the spiritual world was actually real.

I began to see angels, real angels. I could see a circle of angels above me.

Another time is when I was sitting in the National Airport and my deceased father appeared in front of me. It was as if he was still alive and he told me in a very clear, audible voice that my twin brother was having issues with alcohol and that I should try to help him. That proved to be true.

I started meditating and after awhile I began to travel in my mind down a long road. There I saw the Master Jesus Christ.

These kinds of experiences have now become a part of my life, and over the years I have had many experiences that were related to spiritual consciousness. I consider myself blessed to have had these explicit experiences.

Shirley told me that these forces have been with me for my whole life, but that I was now ready to acknowledge them and use them. Shirley became my spiritual mentor; I read books, visited places, and became open to this new view of life. In fact, my life finally made sense to me and I have now been able to express it.

*   *   *

Doug and his partner, Katelyn, believed that the quality of their own personal transformation assisted them with their goals to grow the company's bottom line while still upholding a high level of personal and professional integrity. Awareness, mindfulness, and balance were the main ingredients in their transformation. So they decided to create an "employee satisfied environment" by including a broader range of holistic services in their company as well.

Their company promoted equality, inspiration, commitment, and teamwork, and they produced high quality products and services for their clients. This was a productive change started by one man and his partner. They chose to better themselves then focused on creating a business environment that incorporated the credo; every employee of ours is a valuable and equal part of our organization. Doug and Katelyn became forerunners in higher levels of consciousness in the corporate world.

Doug wanted to engage and develop spiritually as an ongoing practice, so he and his wife, Cheryl, opened their home to a group that wanted to develop spiritually. People in this group came from diverse backgrounds, both professionally and culturally. They represented business cultures in finance, social work, government, corporations, and the medical and health fields.

Several members of this group would consistently attend these sessions. The personal bond and the spiritual synergy they created were powerful. The reason why I bring this up is because one particular day during our insight meditation, we had an unusual experience. I will never forget this group session, which proved the power of group consciousness in our world.

At this particular group session, there were seven of us who came together for the program. The day started out like all our daylong programs; we met in the morning, and the group would chip in and bring the food that would be served for breakfast and lunch. First we would have a light breakfast, chat about our lives and what we had been doing for the past several weeks, and then begin the program. I was particularly quiet that morning and hadn't much to say; usually I would be a chatterbox, but I felt something of a disturbing nature, in the air.

The group settled in, and we began with our normal transformational work in the morning, each one of us participating as facilitator as well as being facilitated by the others in the group. I never began the session with a meditation, because I believed in the concept "show up as you are." This was half the reason the program was so successful. There was trust between the participants in this group; we could just be ourselves and work on our life issues, without feeling restricted. In this way we could engage, in a transparent way, in the process of spiritual transformation that helped us see clear to our weaknesses as well as strengths in order to make change within ourselves.

After the transformation work, we all took a break and had lunch. Instead of eating lunch, I chose to take a walk instead -- a quiet walk. That was very unusual for me, and looking back at this now, I believe it was in preparation for what we were about to experience.

As we began to settle down for the guided meditation after lunch, I felt heaviness all around me, something that I couldn't quite put my finger on, because I usually felt light, joyful, and focused. I delivered the guided meditation in the name of Christ Consciousness, as I usually did, and then it began. To make this concept clear for you, not everyone in a meditation group experiences and perceives information in the same way. In this particular group, some would see colors while others would just see white light. Some could visibly see spiritual guides and angels, while others just felt their presence. But all of us could feel the shift in the room when we meditated, as if we were aligned with a higher, more refined level of knowing.

We had visions and insights into spiritual consciousness that filled us with wisdom and knowledge, and the experience usually left us with an uplifting feeling. But as I mentioned before, this day was different. We felt the energy of Christ Consciousness protecting and guiding us through the meditation when, two specific visions appeared to two of us, while others perceived the feeling of something tragic in the air.

We saw a city with tall buildings on fire, filled with smoke. People were running everywhere. I don't know how long our inner senses engaged in this awareness, but before another vision was given to us, Doug stated that he believed this was in New York City. We all agreed. Then, the experience shifted and we saw a tidal wave flooding a different continent in the world.

It was completely unexpected for us to experience the devastation and the changes that we saw and felt during our meditation. After it was over everyone in the group seemed subdued for quite some time.

This experience never left me. I personally engaged in prayer for these catastrophic events, even though there was no factual evidence that they may even occur in the future. I had realized throughout my spiritual awakening that the universe does respond to all our heart's desires and needs, but from this experience I began to realize something more. The universe was asking us to respond to the universe's needs as well. To me, this meant that there is an infinite loop of giving and receiving from one another and everything in the world and beyond.

This experience from our meditation brought me to a greater understanding that the universe, is communicating to us directly.

I believe these two events to have been September 11, 2001 and the great tsunami of 2004. At the time, we couldn't have known how the events of 9/11 would impact our lives, our country and our security. But our spiritual consciousness was showing us what was coming our way.

* * *

I realized from this experience that most of what we receive daily through subtle levels goes unnoticed, or if we do become aware, we are challenged to understand how it fits into our lives.

Because of this, I now share with people that if you can't do something about a situation that your insights are guiding you toward, then pray, or ask God for assistance to be available to you, and to those that may be affected. Your thoughts and prayers do have an effect on events and those who are involved.

Chapter 13

One Small Change

As I became more proficient in my spiritual understanding of wisdom and love, the universe brought me greater opportunities to share what I had learned.

Many times I would receive phone calls from people who were going through various spiritual awakenings. Illness, financial challenges, relationship issues, as common as these are, can be the impetus for transformation. The desire to find a better solution is a key ingredient for a spiritual awakening to occur. What we seek with true intent shall be revealed. But instead of recognizing these situations as opportunities to begin awakening to our abilities to heal and prosper, we might choose other ways to cope instead.

The coping mechanisms of my clients ran the gamut from overdosing on prescriptive medications, overindulging in food and alcohol, or taking their stress out emotionally on their partners, or their children. Most of us engage in these behaviors in order to keep our momentum up to succeed in our commitments, accountability, and responsibilities.

These behavior patterns eventually become unhealthy habits leading to outward manifestations that would eventually break down our health, relationships and our ability to work efficiently. Once a person hits their limit with these indulgencies other mechanisms must be found to succeed. This can become a vicious cycle. I have worked with successful professionals who have confessed to stealing business ideas from colleagues because they couldn't keep up with what was expected from them. Clients who exhibited these behaviors, eventually crashed and burned. The thought of utilizing wellness modalities to most was never even considered as a viable option. This is why education in how our physiology and consciousness works together is important.

The more my clients included a practice of self-inquiry and mindful techniques in their daily routine, the healthier and more balanced they became. The more balanced they became the easier it was for them to deal with life challenges in a way that was positive, productive and respectful to themselves and to others. They were transforming their lives.

My clients who dropped the façade of their ego were able to move past their persona of being strong and their concerns of what others might think, allowing them to engage in wellness programs that fit their unique criteria. Once they realized their addictions and dysfunctional behaviors were getting in their way of living a great life, they were, finally, able to commit to change.

* * *

A new client, whom I will call Josh, began his session by telling me how he felt when he woke up every morning. Heaviness in his body with a foggy, muddled mind was how he described it. He explained how he struggled with many aspects of his life even though he thought he was doing quite well professionally. He had just given up alcohol and began a spiritual practice that included prayer, meditation, and techniques that he learned from reading self-help books.

Several months later, Josh booked another session. He began his session by telling me that he had lost his job. As we talked through the events that led up to him being fired, he realized something very important. He was zoning out of his problems and tuning into only positive thoughts.

"It felt good," he said. "My meditations were blissful and gave me a sense of confidence in myself."

However, he was missing many of the cues indicating that something was going drastically wrong. Now he understood how he went from using alcohol that allowed him to zone out, to a new coping mechanism, spiritual development that also allowed him to zone out. As the session went on, his core issue became clear to him: conflict avoidance was the cause of many of his unresolved issues.

Other clients recognized that they were biting their tongues while emotionally seething inside about situations that they believed they had no power over. Gossip and twisting the truth were only a few of the deceitful actions they became involved in to succeed. They realized that they were creating a field of negativity and if they did not change, this would continually affect their lives in a negative way. There was no winning at this game.

One day I was in a corporate meeting with several managers to address an issue in conflict resolution and strategic planning. One manager out of nine was pushing back on what the other directors were asking from his division. I abruptly stopped the meeting and asked the team if they were open to answer an unusual question. I asked them to write their answer down, and if they felt inspired, share their answers with the rest of the group.

The question was, "While you were listening to what was being presented at this meeting today, what were you thinking in the back of your minds?"

After a very brief moment, they began to write down their answers. One man laughed and decided to share his answer.

"I was wondering if Kristen had told Max that I believed he is a total jerk when it came to his management style. And that's not all," he said. "I was thinking she would use this to position herself as being more reliable, since she was on unstable ground with him because of her recent work performance."

I thought to myself. *The company these people worked for prided themselves in hiring the best people in the industry, yet from this one question they were able to look deeper into the type of business culture they were creating.* This is what came out of the rest of their discussion:

> Their greatest frustration: Upper Management
>
> What they did about it: They complained to colleagues to relieve the pent-up frustrations from believing they had no power to change the decisions of upper management, and once they complained they believed this may come back and be used against them.
>
> What they recognized they were creating: They were creating their work to be a battleground for their insecurities, competitiveness, and deceptive behaviors, giving credence to the view that you can achieve more if you are deceptive.
>
> Prognosis for success: Their minds were not on work but were on the trivial situations that went on in the office, leaving them with less productive time. Therefore they were not achieving the goals that were expected of them.
>
> Behavioral Change for success: They needed to change from these types of behaviors to productive and intelligent thoughts and actions. This would help to create respectful relationships among their peers and allow them to become better team players.

These corporate employees had the courage to face the negative impact they were creating in the company and themselves. By being honest and open, they were able to make one small change, which led to a greater and long-lasting impact, to change the dysfunctional behaviors, by creating a code of honor in how they would behave and respect one another.

From these experiences, I chose to incorporate educational concepts in personal development. I had come a long way from the practice of prayer and hands-on healing that inspired me to understand our human potential.

Yet there was more to learn about our evolution in consciousness and how we affect our world, and when I was ready to learn more, the right circumstances came my way.

* * *

A client of mine who had just been hired by a fortune 500 company that was located west of Boston called me to be interviewed for a consulting position to their Vice President and senior management team.

I was hired after the first interview and started my consulting position immediately. After meeting individually with each of the managers I realized that what had happened in the company affected each manager deeply.

Jim, the new Vice President explained it to me this way, "Shirley, the last Vice President, (whom I will call Dan), was charismatic. Everybody respected his leadership ability and his principles about employees all being equal and the most important asset to the company. But he left abruptly taking with him 13 of our top experts, all leaving without giving sufficient notice or explanation. Later the company found out that Dan started a similar company, which was already in the process of becoming a profitable business. This left our organization in turmoil and the need for support with the transition we are going through."

The managers I had interviewed believed in Dan. His ability to lead took him quickly from the lowest ranking job to being Vice President. Under Dan's management, the employees were happy, productive, and worked well together. One manager said, "Dan made me feel that we were a family, a family that I never had experienced before in a working environment." The managers expressed how numb and shocked they were, especially because of Dan's leadership and code of business ethics he taught. He was outwardly positive and seemingly committed to the company, right up to the day he left. He hadn't broken any laws, yet the way he handled his decision to leave the company had a severe negative impact on everyone.

So you can imagine how these people felt when Dan and the other employees left the company. Outwardly, these managers and the rest of the employees had to work efficiently and productively to uphold the company's business and bottom line with a greater pressure of feeling betrayed. Also, Dan had created one of the best business strategies that made this division the best in the nation. He would give his managers the strategy at weekly meetings so they had no idea what next actions steps to take on their own. The internal environment had plummeted to a negative place from one man's power and influence. Many were left shocked by his hidden agenda.

I decided to start by bringing the managers together at an off-site daylong program where they could feel more relaxed. The program was hosted by one of the managers at her home. The theme of the day was on finding solutions to rebuild their leadership skills.

The discussion on leadership began yet there seemed to be a feeling of heaviness in the air. I decided to stop the program to take a break and let the managers talk about anything they had on their minds. The topic that came up for everyone was Dan. By all accounts, they believed he had been what made the company successful. The power of success, in their minds, still belonged to Dan.

The more they talked the angrier they became and the energy intensified among the group. Suddenly music began to play in the room. Our hostess went over to her stereo system only to find the stereo system panel showed that is wasn't on. She then pushed the on/off button a couple of times but the music continued playing until she pulled the plug out of the electrical socket, then it stopped. Everyone was bewildered. The emotional impact from the managers had created a poltergeist activity.

Because I understood the science behind matter and energy, I took the opportunity to educate the group by explaining what had just happened. I encouraged them to recognize where their energy was housed in their body as they spoke about Dan. Some felt it in the area of their chest. Others felt it lower in the area of their solar plexus. Some felt intense constriction between their eyes, while others felt tightness in their heads. Mostly everyone felt tightness in the back and neck region. The power of their emotions and thoughts created, what is called in scientific terms incoherence that triggered a sound system to dysfunction! This experience was very powerful for the group and I used this understanding to lead them into the dynamics of corporate leadership.

Energy is energy. Helping them to redirect their emotional energy and thoughts was the key to self-empowerment. I wanted them to experience how they could use this collective force to move themselves and the company forward.

At the end of the day one of the managers used the technique of splitting wood with his bare hands to demonstrate the power of mind over matter. Everyone decided to try it and they all succeeded. It was a powerful ending. Everyone realized they could move forward and uphold their commitment to the company by being positive and letting go of something they could not control.

The human condition of emotion cannot be left outside business doors. Our physiology doesn't allow it. Our feelings play a vital role in our physiology. An integrative approach to understanding the power of our consciousness plays a key role in our ability to create success in the companies we work in.

By the end of the year, my contract was nearing completion, and the management team was integrating their newly developed skillsets and agenda into their performance. All in all they were ready to move on without my assistance.

Just three weeks away from the end of my contract, Jim asked me to meet with him in his office. I pulled up a chair to sit in front of his desk. His eyes looked dull, completely different from what I had expected, since his team was doing so well.

Gazing out the window, Jim turned toward me and said, "So how do you feel the management team will do without you?"

"Very well," I replied. "In fact, you have a great group of managers here, willing to improve themselves and move the company forward."

He nodded his head in agreement, and then I asked, "How are you doing?"

Jim leaned back in his chair and thought for a moment.

"We have a bigger problem in the company that I've been dealing with," he said. "Our multimillion-dollar computer system keeps crashing."

He scratched his head as I began to listen more intently. "We've had the best IT techs dealing with this, and they are able to get the system up and running, but a few days later, it crashes again."

There was silence between us for some time, and then I responded, "Jim, I know you hired me as a consultant to pull your team together, but I believe I can help you with your systems problem."

Jim looked at me inquisitively, and I continued, "I have a great capacity in understanding not only the energy of people but of circumstances that surround situations which may still be affecting other aspects of the business. I would be more than happy to take a look at the system and see if I can find a solution."

Jim stood up and walked around to the front of his desk; he leaned his back against the desk and said, "I heard about what happened with the managers at the day-long program. What do you need in order to accomplish this?"

"I need access to the computer itself and someone to show me the main electrical system the computer is connected to throughout the building. Then I will have to be left alone with the system itself without distractions."

Jim shook his head and replied, "Under company protocol, I cannot leave you alone in the systems room. No one is allowed to be in the computer room without an authorized person."

I nodded.

"Oh, and one more thing," Jim said as he walked me out of his office. "I would rather no one know that you are doing this for me, if you know what I mean."

I understood Jim's concern because I knew what I had gone through with my own doubts and disbeliefs about energy and what other people may think. The next morning, Jim and I met in front of the systems building. He acted like we were just going over the company's standard procedures. That put me at ease.

It was 5:30 a.m. when we walked into the building. No one else was present. Jim turned on the lights as we walked through the massive metal building.

"Here we are," he said as he keyed in his code to enter the computer room. As we walked into the room, Jim put out his hand as if he was introducing me to someone. "This is our computer's brain," he said.

I walked over to the computer and placed my hands on the system. Jim explained that the computer system was functioning but some part of it was still having problems.

After I assessed the computer energetically, I turned to Jim and said, "Okay, that's all I need for now. Can you show me how the computer interfaces with the rest of the company's database?"

Jim and I walked into a smaller room off the computer room where there was a large board. Again, I assessed the system. This time I could feel that there was something wrong. The database system felt fine, but I could hear a screeching sound coming from the energy emanating from the computer.

I turned to Jim and asked, "Do you hear anything unusual?"

Jim leaned over, listened for a moment, and then said, "No, I can't hear anything unusual, just the usual low humming sound."

I took a mental note not to forget the screeching sound that I heard. "Is there anything else you can show me?" I asked.

Jim and I walked down a long open space under the wire cables that hung from the ceiling and went into the other buildings. "This is the only other thing I can show you. These are the cable wires that go into the buildings to feed the computers."

I knew I still didn't have the information I needed to resolve the problem. As we left the building, I asked Jim if we could go into the computer room one more time.

Jim opened the door and said, "Shirley, I've got to get back to my office, so just make sure the door shuts tightly when you leave."

I smiled, thanked him, and went to work right away. As I stood in front of the computer, I placed my hands on it and asked what the problem was. As soon as I asked, I heard a loud screeching sound come from the other room. It was the computer board, so I went and asked for the energy to be released. The screeching sound ceased.

It wasn't until a couple of years after my contract ended I decided to call one of the managers and ask how they were doing. I asked if they had any other computer problems after I'd left the company. Her answer: "As a matter of fact, Shirley, we haven't had any unusual computer glitches since the reorganization of the company."

Now I know this story might have been a bit of a quantum leap forward about how powerful we are even enough to trigger malfunctions in the electrical and technical systems, but just think how the synergy in a group of people with similar intentions and goals can bring about greater and healthier solutions. This was a great experience to increase the understanding about how the energy of a collective group, such as in a corporation, can affect the material world.

* * *

Spiritual consciousness transforms every cell in our bodies. Because we are spiritually advancing and going through a transformation, we impact the connections we have to everything in our lives. During the transformation of our planet, electrical systems such as lights, computers, cars, and televisions can, at times, be affected by the earth's energy grid, and sometimes so can we affect these same systems. Learning how to stay balanced, mentally clear, and stress free can eliminate the negative effects that can affect everything in our lives.

* * *

A couple of years later, I was a presenter at a Mind, Body Conference. My lecture was titled, "You Are the Gift," and it was all about our healing abilities. The conference lasted three days and the morning after my second lecture was given, five participants approached me while I was leaving the lecture hall.

One of the gentlemen spoke first. "Hi Shirley, I'm Joe and we all want to thank you for yesterday's healing meditation."

"You're very welcome," I replied.

A woman from the group spoke up next as if Joe had left something very important out of his greeting. "All of us wanted to share with you what had happened for us after the meditation was over." She looked at the others in the group and continued. "Shirley, I had a healing of my skin yesterday. I have had a rash for the longest time, and the creams that I had been using weren't helping to alleviate the problem." She then held out her arm to show me that she had clear skin where her rash had been.

Joe himself explained that his recurring back problem was gone, and for the first time in years he had been able to sleep through the night without being woken by pain.

The others shared how their joint problems were cured, their eyesight improved, and a man's emotional trauma had been healed during the meditation.

The reason why I have shared this story in this chapter is because I did not heal them. The intention for healing from all the participants in my lecture allowed the synergy of their collective heart energy to create the healing. What was the meditation I instructed them on? It was a meditation focused on their hearts. As I have said before, "The healer resides within all of us."

The other extraordinary aspect of this event was that two of the five people did not know the other three before the program, but they ended up sitting at the same table during breakfast. From their healing experience, the synergy of their energies created a powerful attraction.

So this brings me to a point of discussion: why are we not expecting ongoing health and fulfillment in all of our life activities? What is the difference between being at a healing seminar and being at work? I give these two examples to show that in the case of a healing program such as "You Are the Gift," people's attention for the weekend was on what was being presented: that of spiritual consciousness and healing.

So why is it so easy to give me, the presenter, the "achievement award" for the healings instead of looking at ourselves and recognizing what had to occur within ourselves in order for this to happen? What happened at Jim's company? The managers were giving the "achievement award" to Dan, without recognizing that they had the power within themselves to lead and excel. The same belief system had occurred in both situations.

* * *

The subtle collective consciousness of beliefs is a powerful force that drives families, companies, communities, and cultures. When we are consciously focused on one aspect of our lives, like our jobs or our families, the collective consciousness of the group is the driving force. When we become spiritually aware and conscious of this, we have more choices in how we want to interact that may change the way in which outcomes can occur for the better.

Who will decide not to just go with the flow and instead bring solutions to situations and to bring about healing and greater moral and ethical values in your life? The story you are about to read is a great example of how one person had the courage to use the power of love to create a miracle.

* * *

Dottie was one of my closest friends, so when I was awakened by her phone call at 4:30 in the morning, I knew right away that something dreadful had happened.

"David has been in an accident," she said frantically, referring to her son. "Stephen and I are at the hospital. Please, Shirley, tell me he's going to be okay?" What do you say when one of your best friends asks if her son is going to be okay?

"Dottie," I said, "no matter what, *believe* that he is going to pull through this and *believe* this with all your heart."

That call would be the first of many conversations Dottie and I would have within the next several weeks. That early morning call led me to pay close attention to my friend and the severity of her son's condition.

David was a senior at Assumption College in Worcester, Massachusetts at the time of his accident. He was driving back to campus from a dance on a snowy December evening when he hit a patch of black ice and crashed into a tree. The first prognosis from the surgeon was that David had a severe head injury and his brain was severely damaged; "We don't think he is going to live." He said.

Dottie wrote this in her memoir, *Stay Gold*, about how she and her husband, Stephen, were told of the prognosis:

> I heard the most horrible sound come out of Stephen.
>
> He was crying, "Why, God? I thought I was a good person."
>
> I looked at him surprised. I couldn't let him think this was a punishment.

Then Dottie writes, "This is not about you. This is a journey that David's soul is on. You can't start feeling guilty. That's not going to help David."

That was when Dottie realized that she had to take charge of David's surroundings to help him heal. The following day there were over twenty students from David's college there in the hospital to support him. Dottie asked everyone to engage in positive thoughts for David's full recovery. She shared her belief in the power of positive thinking and explained that when more people think the same way, the more powerful that thought would manifest.

As Dottie explains in her own words, "This was my metaphysical training coming out. I had been studying for about five years but I didn't talk about it much to people because it's a bit of a different belief system. Well, now I was running on automatic and it just took over. It made sense in the deepest part of me like something you already knew but didn't know how you knew. It became my truth."

Dottie stayed strong in her spiritual beliefs even when doctors would report back to her with negative news. She was determined to make sure that everything she learned about spiritual consciousness and healing would be applied to her son's full recovery. She was diligent in playing positive affirmations and healing CD's in his room. And she demanded that everyone who entered her son's room, including the medical staff, only spoke positively to him about his recovery.

As Dottie and her family worked daily at David's bedside with great care and love, I was experiencing a connection on a subtle plane of David's reality; an experience of his soul.

I remember the first night I was awakened by David's spiritual energy in my bedroom. I was in complete shock, as this was the first time I had experienced someone in a coma being able to communicate spiritually.

David's life force was strong and brightly illuminated. I explained to him that in order to heal, he had to choose to live. He then asked me how long would it take for him to recover. I told him that it would take time and perseverance, but he could recover fully. What was so unusual about his spiritual presence is that he was just the same as if I were in touch with him on earth: joking, laughing, yet I believed he was in a place where he and God were making the decisions about his future.

That day, I told Dottie that I had a visitation from David, and she asked me what I thought would happen. Everyone had been praying, masses were being said, and friends would sit in the waiting room at the hospital just waiting for news.

Michael, his brother, was there consistently, along with Dottie and Stephen. Their whole world was focused on David coming out of the coma and being healthy again.

I explained to her how she and everyone that loves David were creating an energy field of love around him for his recovery. I believed he would be out of the coma before Christmas.

David showed small signs of trying to communicate with his family before Christmas including holding his thumb up, but the doctor and nurses recognized his actions as "posturing," which are uncontrolled brain movements that can occur to patients in a catatonic state.

But Dottie, Stephen, and Michael believed it to be more. Dottie wrote, "I could take a twitch as posturing, drooling absolutely, not a thumbs up. We knew he was there. Our hope was renewed. We were filled with new strength."

Dottie shares in her personal memoir, an incident that happened right before Christmas.

Christmas was a very special time for their family. Every year Stephen would play Santa Claus to a couple of hundred children at the Centerville Christmas Walk, and he was committed to doing it again this year, even though his son lay in the hospital in a coma. Michael stayed with David at the hospital and called his mother that evening with good news. When the doctor came in to visit David on his rounds, Michael asked David to give him the thumbs up sign, and a few seconds later David did.

Dottie asked Michael, "What time did this happen?"

Michael responded, "Nine o'clock; why?"

Dottie responded, "I was giving your father a thumbs up at the same time. I had looked at my watch because I wanted to go home. Mike, we were doing this at the same time."

The power of love creates a synchronicity and a communication from our spirit, through a web of divine love that bonds us together. Love is the glue that gives strength and resilience to our desires, guiding us in our actions to manifest what we want the outcomes to be.

During David's second visit to me, he explained how he could see everyone around him. He could feel their love and care but could not hear what was being said, but he knew that he was going to be okay.

The octaves that were not of love and positive thought never reached David on the soul plane. He could only feel that which resonated to him of comfort and love, even while he was in a coma. I believe that Dottie's determination to allow only positive conversations around David during his recovery is why he only felt these positive feelings.

"What you feel are the feelings of those around you," I responded. "Through your feelings and through the feelings of those that love you, you are connecting to one another."

Then he asked the question about who would decide his fate. Will he come back to earth or stay in heaven? And I responded, "That decision is made between you and God and from the desire of your heart."

David visited me one more time before coming out of his coma. This time his presence was so subtle that I could hardly see him at all. I believed this to mean he was more in his body than he was on the soul plane. The last words I heard from him during that visitation were, "I've made a decision. I'm coming back." Through a six-month period of time, David slowly came out of his coma and began his healing process.

After her son's recovery, Dottie wrote, "We always believed in miracles. We just didn't know how to make a miracle occur. Now we do. The fundamental component is love."

Dottie goes on to say, "We are not helpless beings that life happens to but willing participants in all experiences that come to us. I have come to believe very deeply in the power of prayer and the power of self. The self, is the part of us that is God, because there is a piece of him in all of us."

*   *   *

How many times have I been asked these questions: "Why did this happen to me, to my family? Why did someone have to get ill and have to die?" At times there is no understanding why these occurrences happen, except to understand this is a part of living.

There are many factors that play a role in our lives. Genetics, our environment and our stress levels. Accidents do happen. There are global situations that are occurring right now, natural disasters are affecting thousands of lives every day. Life has many variables in it, and we are all participants in life. But the way we choose to participate in life can make all the difference in creating a better outcome.

A man I met at a conference shared with a group of colleagues and me that he had just lost his wife to an illness. In the spirit of good food and company, he presented a very thought-provoking question: "What is the meaning of life?" I didn't respond to this question at that moment, but for me "The meaning of life is what we give to life!" Will it be love, compassion, appreciation, and understanding, or will it be cynicism, impatience, and anger? We affect an outcome by the energy we give to it.

I cannot give justice to David's story in this short space. The gift of David's healing can be found in the truth of his mother's love that inspired a family, a graduating class, and a community to come together as one. This is how they created David's miracle.

Now, what will you choose to give to life?

*   *   *

The stories I've shared with you in the this book show how one small change benefited others as well as helped to shape the future in how we make the world a better place to be in.

Grace looked at her organization as having a soul, and she viewed her business as an integral whole, through which the values and integrity of everyone involved made the business successful. When faced with a moral and ethical conflict of differences in her business, she decided it was better to leave the organization she founded and start over again, no matter how difficult a task that would be.

Doug strove to be a force of good by understanding how his spiritual consciousness worked in his life, and by doing so he was able to make decisions not only on the grounds of creating financial gain but also for a greater purpose in integrating the importance of ethics and integrity in his company and life.

The collective empowerment of the Fortune 500 Company was almost lost when Dan broke his own code of ethics by leaving the company and taking several employees with him. But instead, they found their personal power and strength within themselves, which allowed them to uphold their own professional integrity and create a positive outcome.

The strangers that came together at the conference had the courage to share their instantaneous healing. They were energetically drawn to one another and shared their personal experiences when they sat down together at breakfast.

Dottie was the force behind a miracle. She used her spiritual beliefs and her perseverance to inspire her family, her community, and her son's graduating class to come together in a bond of deep love and positive thoughts; together they created a miracle.

*   *   *

We are going through a major change on our planet, a time of reawakening that many spiritual teachers and scientists have spoken about for years. As for myself, well, there is always more to learn; I was on one of those learning curves. I had been blessed with meeting so many people that were in different professions, communities, and cultures that taught me the value of sharing our stories and the solutions we have found that have changed our lives for the better.

So what was my learning curve? We are no more spiritual than what we can be in our humaneness.

Chapter 14

My Way Back Home

Every experience I had with others brought me closer to listening to my own heart. They helped me to realize how I kept bypassing true feelings about my happiness and how I gave more importance to my professional career than I did to my personal life. I was sad and unhappy. To compensate, I traveled to visit my children even on the days I was not supposed to see them.

It was horrific not having a home close to them where we could go, so frequenting restaurants and sitting in the car to talk were the only options I often had. But even though I was under these constraints and had to travel 90 miles to see them, it was well worth it to me, even if I saw them for only a half hour.

I spent hours on the phone every evening, helping Laurie with her homework. Krysie would share the difficulties she was having in facing conflicts with her friends, and Melyssa would pick up the slack for my not being there; she made sure the household ran smoothly.

Everything was wrong with this picture, because I was missing the most important experience in my life: my children. I missed helping them get ready for school in the morning, making dinner for them, and helping them with their homework. I missed being there to cheer them on during their games in sports and participate with them in after-school activities. And most of all, I missed all the wonderful ways their innocence would touch me like nothing else could.

Finally, I couldn't drown out my feelings any longer. So one Sunday after I brought the children back to Jake's house, I decided to attend the Sunday service at the Spiritualist church where Reverend Harding was the Pastor. I hadn't been there for a few years, so I felt it would be nice to sit in their healing service that I desperately needed.

For me, there was never a disappointment in these services and healing time. First there would be an opening prayer. Then came "Laying on of Hands," healing by the ordained healers in the church. I chose to participate and I sat in one of the healing chairs in the front of the church. While the healer placed his hands on my shoulders and prayed, streams of tears came down my face as the energy moved through my body. Then I felt a sense of peace come over me. My breathing became rhythmic and my mind became clear.

The next phase of the service was a sermon given by one of the junior ministers, who talked about infinite intelligence and how this intelligence is expressed through the phenomena of nature, both physical and spiritual. At the end of the sermon, the junior minister talked about the church's community calendar and the upcoming events and guest speakers.

As the junior minister left the pulpit, Reverend Harding stood up and took her place to give spiritual messages for church members and guests. She was always clear and present when she shared her attunement to spirit. I could always feel the presence of angels when she spoke. As I was thinking this, I heard her voice break into my thoughts as if trying to wake me up.

"The young lady wearing the white blouse in the fifth row," she called out.

I was a little startled but raised my hand and said, "Yes?"

She went on and said, "There is a great being that is standing behind you. He is from the angelic kingdom and he wants you to know that he is with you whenever you are in need of his protection and guidance. Do you understand why he would present himself today?"

As I nodded my head, I responded, "Yes, yes I do. Thank you, Reverend Harding."

On my way back from the Spiritual Service, I began having flashes of events from my past. I remembered the poltergeist event in the kitchen when I heard a voice say, "This is a gift. Use it wisely." I remembered the voice that I heard when I was with Ann in the Philippines that left me when I was calm enough to trust my own knowing that directed us to safety. I remembered when I was at my darkest moment, caught in a rainstorm when I rejected help from a being who gave me permission to use his name as my own. I then heard a voice say, "I am St. Michael."

* * *

I did not know that there would be difficult decisions to make and challenges to overcome on my way back to where I belonged; I would have to heal what I had created and I was now taking full responsibility for my life and how I was going to live it.

My relationship with my brother Billy and his wife Rita remained intact during those challenging years during my spiritual awakening. At the time I had decided to move back to Cape Cod, I was contracted to write a book on spiritual consciousness. The deadline for the outline of the book had already passed, and I was still not able to complete it. What was even worse was that Billy and Rita were both personally involved in the financial backing of this book. I will never forget that day when my brother walked into our condo in Boston and asked me directly why I was late with the book's outline.

Billy is a tall, lean, handsome man with a great sense of humor, but when there was something that he felt was not being respected ... watch out! His body would stiffen and his glare could be deadly. When he was angry, his jaw would tighten and the tone of his voice would deepen, as if he was having difficulty getting the words out. After I greeted him at the door, he and I sat down in the living room.

"Shirl, what the heck have you been thinking about?" As usual, our "brother and sisterly" talks weren't always of a lighthearted nature, but they were educational and honest, to say the least. Billy always helped me to stand my ground on what I believed, not because he agreed with me but because I knew no matter what, his love would always be there for me. So I sat there in silence and listened to what he had to say. "I don't get this!" He stood as he spoke. "You have a great opportunity and you're blowing it!"

Billy waited patiently for my response.

"Place me in front of a lecture room or on weekend retreats as a facilitator," I began, "and the experiences are successful." I then paused for a moment. "Yet when it came to writing this book on spiritual consciousness, something is holding me back!"

At this point, I stood up and began to walk around the room. I then stopped, turned toward Billy, and said, "So you want to know what I'm thinking about? I'm constantly thinking about my children. Living the way we are is not the way I believe our lives should be!"

Billy closed his eyes for a moment and then gestured for me to go on.

"I'm on the phone every night helping Laurie with her homework, listening to Krysie talk about the growing pains she's going through with her friends, but I'm not there to comfort her during these painful experiences. And Melyssa, even though she has great judgment and incredible fortitude, she shouldn't have to take my place while I'm living so far away from them, just because she's the oldest!"

As I said this I could feel my body getting stronger and my mind becoming clearer.

"I know I have great opportunities in becoming successful, but what is missing is what I value the most, and it can never replace the importance of my being with my children. They are young and they need me, not five years from now when I've become a success!" I finally stopped talking.

It was obvious. I was torn between the world of being professionally successful and the world of being the type of mother I knew deep down I wanted to be.

It might have been a different story had the children lived with me in Boston, but that wasn't the case. I was, by our divorce agreement, a divorced parent, and one that had her children every other weekend and at the most, twice a week after school hours.

"How can I teach anyone else about what I know if I can't teach my own children?"

Billy looked at me with deep concern and said, "Then Shirl, go back to the Cape and be with your children." That was the end of our discussion.

It didn't take me long to place my furniture in storage and lease a furnished cottage fifteen minutes away from Jake and the children. Everyone was shocked at my decision, yet I knew in my heart that this was the right choice for my children and me. Jake and I agreed that the children could stay with me whenever they wanted. Melyssa had an opportunity to enroll in a Catholic school in Kingston, Massachusetts, just thirty miles off Cape Cod, so I was busier than ever, car pooling and participating in all the children's activities on a daily basis. And I was able to continue my workshops and consultation by traveling to Boston once a month.

Spring came and it was time to pay my taxes, and once again I was financially strapped. I had slowed my workload down to balance out my life with my children, so my funds had dwindled.

I then had the idea to sell my beautiful furniture in order to pay for my taxes. When I called to retrieve all of my belongings, I learned that my furniture had been sold.

"What do you mean you sold my furniture?" I asked. The receptionist at the storage company explained that because I was late in paying my bill, they had the option of auctioning off everything that I had stored. During this same time, my mail stopped arriving at the post office. Then when I called the IRS to find out the amount I owed on my taxes, they could not find my name or my Social Security number in their system. This once again seemed to be impossible challenges to overcome.

Then one day Melyssa and I were driving in the car when she asked me, "Mom, what's wrong?" There was no hiding what I was feeling. "I don't have the money to pay my taxes," I sadly told her. There was silence between us only for a moment before Melyssa responded, "Mom, you have money in an old bank account."

"What do you mean, Melyssa?" I asked.

"You have an account that has money in it."

She was right! I did have an old account that I hadn't touched since I returned to the Cape, but I knew there couldn't be more than $100 in it.

"Well, I do have an account that has about $100 in it," I said.

"No Mom, ask them at the bank to check to see if you have any other accounts opened in your name."

I began to respond in an anxious way when Melyssa interrupted me and said firmly yet lovingly, "Didn't you tell me to listen to the angels?"

"Yes," I replied.

"Well, they are telling me to tell you to ask them at the bank to check on an account that was opened in your name last summer."

I agreed to do this, and Melyssa and I drove to the bank.

The teller that assisted me was an older woman, and she told me this account had over $5,000 in it. "You must be mistaken," I replied.

"No, this is your account, Ms. Beauman."

Oh my God! Can this be true? I thought to myself. Just then a phone call came in for the teller, so a young gentleman came to my assistance next. I again spoke of the concern that this was a mistake and that this was not my money. This young man retreated into another room and about ten minutes later returned with a slip in his hands. He showed me a printout of the deposit made in June of the previous year.

Melyssa knew nothing about my being in financial straits, yet she was receptive enough when I told her about my financial dilemma that she was open to receive the divine guidance needed in this situation. That money gave me financial support for three more months, just enough time to hire an attorney to look into the sale of my furniture by the storage company and legally change the children's custody agreement.

Brian was a young attorney and was very intent in listening to my reasoning for having the children live with me; he also agreed to see if I had a case in recovering my sold articles from the storage company.

It only took a couple of weeks before I heard back from him. He had found a loophole in the agreement that the storage company had missed. By law, the company had to place a notice in the local papers that they were auctioning off my furniture. They neglected to do this.

And just as the IRS found my information in their system, I received a financial settlement from the storage company, just enough to pay my taxes and my legal fees to Brian.

All of these events led up to a better conclusion than what I could have ever expected. My mail being disrupted, my furniture being sold, and Melyssa's divine message allowed everything to fall into place.

* * *

How many times have you been in a position knowing you had done your best yet found yourself in circumstances that weren't as healthy and perfect as you had wished, then when looking back at it, you realized that the best outcome had happened after all? The universe responds to all of our heart's desires and needs, if only we are open to embrace the many different ways in which the answers come.

* * *

Mother's Day had arrived, and the children and I decided to travel to Worcester to visit my parents. Every time I would visit them, they would give me the unconditional love I desperately needed. The love from them kept me strong, and this would carry me through until the next time the children and I would visit them again.

My mother always made sure she had plenty of food to offer us. She would go out of her way to make Krysie her favorite blueberry pancakes in the morning and she would let the girls stay up a little later to watch their favorite television shows. Dad, still as quiet as usual, always took time to play with the kids and talk to them about the things they enjoyed.

I knew my parents were unhappy about my divorce, especially because being Catholic to them meant staying together through thick and thin and doing your best no matter what. I also knew that my father was very happy that I had moved back to the Cape to be closer to the children again, so when I shared with him that I was seeking full custody, he asked me a direct question.

"Shirley, why do you want to change where the children are settled?" The question was a good one, and I replied without hesitation.

"The children are always at my house, Dad. Every time they are sick they stay with me. When there is a problem that only a mother can answer, I end up driving over to Jake's to pick up the children, and keep them with me for a couple of days. I know this was a difficult decision, but Jake and I need to acknowledge that the children are growing up and becoming young ladies who need my guidance as their mother."

My father sat quietly and thought deeply about what I had said. "Your children are the only ones that are important here," he said. "Whatever will benefit their happiness and stability is what should happen."

My father was my guardian angel on earth to my morals and my personal values. He had lived by this foundation. Even though he had his own rough times throughout his life, he admitted openly about breaking the golden rule because of his own weaknesses.

My father also loved Jake very much, knowing him since he was twelve years old; he treated Jake like his own son. These types of bonds can never be broken; even though time and space may come between us ... the true nature of our hearts keeps the threads of love forever.

It was time to come home ...

* * *

I was about to take on the biggest challenge in my life, and I couldn't believe the resistance I received from Jake.

This man that I had known since childhood, who had been a supportive husband and friend, was now in a different place than I was. Making a change with the children was not a part of his plan.

We now had completely opposite opinions as to what was important for the children. This was the piece of my puzzle in life that didn't fit quite right. The mother that I wanted to be to my children was not the mother I had become.

It had not been fair for me to live so far away from the children, and every time Jake and I talked about the children living full time with me in Boston, the discussion had not been well received. I had agreed that the children should live in a healthy environment near the ocean, where they could be educated by its natural resources, and this was our plan right from the beginning when we moved to Cape Cod.

There was a provision in our divorce agreement that allowed the children to live with either parent. When we both realized that we could not come to an agreement, the only way to resolve this issue would be through the legal system.

It was a natural part of the process that when a child custody case was brought in front of the courts, Child Services would investigate the situation and make their recommendations.

This was a difficult time for all of us. The focus ended up being on whether or not I was a fit mother in the eyes of the court.

The investigator from Child Services (I will call him Mr. Atkins) met weekly with the children and me at the house that I had rented for the year. The interviews were long and draining.

Mr. Atkins who was always kind and pleasant to the children would meet with them for several minutes individually during his visit. Then it would be my turn. He then explained to me that he was going to ask me a battery of questions that might not make sense but reading in between the lines; I knew these questions were actually a psychological test. How I responded would make all the difference in the outcome in deciding whether I was fit to have full custody of my children.

During one visit, Mr. Atkins showed me the claims Jake was using to defend his reasoning why he should be the one to care for the children full time. There it was, right in front of me, in Jake's written statement! After reading it, I felt I was already defeated. Here I was a mother of three young children who wouldn't or couldn't stick to a normal job, who experienced paranormal situations, who traveled to the Philippines in the middle of a civil war, and who had an unusual ability to heal others. I truly believed I didn't have a chance.

I was concerned how the courts would look at this because Jake was; in fact, correct about all the facts he presented. I also knew that Jake, deep in his heart, was concerned for our children's well being. This is where he and I never parted ways.

This was not just about my being a fit mother. This case was about my having the right to believe in what I believe, to use my talents and gifts, even if others looked upon them as unorthodox. Every part of my life and what I did and had experienced was being questioned. And I was the one that created it all.

* * *

The interviews were finally over. It would take Child Services several weeks to complete their investigation for the courts. The waiting was horrific. This was now in God's hands.

I went back to one of the places on the Cape where I felt nourished the most. This was a spa in one of the nicest hotels in Hyannis, where Jake, the children, and I frequented during our marriage.

This is where I found the greatest reassurance in my self-esteem and strength … from the women that frequented the health spa. It was like a hidden perk that you didn't pay for in your membership fees. All you had to do was show up, be present, and be open to a learning circle filled with knowledge and wisdom for your taking.

* * *

The women at the spa were independent, strong, successful, and caring. Having a few life battles they had gone through themselves, they would gather together in the women's locker room and talk about many different aspects of life. So different were their personalities and their opinions, which came as a shock to my limited ideas and concepts on life issues. But I had to admit I loved the way they could stand their own ground in debates and discussions, completely disagree with each other, and still walk out of the spa, side by side, happy and energetic.

This is where I was reminded of the importance of independent thinking, how to respect the differences of others' opinions, and learn from them at the same time, just by being in and around the conversations of other women ... all here at a health spa on Old Cape Cod.

*   *   *

I was exhausted and depleted from my transition. Settling in again with the children's schedule and keeping my counseling sessions on track had taken a toll on me. When I first started to exercise again, no matter what I did, I couldn't get myself up to a healthy vigorous workout.

One day I was walking on the treadmill, and another woman stepped on the treadmill next to me. I hadn't noticed it at first, but as we were walking, we both began to walk at the same stride and pace.

I walked quietly she walked quietly until she looked at me and said something unfathomable: "My little girl died."

I was taken aback by her transparency. "I am very sorry," I said. I hesitated before asking this next question: "May I ask what she died from?"

"She was hit by a car while walking home from school," she responded. "The trauma was so severe ... Well, she died instantly."

She went on to explain that she was from Connecticut and also had a house, here on Cape Cod. She said she always felt good when she came to the Cape and decided to just get away by herself for a couple of days. It had been over a year since her child's death; the energy of the ocean always helped to calm her.

It felt like hours had passed in my mind before I knew what to say next. From working with others in traumatic situations, I knew to speak to her as if we were having a normal conversation but with great compassion.

It was difficult to speak to the fact of grief and loss, especially when it came from the loss of a child. Life sometimes isn't fair, and sometimes we can't understand the reason for a tragedy such as this.

Then I saw a small point of light around her head, and a thought came to me to ask this question: "Do you ever have dreams about your daughter?"

The woman looked at me, with a surprised look. "Why yes, yes I do," she replied.

"Are you in the dream with your daughter or are you just watching the dream?"

She paused and then responded, "I am in the dream with her."

"Do you sometimes think you are making this dream up and that it's only your imagination?" I asked.

"Yes, I do," she exclaimed. "That's why I never say anything to anyone about my dreams of her."

"What do you do in your dreams with your daughter?" I asked.

"We play and talk about things we've always enjoyed." A slight smile came over her face.

"And during that time, does your experience feel real?"

She looked over at me again. "Yes." she said with a smile on her face. "Yes, it does."

"Well," I said, "isn't it wonderful that God made a way for you and your daughter to be together, through your dreams even though she's in heaven and you are here?"

Not one more word was shared between us.

Instead of answering my question, she just gazed off at a distance just before focusing back on her walk on the treadmill. But this time I noticed we were walking a little differently: a slightly faster pace, a longer stride, yet still, the same as one another's.

We had left one another to be in our own private thoughts from our discussion, and then we went our separate ways.

I was in awe of God's presence! What a chance meeting. What a moving conversation. Here was a woman that had lost her daughter in a fatal accident ... Here I was, sad and depressed because I wasn't living in the same house as my children. Here her daughter was taken instantly from her. Here I was, with my daughters healthy and living on Cape Cod. "God, what's wrong with the way I'm thinking?"

I believe God had sent me this living angel to remind me how very fortunate I am in my life! And maybe on some level she had walked away with something special as well. I thanked God and realized during the next several days that my level of concern had been lifted and I was now feeling more optimistic. And best of all, I realized if the courts found the children to be happier living with Jake, then I would be there with them as well, just not in the way I had envisioned.

*   *   *

I was feeling healthier after my conversation with the woman on the treadmill and began to pick up my exercise pace because of it. Another woman at the health club, by the name of Ruth, who was in her mid-sixties was vigilant in going to the spa for her daily exercise routine. No one had seen Ruth for a couple of months so everyone assumed she was on vacation until Jen, who managed the spa for the hotel, told us that she had been very sick.

One day as I was running down the hall of the health spa to join others in an aerobic class, I spotted Ruth walking on a treadmill. Hurriedly, I stopped and poked my head around to the front of the treadmill, where she could see me, and in a kind gesture I placed my hand on her back and said, "Ruth, I am so glad to see you again, I've missed you." And off I went to the aerobics class.

I love aerobics! It always felt good to be using music and dance techniques to strengthen my body as well as my heart. We were past the warm-up phase and into a slight jog when Ruth entered the room. Now just to let you know, no one was allowed to enter a class while it already started, unless you quietly came in the back door and took your place in line so as not to disturb the others. But Ruth came in the front door. I was positioned in the middle of the front row. Ruth then came directly over to me, stood in front of me, and placed her hands together as if in prayer and bowed gracefully in front of me ... then walked out of the room! Now that was a surprise!

I didn't see Ruth for the rest of that week, but when I did finally see her, I asked her what she meant by her expression of gratitude.

"Shirley, you healed me," she remarked.

"What do you mean, Ruth?" I replied.

She then told me that she had been very ill for a couple of months. She explained how she became exhausted very easily and couldn't think clearly. She told me the morning that I saw her at the spa she had forced herself to go there only because she thought it might do her good to move her body and sit in the steam room for a while.

Then she said, "When you placed your hand on my back and told me you missed me, I could feel something lift from me, and instantly I had renewed energy! From that moment on, I've been well!"

Wow! I said to myself. *How could this be?* I had had no stamina for the past several weeks to do much of anything! Also it was only in a few cases that I had used the hands on healing technique for someone: actually since I had moved to Boston. So I started to review what had happened to me in the past couple of weeks when I remembered the conversation I had had with the woman on the treadmill.

I then realized that from our conversation, she helped me to reconnect to my heart. I had been closed off from this part of myself, and without my realizing it; she helped me open up to it once again.

Ruth owned a bookstore, and she invited me to her store, where she thought we could talk more in depth about what had happened. As I walked into her bookstore, beautiful music was playing and there was tea and small cookies on a small table next to two sitting chairs. I shared with her how peaceful her store's atmosphere was. She thanked me and said, "I want people to be able to come and feel that they can take their time to browse so they can find the books they are searching for."

We sat down, and she began to explain how she had studied the beliefs of many religions, including the esoteric aspects of them as well. Ruth herself was Jewish, yet she gravitated toward and practiced daily the disciplines of Buddhism.

"You have good karma," she stated.

"What do you mean?" I asked. At this stage of my spiritual growth, the word "karma" perplexed me. I had heard it used so many different ways at times, so I always made sure I asked whoever used it what they meant.

"In your situation it means the effect of your actions brings goodness to you and others," Ruth answered.

"Ruth, I was just happy to see you and I placed my hand on your back! That's all I did!"

Ruth went on to explain the belief in some Eastern spiritual philosophies that a person is gifted with spiritual abilities depending upon how they have lived their previous lives and how they live in their present life.

I knew from my research and experiences that there were many beliefs in consciousness, and I believed that every situation I had been in had a greater outcome because of the bond of love between the people involved.

So I smiled at her and said, "Even though I have read of some of these beliefs, I still believe that all religions were created from the same spiritual laws and foundational beliefs, the main law is to love one another and help one another. That is our natural divine state. Anything less than this is less than what we are meant to be."

Ruth agreed wholeheartedly, and she shared with me the similarities she had found while studying the main religions of the world. It wasn't until later when I came upon a book by Huston Smith called *The World's Religions* that I understood this concept more fully.

Chapter 15

The Eternal Gift

It had been a long six weeks while going through interviews with the investigator from Child Services. Right after the completion of the interviews I received a call from another movie producer, named Phillip, whom I had met while working with Zach on the writing of his screenplay. Philip had several guests coming into town who were interested in meeting with me. I decided this would be a good time to take a break from all of the pressure and fly out to California.

When I was preparing for my trip I, while driving to the Cape Cod Mall, saw at a distance in the sky, a figure of a young man in spirit, wearing military fatigues, with others standing long with him. As I focused on him intently, a thought came into my mind, "Don't forget us." Otis Air Force base was located nearby so it made sense that those whom have served may be here in spirit. Yet I still could not understand why they would choose to present themselves to me, so I let the vision and thought, go.

This trip was eventful and packed with meeting people, mostly from the entertainment industry. I was looking forward to meeting the film producer, whom I will call Mr. Meir, from Universal Studios. He was the producer who had hired Zach to write the screenplay. As I mentioned before, I had helped Zach by sharing my perceptions of heaven from the perspective of a healer. I had agreed to work with Zach on the screenplay in exchange for delivering a message to Suzanne Langley. Mr. Meir was very interested in spiritual consciousness and wanted to meet the woman who had the chutzpa to make such an unusual request.

Universal Studios is a large complex, and I was directed to a certain building where the meeting would take place. Mr. Meir was very successful in his profession and well respected by his peers. As I walked down the long hall to his office, I couldn't help but notice the pictures of famous movies and actors that lined the walls.

When I entered his office, a tall, handsome, grey haired man stood up from his desk and walked across the room toward me. As he extended his hand out to me he said, "It is nice to finally meet you, Shirley, I'm Mr. Meir."

"Thank you, Mr. Meir, for seeing me," I said.

"The pleasure is all mine." He commented.

He gestured for me to take a seat in front of his desk, and he took the chair beside me instead of sitting behind the desk. Our dialogue was light as we discussed spirituality. He expressed how important it was that the studio would bring to their audiences both entertainment and the reality and a truthful perspective of the subject matter they were filming.

In the case of the screenplay I had worked on with Zach, he wanted to create the perception of multi levels of consciousness and the different spheres of creation; the main character, after leaving the earth plane, visits all the spiritual planes yet moves on to the level that his beliefs resonated with at the end of his life. What he had learned and what he held as true in his soul was where he would once again live and learn in the realms of heaven, exploring the belief that life goes on and never ends.

* * *

During my stay in Hollywood, I met with several other professionals who worked directly with filmmakers. Elaine and Zach had set up all these meetings so I could get to know the culture of the film industry. I was amazed at how welcoming and caring these people were. They were producers, writers, stage developers, wives and girlfriends of actors, and well-known celebrities, some of whom became my clients.

One of these new clients was a well-known psychic to many of the people in the film industry. She told me she wanted to become a vegetarian, yet she was having a difficult time in doing so. She went on to explain her year-long attempt only left her feeling lethargic, and her weight had reached an unhealthy level. As I sat with her, I explained that her body was rebelling against the drastic change she had made to vegetarianism. I suggested that she should educate herself by going to someone who had more knowledge on this transition so she would cleanse and purify her body in a way that was safe. I then asked what her intention was for this change in diet. She said she had feelings of guilt toward sustaining herself from the animal kingdom.

"Pray over your food before you eat," I said. "Ask God to guide you and give blessings and thankfulness for any nourishment that you are about to consume. God no less blesses you because you eat meat. It is in the way we respect the gift of their energy that is important."

A few days later, I met with her again. She was elated at the change that had already occurred. She had more vitality, and she had lost several pounds of excess water weight after adding some animal protein back into her diet. We became instant friends. In return for my helping her, she invited me to a Sunday service at the Self Realization Fellowship Gardens of Paramahansa Yogananda in Hollywood.

I had never heard of Paramahansa Yogananda, yet I soon learned of his great devotion to God and mankind. His teachings speak of God, and fellowship with all mankind. And another admirable comment made by Dr. Wendell Thomas, "…he became Christian and American without ceasing to be Hindu and Indian." This resonated as a truth that I had found of the teachings of Christ, that the divine lives within all of us and that Christ consciousness dwells in all religious beliefs

The organization respected many spiritual teachers. The gardens that surrounded the temple were beautiful, and inside the meditation room were pictures of several beloved spiritual teachers, one of which was Jesus. Needless to say, I felt at peace in these surroundings.

A well-known actor, who was a twenty-year member of the Self Realization Fellowship, gave the sermon that afternoon. I was about to learn some of the most important wisdom of my life. Before the meditation, he began to describe the cosmic reality of consciousness. He explained it very much like I had heard through the teachings of Jesus.

"There are many mansions in God's kingdom," he said. But he also explained the importance of protecting yourself while meditating because of the many spiritual forces existing in and around our consciousness that can influence us in many ways, both positive and negative. He made sure everyone understood this and said that most people that have prayed and meditated for years understood that these forces do exist.

I knew what he meant. As I sat and listened to him, I thought about cases I had worked with pertaining to the paranormal aspect of spiritual awakening. These occurrences happen to those who are highly spiritually attuned as well as to those who had no understanding of anything beyond their five physical senses.

The reason why I chose not to recount these experiences in this book is because the solution in working with these experiences is to understand that what you give power to and what you focus on creates the outcome of any situation in your life. Because these are usually complex situations, getting expert advice is imperative.

As I have suggested before, if we are engaging in a continual behavior pattern that creates a severe imbalance in our physiology and psychology we are bombarding ourselves with negativity. This can create energetic openings that allow us to resonate with invisible forces of a lower nature than what we were intended to resonate with.

I watched a TV interview with a well-known producer. The producer, his crew, and actors were filming a movie about paranormal experiences. The reason why I bring this up is because this is a good example of how the world of invisible forces aligns with our thinking and feelings connected to similar natures that are within us. The producer, along with his crew and cast, had real time spiritual experiences, where these forces played havoc with them on the set, creating days of lost time and money; many of the main actors became physically ill while shooting this film. Because this movie was about the paranormal, the collective consciousness aligned with these natural forces. So if anyone is having a negative experience that they do not understand please get in touch with experts that can assist you.

* * *

After my trip to California, I realized the importance of feeling at home in my own skin. Here I was, trying to find a place where I would be accepted by others and with those who had the same perceptions and beliefs as mine in life. Mr. Meir had shared with me from his years of living that what is important about spirituality is how we emanate this in our everyday lives, and how we live our lives is the outward manifestation of what we have learned through our spiritual growth. This was a great piece of wisdom given by a great businessman.

* * *

While waiting for the decision from the courts, my mind often drifted to the one dream that still stayed with me about Max.

One day, when I was visiting my parents a family member showed me an article of a man whom was being rewarded for his long-time contributions to his community. The article was about Max. This was the beginning of my memory returning surrounding the events that triggered my fears and confusion as a teenager.

This is my story: It was the summer between my sophomore and junior year of high school. I was vacationing with my family at Hampton Beach in New Hampshire. It was a hot sunny day when I met Jamie. He was playing kickball on the beach with his buddies, and as I watched them play, Jamie looked up at me. While on their break, he came over and we started a conversation.

It wasn't long before we were talking on the phone daily and since we lived in different states we made plans for him to visit me in my hometown of Worcester. What fun we had together that weekend, walking in my favorite park, talking about travel, his future dreams and goals, my future dreams and goals and making up scenarios how it might just happen that we would someday be able to do this together. We had a good relationship and cared about each other deeply until one day my father came to me to let me know that I could not date him anymore. Jamie and I never gave importance to our age difference but my father did. Our relationship was over.

It wasn't long before my life began to change. So, there I was, 17 years of age, attending a great school with awesome friends, I had just landed my first part time job, and to beat it all, I met a great guy named Max. This was a time when friends were more vital to life, more so than family, and that the strength that became my backbone came mostly from the influences from my teachers and classmates. I was taught that challenges that came in life are opportunities to see what I had learned and if looked at properly, they would help me become the person I wanted to be. Life was great!

Several months, during this time, went by, when one afternoon, my mother handed me a letter postmarked from another country. It was from a guy whom I didn't know. The letter went something like this.

Dear Shirley,

You don't know me but I am a friend of Jamie's. Because of our situation we have become very close. He would talk about you and the wonderful weekend he had before we were shipped overseas.

I am sorry to have to tell you this, but Jamie was killed in action a month ago. I know he would have wanted you to know. He died instantly......

I don't quite remember how I felt. Shock is the only word that comes to mind, and it only took a few months before I became ill. Jamie was only 21 years old He had joined the army right after high school for educational purposes and service. Looking back and remembering the spiritual presence whom I feared for months in high school, could this have been Jamie?

Then there was Max. One day I saw the same spiritual presence hover over Max and that is when I decided I had to stop dating him out of fear that this presence may bring him harm. Because of these experiences, I hid my fears for years. And maybe if I had sought help back then, this book may never have been written.

I now had the strength to tell my story. So, I looked up Max's contact information and reached out to him in a letter explaining what had happened and if he would forgive me for hurting him so deeply. Of course, years later and happily married, he, not even giving what happened a thought, understood my intention and forgave me. As for Jamie, I chose to honor his memory by placing a tribute to him on the memorial site for veterans. This experience taught me never to allow my fears to overshadow me and to remember that love is what opens the doors to the knowledge and wisdom we need in all circumstances.

* * *

When I thought of Jamie and the thought that came to me, "Don't forget us," I instantly thought of other times when spirit presented themselves.

I was in a bank opening an account. The lady whom was assisting me was pleasant but very to herself. As I sat there a beam of light appeared on her left side and from this light came the image of a man wearing a police uniform. I knew he was going to ask me to help make a connection to her. Because I never liked doing this, I said telepathically, "Please don't ask me to do something for you."

Then telepathically I heard, "Please, just ask her about her jewelry."

This struck my heart. As she was processing my information I had a feeling to ask her if she had lost someone in her life recently.

"Yes!" she exclaimed. "My husband died several months ago."

"I am so sorry," I said. "I know you don't know me but there is a man in spirit who is wearing a policeman's uniform, whom is present with us. He wants me to ask you about your jewelry."

Taken back by what I said, she exclaimed," Oh! That's my husband. She went on to explain that her husband had died of an illness. With tears in her eyes she went on to say, "He always bought me jewelry. He never wanted me to tell anyone because he was afraid the guys at the precinct would tease him about picking out such beautiful pieces."

Then to my surprise she asked, "Could you please ask him if he can hear me when I am talking to him and what is the answer to my concerns?" I listened for a moment to the spirit, then responded, "You will be married again so do not worry, he is fine with this and you will be happy, once again. He is watching over you, the kids and helping guide other fellow policemen." I walked out of the bank, knowing that our loved ones are near and helping us in our lives even though we can't see them.

The most important personal experience I had, was when I had a very close call with death. I had a cracked tooth hidden under a crown, that went undetected by my dentist and became so infected they had to remove the tooth. As I sat in the oral surgeon's examining chair, a sharp meteor like light came into the room. There appeared in front of me, an older man in spirit. I wanted to stop and ask the others in the room if they could see him but something inside wouldn't let me do this. As this man from spirit came closer to me he said," You could die from this, you know." And with that, he quickly returned the same way he came. I was astounded at the way the light came through. So hurriedly as if there was no time to waste and the message was direct and alarming. But I soon forgot about it since the following day was my surgery.

The day after surgery, I awoke with a horrific pain in my mouth. While taking my pain medication, a beautiful young girl in spirit suddenly appeared to me. And she also didn't waste any time in giving me a message.

"You are going to go through a horrific time. You need to be strong. You will get through this but it will be difficult." Then she disappeared.

Several hours later I landed in the hospital. Allergy to the medication I had been prescribed they said. I should be fine. All went well for the next couple of days after this episode, until the fourth day.

It was around 10:00 p.m. I suddenly felt incredible nausea and began to vomit, profusely. I couldn't stop! This went on for an hour when I finally realized I felt I was being pulled by a force into a vacuum like energy within me. I called 911 and while being driven to the hospital the pull of the force became stronger. I could see a beautiful golden white light very far away from here and the pull to it was unmistakably powerful. I looked at the MT and told her that if I become unconscious, I won't be back. While in the cardiac unit at the hospital I had to fight all night long from this force taking me and then by morning my fluids and extremely low blood pressure came back to normal. The storm within me, was finally over.

During my last visit to the surgeon's office, while sitting in the waiting room, I started to notice the plaques thanking the doctor for his dedication in helping children in third world countries for his time and service. Then something unexpected happened to me. While I was in the examining room, the assistant left the room while the doctor finished writing his findings. Suddenly, a light so beautiful expanded above my head and I knew I had to say something.

Dr. Rosemont, may I share with you what happened to me while I was going through my recovery. "Yes." He said. I began to tell him of the young girl in spirit that warned me of what was going to happen to me and that she told me to be strong. He began to listen more intently. Then surprisingly I said, "This wasn't your fault." What? He asked. "This young girl, she died from a situation similar to mine. She says you were her surgeon."

The doctor gasped and said, "Oh my God! I know who you are talking about. Her name is Sarah." Sarah went on to tell me that he and others were left with guilt since she was under his care from what had taken her life. She wanted them to know it was not their fault. And then she left.

Healing comes in many ways and if we are open, the universe will respond to all of our heart's desires at the right time. Isn't it amazing what we hold within ourselves which hinders us from being happy. Forgiveness is vital in our lives, whether we need to forgive ourselves or forgive another. We may not forget what happened in our experiences, yet the conscious effort in forgiving allows the release any negative impact this may have on us and allow us to understand what we needed to learn.

I believe that we are all evolving in consciousness and that which used to be for the gifted and spiritually attuned is now happening to all of us. These stories I share tell a greater story of how the world of consciousness is within all of us.

* * *

The call finally came from Child Services. The judge wanted to interview the children and speak with Jake and me. The moment had come. I knew whatever the children said would greatly affect the outcome of the court's decision.

The judge chose to interview the children separately, behind closed doors. Even though I never asked, I knew that the children loved us both and that the intention of this was to ensure the children had rights to choose what they felt best for themselves.

I could feel myself letting go of the outcome. All the information that the judge needed was finally uncovered. It now was in the hands of the court, and the judge would be the one to make the final decision. When the decision arrived, there was no courtroom drama, no battling over power, just a visit from Mr. Atkins from Child Services at my home.

As he sat down at the kitchen table, he opened his briefcase and pulled out a document. My heart started to race. He then looked up at me and said, "Shirley, the courts have established you as competent to take care of your children; you will share custody rights with your ex-husband. It will be up to the children as to where they wish to live full time."

I didn't know what to say. I remember waiting for him to say that there would be certain stipulations, but that wasn't the case. It was agreed the children would live with me full time, and Jake would have visitation rights anytime he wanted. I remember feeling that the children would finally have the motherly guidance that they needed.

During the following year I leased a home only two miles from their school. The children seemed very happy there. Not much had changed for them, and Jake thought it best that their dog, Bruty, should live with us, and so he did.

For me, it was time to visit with a therapist who could help me focus on healing the pain I still carried from the choices I had made since my spiritual awakening. This time I would look for someone who was skilled in family therapy but who also had an understanding of spirituality. So I asked my friend Mary Anne if she knew of someone with these qualities. Mary Anne had been such a dear friend and colleague through all of my trials and experiences. She directed me to Corrine, a therapist who often came to her bookstore.

Corrine opened the door and invited me into her private office. With a smile on her face, she approached me and shook my hand. Her office walls were painted in a soft pastel green, and the natural light coming in through the large windows felt soothing to me. Several statues of angels were dispersed throughout the room.

"It's so nice to finally meet you," she said. I must have looked a little surprised to hear this. It wasn't in the words she said but in her tone that I felt something. I thought she already knew something about me.

"You look a little confused." She said.

"Yes," I replied.

"Well, you probably sensed that I already know some things about you."

"Yes, I did have a sense of that," I replied.

"I probably shouldn't have taken you on as a new client," she added, "but I thought it would do both of us good to meet one another."

Now, I was very confused.

"I'm sorry, Corrine, I don't understand," I said.

"I will explain," she replied.

Oh boy! Here it comes again! I thought. I took a deep breath, preparing myself for another situation where I would have to explain something or I would have to defend myself as to why I became a healer. *How much more of this can I take?* I thought to myself.

"Shirley, I was one of the psychotherapists on the investigating team for Child Services," she said.

I was shocked! I didn't know what to say!

She went on, "Under the law I can't tell you what we found in the investigation, but I can tell you what I walked away believing."

Oh my God! I thought. *This cannot be happening to me!* I wanted to run and never look back. But I just sat there as still as I could. No facial expression did I choose to give, no gestures, just me running around in my head again!

Corrine then went on.

"I believe that you are saner than what we understand sanity to be." Corrine paused, leaned slightly toward me, and said, "You have shown by your beliefs, prayers, and the way you care and love that healing the impossible, is possible, and that to me is saner than believing otherwise."

My eyes began to fill with tears.

Silence filled the room. Not just any silence, but a peaceful silence. Corrine and I talked a little more, and then I thanked her for her honesty and we said good-bye. I never saw her again, but I was thankful that she had the desire to meet and share with me what was going on behind the scene of my children's court case. In just one meeting and with this one comment, my fears were dissolved.

As I drove home, I thought of the people who had come into my life as if it were orchestrated by an invisible divine light. Every time I needed help, there would be someone or some being there to guide me on my way. I thought of the new awareness I had come to know and experience; it wasn't important if I ever saw a glimpse of energy because what I came to understand was that the gift of this all was in the way love was exchanged from one person to another in every situation.

Most important, what I found to be true is not that this energy of divine love is there for all of us but that we, along with those on spiritual planes, are the ones creating it. This is the eternal gift of life: that we are an important part of the creation. My beliefs, my choices, and my actions helped create what had happened during these phenomenal experiences. I believed in my christian faith and in Jesus, and even though I never saw or heard from him as I saw and heard from others during my spiritual awakening, I knew he was the force guiding me through it all. Christ's Conscience showed me that there are no barriers when it comes to love. What is known as Christ Consciousness lives within all of us, those of different faiths, those with no faith, through the love and the actions we take in our lives daily.

* * *

It was wonderful to be living with my children, having them and their friends running in and out of the house. It was great to catch up with the parents in the community, talk about natural foods and to attend all of my children's sports games. It was all so wonderful!

One day the girls and I decided to go to the ocean and sit on the beach where our neighbors would often congregate. As the girls played with their friends, I sat with one of the mothers, who had greeted me warmly. She and I had a discussion about the work I was doing and how great she thought it must feel to help others in that way. She was very open to discussing the power of thought, and as we were talking, her son Timmy came up to our blanket.

As she straightened out her son's sweatshirt, she looked at me and asked, "Shirley, do you know anything about children who have invisible friends?"

I smiled slightly and answered, "Yes, I do."

"Well," she exclaimed, "Timmy has been driving me crazy with a notion that he has an invisible friend …"

I finished her thought: "... who plays a flute and couldn't come with him to the beach today."

It was obvious from the look on her face that she was shocked. Then she looked at her son and asked, "Timmy is your spiritual friend with you today?"

"No, Mom," Timmy replied. "He couldn't come today." As Timmy's glance shifted from his mother to me, I lovingly smiled at him. He then turned and ran back toward his friends.

It seemed like forever before she asked me another question: "How did you know he played a flute?" We both laughed and then gazed out at the ocean near where the children were playing.

I remember saying a special prayer while we sat there watching our children play in the waves of the ocean.

Thank you, God. This is finally over.

And then I heard a voice reply:
"No Shirley, this is just the beginning!"

The Beginning

Remember, we are living in a time of dynamic change. That, which we thought as impossible, is in fact, possible. No matter what you choose in seeking how to make your dreams a reality, the world is filled with many different paths to get you there. May your journey that takes you inside your heaven's door be as wondrous and fulfilling as mine has been for me.

Shirley St. Michael

Personal, Group, and Book Club Transformational Guide for Inside Heaven's Door

If you are interested in taking the next step toward your own transformation, please visit my website www.shirleystmichael.com. Click on Inside Heaven's Door and go to Personal, Group, and Book Club Transformational Guide for discussions and self-discovery.

Acknowledgements

This book would never have been written if not for the richness of talent and diversity from the people who came into my life during the five years of my writing this story. Being a self-published author I had the opportunity to choose what company I wanted to work with. Because of the pristine reputation of Louise Hay and her incredible talented authors from Hay House, I decided to hire Miss Louise's self-publishing company, Balboa. I wanted to create the best book I could possibly write and Balboa didn't waste any time putting me to task.

My sincerest gratitude goes to my two check-in coordinators from Balboa, Madison Lux and Heather Perry. Madison, thank you for your unquestionable knowledge and guidance that directed me during the initial stages of development, ensuring that I would give my very best to this project. Since my book was my own personal story, you also encouraged me to send excerpts to each person it pertained to, to validate the storyline for its authenticity in striving to keep the integrity of truth throughout the book. This task alone showed me Balboa's level of professional integrity and their focus on creating a high quality product.

I also want to thank Heather Perry. Not only do you have an exceptional ability in keeping me focused and steadfast to details but you came to my rescue so many times in understanding the process of book publishing and what steps needed to happen along with the why's and when's. You also took the time to listen to why I chose certain artistic direction and you even made yourself available to speak with others, whom were on my team, but were outside of the Balboa organization. Your high level of leadership and your ability to embrace and incorporate others into the process was beyond my expectations.

And for those whom I have worked more closely with are Sam Clarke, from publishing services, Scott Crenshaw, Anne Summers, Ashley Sutton, Brad Wilhelm and James Aguilar from Marketing services and the very last to Joy Colton and her team from Post publishing services. You all have shown me the dedication you have to making this book the best it can be and how working with you has proven, beyond a shadow of a doubt, that it takes heart centered and highly skilled professionals like yourself to create such good works. Thank you!

Being a novice writer trying to bring a story to life, I came across many unexpected challenges. My first great challenge was when my computer, in the middle of the night, decided to spark like the 4th of July, burning up the hard drive in a matter of minutes. Like I said, being a novice at writing I had no backups to any of my work so one hundred and forty two pages of my manuscript were gone . . . until I met James, a computer specialist who works for the Apple Store in Columbia, Maryland. James, you worked feverishly for two days on my burnt-out computer and miraculously was able to retrieve the one and only document that could be recovered, the manuscript for Inside Heaven's Door. Amazing! Thank you James, you and the rest of the Apple crew embraced my funky computer quirks and rescued me more than I dare to remember.

Others who helped make this book the best it could possibly be are my two dearest colleagues, Dushyant Viswanathan M.D. (Dr. D.V.), Paula Oliver and my great friend Karen Murphy.

Dr. DV, between our busy schedule of running a integrative health center and making sure the patients were given the very best possible care, you made it your job to read and reread my book, sharing the philosophy of integrative medicine and how the concepts of energy and spirituality, found in my book, fit clearly with integrative health and a self care model for patients. Thank you for your time and the encouragement you gave me to present my work to the medical field at large.

Paula, you are by far one of the best professionals I have ever worked with. You took the time, outside of our work at the center to read, and help revise specific aspects of information. Your clarity and ability to take on the role of the interested reader who was new to spiritual and healing modalities, gave me great insight. Paula, you are invaluable.

And Karen, what can I say! Your clear and focused ability to find the mistakes in my manuscript and then re-work them into a greater flow was extraordinary. Thank you my dear friend. I have never met such a loving, caring and selfless woman. The time and focus you give to so many is amazing. Giving without asking for anything in return, for you have found the true expression of love.

As had happened so many times throughout my story, I, while writing, would get stuck on something specific with no clear-cut solutions at hand. During these times, I would pray for help and low and behold at some point, something magical would occur. My deepest appreciation goes to Spirit for the direction as to what to do next, such as guiding me to go to Google, to type in book designer, and drawing my attention to George Foster.

George, I am so happy that Spirit brought me to you! Not only did you create the perfect book cover, emanating the beauty of the story, but you also mentored me through the challenges of a culture that in the beginning was so foreign to me. The beauty and divine energy you brought to this experience gave me hope and peace during times when I could not find my own.

To the heroes and heroines of Inside Heaven's Door, Jake, Bill & Rita, Pat McKenna, Reverend Irene Harding, Cyndy Niblett, Joanie Wisher, Anne Burns, Mary Anne Lucas, Elaine, Doug Gorman, Carol Mann, Dottie & Stephen, David, Michael, Ruth, Karen Mileson, and those that gave me permission to share their stories even though they chose to stay anonymous. If it weren't for you, there would be no Inside Heaven's Door. I learned the true meaning of believing in something greater, determination to find a solution, endurance, fortitude, belief and the ability to give freely in service to others. Thank you from the deepest part of my heart for allowing me to share your stories and to have been a part of your amazing journeys.

And lastly, to my three beautiful daughters, Melyssa, Krystine and Laurie; with deep gratitude and love.

Melyssa, since you were a child you have exemplified the wisdom and patience of a Zen Master and a peaceful warrior. Your ability to embrace others as they are and your love that draws animals and children to you wherever you go has always amazed me. Truly, you have taught me well to remember to seek the quiet wisdom and peace within. May I be able to master this as you have. Thank you for all that you are and the love you have given me.

Krysie, you are the personification of love and stability. I know no other person whom can love, appreciate and support family and friends the way you do. Your clarity and ability to draw out the goodness in people and to allow the rest to fade away from importance, is the precious gift you have taught me. The joy, laughter and exuberance of your being is felt and appreciated by everyone who meets you. Thank you Krysie. I am so blessed to have you as my daughter.

Laurie, you have the incredible gifted talent of always being the one who challenges me to embrace those situations in life that I am the most uncomfortable with so I may have the opportunity to know their true beauty. You embrace the exotic, to the eclectic as well as the mundane, always able to find true beauty and love in everything. Thank you Laurie for showing me your way of being in life. You are so beautiful!

And for those that have been a part of my life both professionally and personally, thank you for all that you shared with me and for the great teachings in love that were free for the taking by just showing up in your life.

For more information and to access the book club questions for Inside Heaven's Door please visit www.shirleystmichael.com

Legal Documentation of Healings Cited in Inside Heaven's Door

DEATHS in

No.	When Registered.	Name and Surname.	Sex and Condition.	AGE. Yrs.	Mos.	Dys.	Occupation.	Date of Death.
1	January 1864	Sayra J. Chipman	Female	3	10			January 4 1864
2		Susan Mayew	Widow	75	6			5
3		Henry Wright		97				6
4		Lewis Lewis Jr.	Mar Male	63			M. G. Ret Maror	6
5		Mary A. Keen	Female		2			9
6		Gideon Ellsworth			1			9
7		Orrin E. Fuller	Male Maror	30			Ship builder	13
8		Elizabeth J. Morgan	Married Single	21	9			14
9		John H. Crocker	Male					16
10		Deborah Roy	Unmk Mar	31				16
11		Celista M. Burt			3			17
12		William Snow	Mar Single				Laborer	26
13		Sylvia E. Rice	Unmk Mar	57				30
14		Thomas S. Tobey	Male	61			Farmer	Feb 4 1864
15		Collis Crowel	Widower	73				11
16		Henry H. Loveitt			4	5			17
17		Effie L. Harris	Female	2	3			18
18		Margaret Hatton		2	6			
19		Ellen C. Loke		4	6			March 6 1864
20		Eledia Ryfs	Male Married	18				6
21		Levinston Tobb	Unmk Mar	79	11	5		12
22		Colen Smith	Widower	75	6			13
23		Hezekiah Lombard	Male	65				20
24		Deborah Nottingham	Unmk Mar	71	11	3		27
25		James McKnight	Male	1	5			31
26		Mary A. Badger	Female	46				April 2
27		Lewis H. Berry	Male Mar	84			Mariner	18
28		Orlando H. Wright		4	2			20
29		Edward Burns		81			Farmer	23
30		Amelia Atkins	Female	6	3			24
31		Lewis H. Crocs	Male Mar	83			Farmer	27
32		Ann Crowley	Female Mar	83	9			30
33		Sarah Nisl			11			May 5
34		Susan F. Atkins		1	7			5
35		James W. Hinds	Male Wido	71	18		Laborer	18
36		Eugene Hasta		12				22
37		Mary B. Barklett	Female mar	36				25
38		Mehetable Nye	Widow	87				25

236

Registrar.

Place of Interment.	Disease or Cause of Death.	Place of Birth.	Name and Surname of Parents. If a married Female, the name of Husband.	Informant.
Sandwich	Teething / Unknown	Sandwich		
	Old age / Consumption			
	Consumption			
	Consumption	Boston / Plymouth		
	Typhoid Fever	Sandwich / Barnstable		
	Small Pox / Small Pox	Sandwich / Barnstable		
	Childbed / Softening of Brain	Falmouth / Sandwich		
	Insanity / Small Pox			
	Inflammation of Bowels / Teething	Sandwich		
	Inflammation of Bowels / Consumption	Sandwich		
	Old age / Consumption			
	Old age / Cancer	Barnstable / Sandwich		
	Dropsy of Brain / Lumbar Abscess	Boston		
At Sea / Sandwich	Drowned / Scarlet Fever	Sandwich		
	Scarlet Fever	London / Sandwich		
	Old age / Inflammation of Uterus	Ireland		
	Scarlet Fever	Barnstable / Falmouth		
	Scarlet Fever / Consumption	Ireland / Sandwich		
	Consumption / Old age	Ireland / Barnstable		

March 29, 1988

To Whom It May Concern:

This letter documents the healing work that I have experienced with
Shirley St. Michael. - Back in 1981, I suffered a compound fracture of
my left wrist which resulted from a roller skating accident. I received
immediate treatment at Beth Israel Hospital in Boston, Massachusetts
and then went through extensive physical therapy at Waltham Hospital,
in Waltham, Massachusetts. At the end of the physical therapy sessions
I still could not turn my hand over. I went to a surgeon at Massachusetts
General Hospital to see if he could help me get the mobility back in my
wrist. I was told that the joint in my wrist would have to be removed.
I then started having healing sessions with Shirley St. Michael to work
on removing the blockage. At the end of the sessions I was able to turn
my wrist at least 60% further than before the sessions. -

Another instance when Shirley helped me greatly was in 1983. I went to
work one morning and within a half hour of arriving at my office I had
developed a severe pain on the left side of my lower back. It was so bad
that I had to lie on the floor of my office to get some relief. I decided that
I needed to get myself to a doctor so I drove to my doctor in Waltham. He
was not sure what the problem was. He thought it might have been some
type of urinary infection. He sent me over to the hospital for tests and gave
a prescription to start taking. While driving home the pain got so bad
that I was having problems changing my foot from the gas to the brake.
By the time that I got into my home I was rolling on the floor with pain.
Shirley psychically tuned in to the fact that I was in serious pain. She called
me and began sending healing energy my way. Within ten minutes the pain was gone
and I had passed a kidney stone.

Please feel free to contact me directly if you need any further information.

Sincerely,

Rita M.

6

Middlesex City
Appeared before me Rita M. _____ - March 29th 1988.
Roberta, Caricatore Aug 1, 1991

July 15, 1984

To Whom it May Concern:

In late 1974, I was diagnosed as having progressive systemic scleroderma, and Raynauds Syndrome. I feel I handled my dis-ease well over the years and though I had many bad times, tried always to have a positive attitude. Last May through November was a very difficult time for me. In addition to ulcers on my fingertips, which I generally had 1-3 at a time, I developed ulcers on both elbows and had to have a blister removed on one finger tip. I became very depressed, with crying spells and wishing I was dead. I had lost all energy and my hands were gradually becoming crippled. I knew at this point I had to do something and my only hope was through diet. I contacted Shirley ████████ last November and saw her several times for nutrition counseling. I improved my diet-mostly raw foods, but still a small amount of fish, chicken, dairy and whole grain products. I invested in a juicer and started monthly colonics. Immediately I had more energy and the swelling I had in my foot disappeared.

In early April, Shirley contacted me to see how I was doing and to ask me if I would be interested in coming to her for spiritual healing. I went to see her once then and started regularly seeing her Thursday April 26, 1984. What I remember about this first channeling session was that I became warm very quickly, but this was not new to me as I had previously warmed up quickly and stayed warm during nutrition counseling when the temperature of her house was about 65 degrees. This is extremely unusual for me as I need a temperature of 75 degrees to be completely comfortable due to the Raynauds Syndrome.

Since Seeing Shirley for Spiritual healing, I have had the following improvements:

(1) On 4/29/84 blood veins/arteries became noticeable through the the skin on back of hands. Skin was also a little softer in that area. Circulation and color of hands much better especially during channeling. Able to make a fist better with right hand, but left pointing and middle fingers have stiffened up.

(2) 4/30/84 outline of bones appearing on back of hands. Skin wrinkling and becoming pliable. Neck range of motion improved, able to bend knees better.

(3) 5/1/84 Discovered scar tissue on sides from shoulder/armpit area was gone. The "cord" I could feel was no longer there and the skin was a normal color as it had been darker in that area. Able to raise my arms higher though still tightness in that area.

(4) 5/2/84 Swollen, darkened area on back on hands close to and through wrist area smaller.

(5) 5/3/84 Face rash improving. Shirley convinced me to stop taking E-Mycin the first time I saw her for channeling. I had only been taking the drug a few days. At this date the condition (which is a type of acne due to hormonal changes in the menstral cycle) is completely cleared except for a slight break out right before I started my period but this clears right up. This condition I have had on and off since the early 70's and has only cleared up when I took telracycline or E-Mycin.

(6) 5/4/84 Skin on forearms very pliable and soft. Especially noted wrist area palm side on left arm.

(7) 5/8/84 Face looks fuller. Skin between pointing finger and thumb softening and also at bend of elbow.

Other improvements which don't have a specific date include:

(8) Elbows have completely healed except for a small scab on the right one. The skin in that area is more pliable.

(9) No more indigestion or reflux. Able to sleep with only one pillow although, if I eat late, I will use two pillows.

(10) Extreme cramping and discomfort with monthly periods which necessitated the use of Motrin - probably 10 pills over 2-3 days has gone to the point of slight discomfort for ½ day and 1 motrin tablet at this date.

During channeling I always experience tingling in my hands, feet and face. (especially lips) due to the flow of energy. I also have experienced intense tingling sensation in the spine, stomach, intestines and rib areas and have had pressure in my ears and rapid heart beat. Around mid May, I got to the point where my entire body has the tingling sensation during healing and I feel warm all over. This is due to all blocks being opened up and the energy is able to flow throughout my body.

One such block was was a torn Ligament in my right knee. I had pulled this last fall while exercising. I never told Shirley about this but she picked up on it psychically. She has worked on this area greatly and though it is healing, I still experience pain in this area if I sit for a long time or if the weather is cold and damp. This tear limited some exercises I used to do, but I am gradually starting to improve in that area.

During the period of healing since April, I have experienced many discomforts which come and go due to the release of toxins. These include: (1) back pain and itchyness on back bone especially near base. (2) sweatiness. (3) general achyness and tiredness. (4) pain on wrist and hip joints. (5) dull ache in lungs during deep breathing. (6) Ulcer on my right pointing finger became more painful but has finally subsided and is healing. On my left pointing finger flairup under cuticle which had become very thick and en-larged due to an occulsion of blood vessel in Mar 1982. This flairup took a few weeks to heal and the new cuticle is much more normal.

(7) April 30, 1984, I developed a large lump on my left wrist, palm side. This was painful at first but at this date is very small with no discomfort. Whenever Shirley channeled healing energy to this lump it would diminish in size, but would gradually enlarge again due to the fact that it is a drain for toxins. (8) In late June, I had swollen glands for 4-5 days then a week of runny nose and mucous in the throat. I still have a little mucous. (9) Skin is darker, especially hand area. (10) weight loss - 10-15 pounds.

I think it would be of interest to note what I am doing for myself with Shirley's guidance in addition to the spiritual healing.

DIET-Juicing 3 times a day, watermelon in the morning, green drinks at noon and supper. -Intake of fluids to total 8 8oz. glasses. To include juices, distilled water, and distilled water w/ lemon first thing in morning and last in evening, one glass rejuvelac. -No dairy products, cooked grain or fish and chicken. Only raw fruits and vegetables, nuts and seeds. Lightly steamed or baked vegetables would be allowed. -Salad dressing made with olive oil and apple cider vinegar with herbs. -Nuts soaked or ground up or chewed thoroughly. Better still made into fermented dishes. -Kelp tablets, 4 each meal. -Protein at each meal. -Combine food properly. -Rejuvelac each day. -No fasting. -If I crave something, have it; Don't make myself misurable. Do this within limits though.

MISC-Use only coconut oil on skin. -Natural products such as tooth paste, deoderant. -soak in epsom salt bath. -Dry brushing morning and night. -deep breathing exercises. -monthly colonics. -weekly enemas, 3 consecutive. -rest. -Exercise at least every other day. -Change to brighter colors, especially yellow and green. -if angry or upset, don't just storm around sit down and think out what is creating the problem, try to talk it over if someone is involved. -Very important, try to be happy. Think positive thoughts, look in the mirror and tell myself I am important. Also say "I am well" every day at least 10 times.

I saw my doctor at Mass. Gen. Hosp., Dwight Robinson on June 14, 1984 and he was very impressed with my improvements. He listed as I explained what I have been doing and told me he wanted to follow my case closely. He did state that my fingertips have shortened due to the bone tips being dissolved into the blood stream and that this condition could not be reversed.

On June 17, 1984, I experienced my own healing energy-tingling in my hands, feet and face. I should be able to do this if I can get myself in a quiet and relaxed state and think positive thoughts. I have been able to do this a few times since then.

Lastly Shirley has told me that in order for the healing energy to flow better I must deal with some emotional blocks due to low self esteem. I must see that I am important. I must do what I feel is the right thing to do, not what I feel others will expect me to do. She is helping me to cope with a stressful job and mood changes which I have difficulty controling. She has gotten me to think about what I want to do in the future and I am started in that direction with hopes to enroll in a nursing program fall of 1985.

I feel 100 percent improved since last fall and have God, Shirley and myself to thank for this. Shirley is a wonderful, dedicated, self-sacrificing and courageous women and I feel so fortunate to have met her.

Cynthia Niblett

Sincerdy,
Cynthia Niblett

Karen Yenckel Mileson
P.O. Box 6997
Snowmass Village, CO. 81615
Telephone 970-923-0696

The first mention of Shirley was when my dentist (Dr. B.) was in the process of pulling my tooth. I did not know if he was trying to distract me or if I was really supposed to be paying attention. He had mentioned me to her and thought because of our similar interests, we may want to meet. As soon as the tooth was out, I totally forgot about Shirley.

In mid-August 1997, the week after having five more teeth pulled, I called Dr. B's office. The woman who answered immediately said, "There is someone here Dr. B. wants you to talk to." It was Shirley. She had stopped by the office (without an appointment) and just happened to be there when I called.

I had felt perfectly healthy until mid-December 1996. I had had an eye exam the week before and my optometrist had wondered what was going on because my eyesight had worsened so drastically. I was not aware of any changes.

During mid-December I woke up one morning with my lower lip twitching. During the next week it moved to other parts of my face and extremities. Since my husband's seizures from brain tumors had begun in a similar manner, I soon called a neurologist and asked for a CAT scan of the brain. It was negative. I soon had an EEG (to rule out seizures) and it was also negative. I also had an MRI of the brain (to rule out MS and tumors the CAT scan could have missed). This was followed by a chest x-ray, bone scan, blood work-up, neurological exams, osteopathic exams, chiropractic exams - all of which were negative.

That was great, except my symptoms were getting worse. At this point some of the twitching was more like jerking in the face and extremities with muscle weakness, chilliness, tightness in the throat, and extreme fatigue. The neurologist could only recommend muscle relaxers or anti-convulsive medications, none of which I would take. I wanted the cause and cure, not suppression.

At that point I thought it would be best to try some alternative therapies in addition to what I was trying for myself. I was aware of problems in my jaw and was referred to a new dintist who could treat these (Dr. B.).

I saw Dr. B. on a very regular basis throughout the year. The facial twitching and dental related symptoms improved greatly, but not much else.

In the Spring I began ultraviolet treatment of the blood. I improved from the first treatment and was almost normal after two months of treatment. Unfortunately, after two more months of treatment, most of my symptoms had returned.

I had also had some acupuncture, electro-acupuncture, herbal, nutritional, and homeopathic treatments, a hair analysis (confirmed copper still very high). None of these provided any lasting relief.

It was at this point on August 18, 1997, that I was introduced to Shirley. We scheduled a telephone appointment for that evening. Her trip out of town had just been cancelled, which gave her time to see me several times that first week.

Between my first conversation and the appointment that evening, my deceased husband contacted her in her car. There were many personal things that he told me through her - that it was his time to die, and answers to other questions I had had about his death - things that nobody else would know.

Shirley explained how I had received some of my strength from him and how this loss could be responsible on an energetic level for triggering my illness. She also relayed information about a new technology my husband was currently working on that would be filtered down to me to make useable on this plane.

She explained about a blockage in one of my chakras, what it represented, and how to work with the chakra system in order to balance it.

Two days later on Wednesday, we met at our dentist's office. My godson, who had been staying with me during part of that year, was also with me. He had also developed some twitching symptoms which made me wonder if there was something else in the house that was causing or aggravating my problems. I had previously corrected a radon problem, added an ultra-violet water system, and made changes to the lightning protection system (LPS) on the roof of the house. She decided that she had to be in the house herself (a 1-1/2 hour drive each way for her).

Shirley visited the house on Friday (thank God her business trip had been cancelled). She felt a problem from the house before she was even in the door. She toured the house and pointed out which areas were the worst. She looked at the LPS on the roof. My godson and I left the house while she worked on it energetically.

Shirley was out again the next day - Saturday. We both knew there was still a problem in the house. Cutting out a portion of the LPS cable was not enough. I decided I wanted the whole thing out and she agreed, so we spent the next 1-1/2 hours on the roof removing the LPS.

My husband was applauding. Installation of that system had been his idea. He kept referring to a cable by the closet that needed to be cut. We did not find that for a few more days. This cable was just outside my bedroom. Shirley stated that this cable was allowing the energy from a vortex underneath the house to travel up into the house. The energy in the house was much better. Even I could feel a difference.

During the following weeks, I talked to Shirley at least once a day. She would give me insight into what was happening and teach me her method of correcting the problem. She taught me how to detoxify and strengthen my teeth and jaw area. I was also trying to use my method of testing to confirm her methods.

She allowed me to test her using my methods. Energetically, she tested better than anyone I had ever tested. This convinced me that I needed to incorporate her techniques into my program.

At this point I felt like I was making progress (I had not had any more teeth pulled), but there were still problems. On one of her visits she was aware of another problem with the house - geopathic grid lines. I had tested for this myself but thought it was from the LPS - it was two different problems.

I had been planning to move out of the area anyway and Shirley suggested I move as soon as possible. I was out in less than a month and living in my vacation condominium where I had always felt healthier than in my house.

Within two months of moving out of the house I joined a health club and started rebuilding my weakened muscles. A week later I started skiing - one of my major goals and passions. It had been two years since I had skied and it felt like it had only been two weeks.

In July 1998, I did have one more tooth extracted which might have been saved if I had been near my regular dentist (Dr. B.). In September 1998, Dr. B. examined and tested my teeth and jaw areas and found them to be healthy.

After the skiing ended, I started playing tennis, golf, roller blading, hiking and kayaking.

I am continuing to rebuild my body but am now convinced that it is only a matter of time until I am stronger than ever mentally, emotionally, and physically. I know that Shirley's help has been instrumental to this improvement.

When I began to think about how Shirley has changed my life, I was in tears - tears of gratitude. It brought back the memories of the trauma I had been in and has reminded me of how far I have come in the past year. She has given me insights and understanding into my life.

Shirley has taught me many things during our almost daily phone conversations over the past 1-1/2 years. She has taught me about our energy system and how to use it to transmute toxins from my body without the use of supplements or remedies. She has taught me: how to bring in the necessary energies for my well being - how I had lost my power and how to get it back - how to keep moving forward and not get stuck in the past - how to get in touch with my feelings. She has kept me focused on what I need to be working on.

I am now capable of doing things myself that I never even thought possible. I have a much broader understanding of my own work and insights into new areas of my research.

Shirley has done some healing on my body both in person and long distance. She has been able to release some of my toxins through this healing. My testing on myself has confirmed this. From our many phone conversations I have also received her support, encouragement, love, knowledge, and insight. I have learned to trust her truth, ethics, and morality totally. Most importantly, I have a new friend.

Karen Yenckel Mileson   1/25/99

Karen Yenckel Mileson   Date

Karen Y. Mileson personally appeared before me at the time of notarization and acknowledged signing the foregoing document.

[signature]

Notary Public

State of Colorado, County of Pitkin

My Commission Expires 09/22/2001

Commission Number and Commission Expiration Date_____

SEAL

TERROR TAMED

• • •

SPIRITUALITY AND SERENITY GAINED

The Everlasting Adventure
of Birth, Life, Death,
Rebirth and Eternal Growth

Norman Edgmon

BALBOA.
PRESS

A DIVISION OF HAY HOUSE

Balboa Press books may be ordered through booksellers or by contacting:

Balboa Press
A Division of Hay House
1663 Liberty Drive
Bloomington, IN 47403
www.balboapress.com
1 (877) 407-4847

Because of the dynamic nature of the Internet, any web addresses or links contained in this book may have changed since publication and may no longer be valid. The views expressed in this work are solely those of the author and do not necessarily reflect the views of the publisher, and the publisher hereby disclaims any responsibility for them.

The author of this book does not dispense medical advice or prescribe the use of any technique as a form of treatment for physical, emotional, or medical problems without the advice of a physician, either directly or indirectly. The intent of the author is only to offer information of a general nature to help you in your quest for emotional and spiritual well-being. In the event you use any of the information in this book for yourself, which is your constitutional right, the author and the publisher assume no responsibility for your actions.

Any people depicted in stock imagery provided by Thinkstock are models, and such images are being used for illustrative purposes only. Certain stock imagery © Thinkstock.

Print information available on the last page.

ISBN: 978-1-5043-8969-3 (sc)
ISBN: 978-1-5043-8970-9 (e)

Balboa Press rev. date: 02/12/2018

Spiritual and Ethical Guidelines....

and Mission Statements

For Public and Private School Teachers

and Students throughout the World

Introduction to the book

Norman Edgmon

We are now living in what many call an "Age of Terror". Even so, each of us can choose for our short, fragile, mysterious and magical existence to be an intriguing adventure of love, service, wonder and discovery or an anxiety filled nightmare of perpetual retreat. This book is about having the blatant audacity to consciously choose to face the reality of our own mortality as well as the specific fears, demons, and worries most mortals tend to deny rather than proactively confront, defeat, conquer and lay peacefully to rest. Those who are bold enough to allow it into their consciousnesses observe that whether in war or peace, every single day is literally a heroic, majestic, near physical death span of existence with not a single tomorrow promised, while the life of the soul is eternal.

Once this is truly understood and completely accepted, we cease attempting to cling to the elusive safety of mediocrity. We dare to plunge into the foreboding, abysmal pit of the dark sides of our psyches to challenge any savage demons we encounter there. We find that their exaggerated and misperceived strengths are abruptly unmasked and their weaknesses swiftly exposed. We learn that whether we win or whether we lose any of life's many, inevitable challenges or battles with circumstances with others or with ourselves, that our willingness to participate, struggle and evolve, makes us stronger than we could have ever before imagined, even in our grandest dreams.

We are able to climb the highest of mountains. Then with wildly beating hearts and throats seared dry with scorching horror, we leap from the summit to create our own wings and fulfill our own dreams. We discover that with power and love, we can confront any evil or tyrant, abroad or at home, bear any burden or sorrow, "Tame Any Terror", and even boldly embrace visions Of that final transitional spiritual journey when we are destined to fly from the darkness into the light, soar above the earth like eagles on wings of unlimited possibilities, and finally joyfully and adventurously roam the heavens with angels.

I believe this book will inspire and comfort many readers at this time of widespread anxiety. It's about having the courage to face the fierce reality of our own mortality and yet overcoming all challenges by calling on the vast reservoirs of our spiritual powers. It emphasizes the values of maturity and enlightenment and the importance of having appreciation and total respect for all religions, creeds and life styles on Planet Earth.

Part One: Spiritual Guidelines
and Lessons

To start this Spiritual Guideline or Journey

I would like to take you in your imaginations

to a time and place to where and when

you have probably never before

had any reason to go or to visit

or to even contemplate

That almost inconceivable time

is before the dawning of creation

in the infinite unfathomable immeasurable past

prior to the actual birth of the universe

and before the beginning of time itself

That almost unimaginable place

or condition of reality

has been creatively envisioned and hypothesized

by some of our most brilliant scientific genesis

with conflicting theories that greatly vary

Many of those scientists perceive

that the preconditions

before the birth of the Universe

were that of an incredibly concentrated

and tiny state of being

encompassed in a mass

smaller than the size of the head of a pin

existing in a form or subatomic particle

containing all the mass of the universe

Others surmise the conditions as being that

of a terribly hot.....heavy.....volatile

dense soup of energy

with an atmosphere and an environment

beyond our wildest imaginings

Still others even outrageously wonder

if our Universe might have been

an off-spring of another older Universe

and that each Universe

has continuously spawned off similar off-springs

which not unreasonably suggests

that God and other Universes have forever existed

Whatever the pre-creation or pre-existing

conditions were with no stars and fire and light

and with no eyes there with which to see...

no ears there with which to hear...

and no hearts and minds there

with which to love or hope and dream...

only silence and deep...deep...darkness prevailed

in the everlasting forever

of the infinite and immeasurable

nothingness of nothing state of being

which had seemingly forever been

and relentlessly continued to be

Then a span of time in the far distant past

so vastly enormous

that the most powerful and advanced computers

could never measure it

and the length of which mankind's greatest geniuses

could only dream

the supreme omnipotent mystical spirit

of unlimited love and power

roared out a thunderous command

and into being came forth

the grand cataclysmic Big Bang of Creation

In a nanosecond

much quicker than a single thrust

of the beating wings

of a hovering hovering humming bird

billions upon billions of gigantic caldrons

of raging fire and gas

were spewed like grains of sand

spiraling into infinity

to their star bound destinations

The incredibly dark void

and primitive state of being

whose ancient destiny

had finally reached its stage of fruition

gave birth to the piercing brightness

of the colossal ever expanding universe

and at that exact instant

the earliest genealogy of all life forms

including yours and mine

had its most primitive chemical-laden beginning

An eternity of uncountable eons

slowly.....slowly.....slowly..... drifted by

Then somewhere in the immense vastness

of up to 300 billion galaxies

brimming with trillions of stars

being orbited by uncountable numbers of satellite

there came to pass on a minor little planet

in orbit

faithfully clinging to its own blazing Mother Star

which inhabitants of that planet called their Sun

there came to pass a most wondrous

and enchanting day

That day held within itself the essence of life

with all of its challenges and creative possibilities

and a voice was heard to say

Welcome to its dawning

This is that very day

This is that very place

located and soaring

somewhere in the immense vastness of a galaxy

called The Milky Way

Planet Earth

someplace on land in the air or on the sea

wherever you might happen to be

Come sip the sweetness of the nectar

from life's bountiful cup of consciousness and being

of doing and creating

of contributing and receiving

Drink deeply

Today…today…today

moment by moment by moment

is God's priceless true and perfect gift

whose infinite value

can only be diminished

by futile attempts to linger

in decaying castles of days gone by

or escape to fathom palaces of unborn tomorrows

which can never be

You know how short the time we have

to explore and experience

on this our resplendent home and boundless stage

the magnificently beautiful blue ship of space

Mother Earth

and once we soliloquize our farewell

exits and disembark

may nevermore return

in the exact same versions

of the life forms that now we are

or at least not in the identical physical vessels

in which our souls now dwell

As we soar around our sun

while it carries us among the stars

through the unfathomable mysteries

of time and space we realize...

that no matter how young...

or how healthy...

how wise...or how wealthy

there is no absolute lasting physical security

or physical existence

yet unceasing spiritual growth

with no predictable final cosmic journey's end

and that each short fragile mysterious

and magical little life

can be an intriguing adventure

of love service wonder and discovery

or an anxiety filled nightmare of perpetual retreat

So with spirits ablaze

let us choose to act even when afraid

Let the hovering haunting shadows

of guilt regret judgement and negativity

of hesitation procrastination and timidity fade

The Book of Life is a treasure

but brief we've learned

and at every sunset a page is turned

Therefore understanding that the number of days

of each of our visits on this planet is limited

and considering God's inexorable natural laws

along with the randomly occurring

vicissitudes and variables of life

we realize that most individuals

whose mortal existence ended yesterday

had not anticipated it the day before

but that he or she who is bold enough

to allow it into their consciousness

observes that every single day

is literally a heroic majestic

near physical death span of existence

with not a single tomorrow promised

while the life of the soul is eternal

Once this is truly understood

and completely accepted

we cease attempting to cling

to the elusive safety of mediocrity

We choose to refuse to be captivated

by the seductive and self-destructive

serpents of fear and anger

or be blinded and paralyzed

by the bitter tears within our eyes

We dare to plunge into the foreboding abysmal pit

of the dark sides of our psyches

to challenge any savage demons we encounter there

We find that their exaggerated

and misperceived strengths

are abruptly unmasked

and their weaknesses swiftly exposed

We learn that whether we win or whether we lose

any of life's many inevitable challenges or battles

with circumstances with others or with ourselves

that our willingness to participate

struggle and grow

makes us stronger

than we could have ever before imagined

even in our grandest dreams

We are able to climb the highest of mountains

then with wildly beating hearts

and throats seared dry by scorching horror

we leap from the summit

to create our own wings

and fulfill our own dreams.

We discover that with power and love

we can confront any evil or tyrant

abroad or at home

transcend any tragedy or calamity

surmount any pain or suffering

bear any burden or sorrow

tame any terror

and even embrace visions

of that final transitional spiritual journey

when we are destined to fly

from the darkness into the light

soar above the earth like eagles

on wings of unlimited possibilities

and finally

joyfully and adventurously

roam the heavens with angels

After roaming the heavens with angels for awhile

perhaps for a few days or a few weeks

or a few months or years or centuries

should strange unconscious mysterious longings

cause our explorations and wanderings

to carry us back to the very place

from where we first began

Our mothers may bare us

It's possible

Other mothers may bare us

and should that come to pass

bursting and trembling with the newness of life

we shall evolve to a fresh beginning

and once more observe

the mystical ethereal beauty

of our old forgotten home Mother Earth

just as if it were for the very first time

With these thoughts gently drifting

reverberating and echoing

in the complexity of myriad pathways

and intricate chambers

that form the unparalleled circuitry of our minds

making each of us a potential genius

if we can but harness the power

let us make that almost inconceivable

upward thrust of consciousness

to a space outside the stifling prison of conformity

where epiphanies of the heart and intuition

blend with that of the intellect

to reveal that our common knowledge

is like a mere pinch of sand

being shifted and revised

as it is swirled up by the winds of change

from the spacious beach of ultimate reality

We then understand

that only those of an earlier primitive nature

confused by superstition

besieged with guilt and anger

and blinded by a sense of revenge

could forge up

out of the frightening darkness of the unknown

and unwisely...and recklessly...

impose upon humanity

the false and most cruel concept

of a jealous... angry... sadistically punishing...

and unforgiving God

and a terrifying...horrifying...

eternal burning Hell

where millions upon millions of condemned beings

of all races... religions... creeds and lifestyles

consisting of the most evil

and many of the very good

who simply by not professing a particular belief

would scream and writhe in excruciating agony

and unbearable sorrow

not for just a little while

not for just a few seconds.....and it's all over with

not for a few hours

or weeks or months years or centuries

but forever and forever and forever

Only the minds of the most primitive of men

could conjure up

out of the frightening darkness of the unknown

and impose upon humanity

the false concept of such a jealous...

angry...vindictive...and heartless God

who would be more cruel than the most evil of men

Instead of such a nightmarish...archaic... barbaric

and garish scenario

many advanced spiritual Gurus throughout

the world intuit and predict all encompassing

and totally revealing

end of life reviews and self-appraisals

that will cleanse and bless each soul

by allowing them to personally feel and experience

the marvelous joys and gratifications

of their caring and loving actions

as well as any devastation...

pain...sorrow...agony...and horror

that they have created in the world

for their fellow beings

Such all encompassing and soul-searing

revelations and phenomenal insights

will create unspeakable bliss as

well as agonizing atonements and just reparations

but with God's unconditional love and mercy

there can only be separations

We participate in a oneness with God and humanity

that encompasses all souls

existing everywhere in time and space

and by our thoughts and actions

we are constantly attempting to fulfill

the bright and shinning visions

of the loftiest versions

of whom we are choosing to be

but yet cannot even imagine

what champions of love

what dwellers in the light

what glowing comrades of God

we are destined to finally become

We then marvel at what enthralling

and spellbinding tales

we shall all surely be able to exalt in telling

as the ever present now moments of today

instantly become the future of all past existence

and simultaneously the past

of all uncountable tomorrows

Thus is created the mystical...magical...

miraculous...merging of all time

into the sacred miracle of now...now...now

whose assumed passing is only an illusion

created by the spreading shadows of evening

and the welcoming rays of the early morning sun

So with planet Earth

as with the vast array of diverse

and exotic heavenly bodies

scattered hundreds of billions of light years apart

throughout the farthest reaches of the Universe

time and eternity is always now now now

and thus shall always be

Therefore may you hasten...hasten...hasten

to gallantly...gallantly...rekindle

and steadfastly pursue

the forgotten... beautiful...beautiful...plans

and golden...golden...dreams

that once belonged to only you.

Part Two: Mission Statement and Personal Guidelines

Do not let this day pass

without sharing

deep unconditional affection

and exhilarating healing laughter

with students family friends and others

while sensing that love for one or many

of all races religions creeds or life-styles

may be inclusive unlimited

immeasurable and everlasting

Do not let this day pass

without striving for integrity

and congruent authenticity

so that your totally respectful

but disarmingly open and refreshing frankness

encourages little wild abandoned celebrations

of unrestrained honesty

wherever you go

Do not let this day pass

without taming your own demons

by recognizing accepting expressing with control

and thereby dissipating

your personal fear guilt sorrow and anger

as you show

tolerance understanding

forbearance and compassion

to all students as well as all of humanity

which includes flawed but fantastic relatives

friends loved ones and others

and your own vastly imperfect

but honorable self

Do not let this day pass

without choosing to activate

The Holy Key of Self-knowledge

which unlocks hidden talents...

unveils false illusions

and revives the forgotten secrets

and desires of the heart

so that your true mission in life

is finally fully revealed

and you faithfully commit

to that which brings your bliss

Do not let this day pass

without seeking the tranquility that

comes through meditating

and communing with the higher self

who dwells within

while rejoicing that those who have encountered

strange inexplicable transitional excursions

through the long dark tunnel

while seeking the radiant light on the other side

have returned with evidence

of bright startling new paradigms

of reality and existence

that change their lives

and thereby ours forever

Do not let this day pass

without honoring the incomparable generosity

of the Benevolent Creator of your mortal

but miraculously and majestically

formed physical being

by respecting your natural longing

for the ecstasy of wholesome

ultra-responsible romantic fulfillment

and your needs for consistent nutritional excellence

and constant superb physical conditioning

so that your splendid journey through this world

may be taken

with devoted and loyal but non-possessive

loving erotic passion

robust unlimited stamina and agile flowing grace

Do not let this day pass

without realizing that the sleeping giant

silently residing within your own inner being

may be gently aroused

by a mere whisper or intention

and that that silent summons

along with your decisive yet detached commitment

to disciplined self-assertive responsibility

shall give you the power

to change the world

And lastly do not let this day pass

without acknowledging your own

and mankind's inclination to be seduced

by planet destroying greed

yet keeping life's circle of generosity unbroken

by graciously sharing the treasures

from the overflowing abundance

of your own eternal wealth and power

so that you might jubilantly and even blissfully

grant to others throughout the world

that which has been so kindly and lovingly

imparted to you

But most of all understand

that the values and principles you cherish

the priorities and written plans you firmly establish

the creative dreams and loving relationships

you constantly visualize

and the often undervalued

but all powerful even miraculous attitude

you freely choose to embrace

will empower either your own personal inner

chatterbox of negativity

or your positive voice of self-actualization

to predominate your stream of consciousness

and produce the thoughts and actions

you habitually choose to think and do

Those constant choices

will surely bind you in proverbial chains

or set your spirit free to gratefully accept

and even fearlessly revel in the everlasting story

of birth...life...death... rebirth

and eternal growth

until you are finally one with the very mind of God

Until that time remember

Kings and Queens on earth

and Angels in Heaven

would weep with envy

were they but aware of the treasures

which have always been your own

Open wide then your eyes

Take not such riches for granted

but perceive those sacred gifts

and your noble existence in the universe

through enlightened visions of appreciation

as you sing a song of joy and daily celebrate

the constantly changing... expanding...spinning

whirling...shining...wondrous...

Dance of Life

SUMMARY

And so it goes

and so one grows

Bravely then let us swiftly expedite

the unconditional surrender

of any dark fears doubts self-blaming regrets

or fierce resistance

to the irrefutable spiritual and physical laws

of God and the Universe

and in turn be blessed and comforted

with the sacred gift of serenity

with depths of peace

of which most souls can only dream

Finally

Forget not this caveat

Enlightenment

without daily anticipation

and articulation faithfully followed by activation

and application bares little fruition

In a prodigious unlimited Universe

of infinite possibilities

in order to evolve create and even

call forth new realities

that appear to be miracles

but which are actually just

unrecognized and underutilized

Laws of the Universe

you must constantly visualize your grandest dreams

continuously declare your sacred word

and steadfastly take actions to fulfill your intentions

Therefore...salute your mentors

with love and honor

as we are all mentors to each other

at different times

in small or great ways

and celebrate new insights as your greatest wealth

but comprehend

that the concealed and most powerful of all heroes

who must ultimately as a Co-Creator with God

forge your dreams into reality

can only be yourself

MANTRA

Now seize embrace and empower this very moment

with love and fire in your heart

Wait not for tomorrow

Each second's a new start

Wherever you find yourself in time and space

notice that the time is always now

and wherever you are is always the place

Remember that today

is instantaneously yesterday's future

and simultaneously tomorrow's past

creating the mystical magical merging of all time

into God's sacred miracle of now now now

which along with your immortal soul

shall always last

TERROR TAMED...

SPIRITUALITY AND SERENITY
GAINED

(The Everlasting Adventure of Birth, Life,
Death, Rebirth and Eternal Growth)